# Employer Branding

## by Richard Mosley and Lars Schmidt

## Employer Branding For Dummies®

Published by: **John Wiley & Sons, Inc.,** 111 River Street, Hoboken, NJ 07030-5774, www.wiley.com

Copyright © 2017 by John Wiley & Sons, Inc., Hoboken, New Jersey

Published simultaneously in Canada

For general information on our other products and services, please contact our Customer Care Department within the U.S. at 877-762-2974, outside the U.S. at 317-572-3993, or fax 317-572-4002. For technical support, please visit https://hub.wiley.com/community/support/dummies.

Wiley publishes in a variety of print and electronic formats and by print-on-demand. Some material included with standard print versions of this book may not be included in e-books or in print-on-demand. If this book refers to media such as a CD or DVD that is not included in the version you purchased, you may download this material at http://booksupport.wiley.com. For more information about Wiley products, visit www.wiley.com.

Library of Congress Control Number: 2016962922

ISBN 978-1-119-07164-8 (pbk); ISBN 978-1-119-07162-4 (ebk); ISBN 978-1-119-07178-5 (ebk)

Manufactured in the United States of America

10  9  8  7  6  5  4  3  2  1

# Contents at a Glance

# Table of Contents

## PART 5: MEASURING THE SUCCESS OF YOUR EMPLOYER BRANDING STRATEGY

# Introduction

When it comes to talent, business is a lot like sports: The teams with the best organization and players win, and these same teams attract the best players, keep them, and build franchises with the momentum to continue their success.

As the global competition for talent heats up, your organization must do more to attract, engage, and retain the talent it needs to succeed. One of the most effective ways to accomplish this goal is to build a strong *employer brand* — a reputation and proven track record for being a great place to work.

Follow our lead, invest the necessary time and effort upfront, and your organization will soon have an employer brand that does much of the heavy lifting required to attract, engage, and retain the most talented candidates in the workforce.

Already have an employer brand? Then this book is also for you. You can apply the same guidance presented in this book to fix a broken employer brand, build a better employer brand, or create a new employer brand from scratch. You also discover strategies for giving a global employer brand local relevance.

## About This Book

Is your organization losing the talent contest? Are you disappointed with the applicants, struggling with high turnover, and plagued by employee disengagement? Then *Employer Branding For Dummies* is the book you need. With this book, you can begin to turn your situation around.

Organized in an easy-to-access format and presented in plain English, this book brings you up to speed with what an employer brand is, how it can help your organization perform better, and how you can build a strong employer brand from the ground up. Here you discover how to lay the groundwork, evaluate your current situation, develop an effective employer brand strategy, communicate your brand through the right channels, deliver on your employer brand promises, and then measure your success with key metrics and make adjustments as necessary to maintain and build momentum.

Although we encourage you to read every single word of this book from start to finish, you're welcome to skip around to acquire your knowledge on a need-to-know basis and completely skip the sidebars (which are shaded gray). Although the sidebars may be too fascinating to ignore, they're not essential.

Within this book, you may note that some web addresses break across two lines of text. If you're reading this book in print and want to visit one of these web pages, simply key in the web address exactly as it's noted in the text, pretending as though the line break doesn't exist. If you're reading this as an e-book, you've got it easy — just click the web address to be taken directly to the web page.

# Foolish Assumptions

First things first: If you're smart enough to pick up a book about employer branding, you're one smart dummy. You're smart enough to rise to a level in your organization where you're involved in employer brand development, but you're not completely confident in your knowledge and skills in this area. That's okay, because that's exactly what this book is for.

Here are a few additional assumptions we made about you and others we hope will read this book and apply its guidance:

>> You're open-minded enough to consider the value of an employer brand and not cemented in the traditional approach of either posting job ads and praying for a good response, or leaving it up to headhunters to deliver the talent you need.

>> Your organization has room for improvement in terms of attracting, engaging, and retaining the best people.

>> You're committed to creating a strong employer brand for your organization or strengthening the organization's existing employer brand.

>> You're willing to invest your time and effort and your organization's resources to reap the benefits that result from a strong employer brand.

# Icons Used in This Book

Throughout this book, icons in the margins highlight different types of information that call out for your attention. Here are the icons you'll see and a brief description of each.

**REMEMBER**

We want you to remember everything you read in this book, but if you can't quite do that, then remember the important points flagged with this icon.

**TIP**

Tips provide insider insight. When you're looking for a better, faster way to do something, check out anything marked with this icon.

**WARNING**

This icon appears when you need to be extra vigilant before moving forward. Here, you find out how to sidestep the obstacles that are likely to trip you up.

# Beyond the Book

In addition to the material in the print or e-book you're reading right now, this product also comes with some access-anywhere goodies on the web. Check out the free Cheat Sheet for tips on making the case for employer branding, developing your employer value proposition, and more. To get this Cheat Sheet, simply go to www.dummies.com and type **Employer Branding For Dummies Cheat Sheet** in the Search box.

# Where to Go from Here

We structured this book so you could use it in a couple different ways. To get the most out of it, read it from cover to cover, so you don't miss out on any valuable information and insight. You may also use it as an employer branding desk reference; when you're dealing with a particular issue related to employer branding, simply look up the topic in the Table of Contents or the Index and flip to the designated page to find the information and guidance you need.

If you're not sure where to start, you can't go wrong with Chapter 3, which is about conducting an employer brand health check. Even if you're not actively engaged in creating and promoting an employer brand, you already have one; your employer brand is your reputation as an employer — the collective perception of everyone inside and outside your organization. You don't know how well or poorly you're doing from the perspective of those who really matter until you collect and analyze relevant data, both quantitative and qualitative.

If you don't have an employer brand, or you have one but need to refresh or improve it, head to Part 2, where you find out how to define your employer proposition, build your employer brand framework, generate engaging content, and develop and implement your brand strategy. The chapters in Part 3 provide additional guidance on how to promote your employer brand through the proper channels — including websites, social media, recruitment advertising, and college campuses.

No matter where you start, this book will help you build a strong employer brand. You simply need to decide where you are in the process and take it from there. Happy branding!

# 1

# Getting Started with Employer Branding

Discover what employer branding is all about and how it can benefit your organization in attracting, engaging, and retaining the right people.

Identify the four steps to developing and executing an effective employer brand strategy.

Clarify your organization's strategic objectives, identify the talent required to achieve those objectives, and gain the support of your organization's leadership team.

Evaluate your existing employer brand to determine how well it's currently perceived and whether it's delivering the kind of talent your organization needs to succeed.

Chapter **1**

# Building a Strong Employer Brand

Employers used to assume they were in the driver's seat. Advertised vacancies would attract a plentiful selection of candidates. Employers would select the best, and the best would gratefully accept their offers of employment. Times have changed. Established companies can no longer assume that the right kind of talent will beat a path to their door. The new economy requires significantly more people qualified in science, technology, engineering, and math than our education systems are producing. The most innovative and entrepreneurial are increasingly choosing to join or found startup businesses rather than join established companies. And the declining birthrate in many countries means fewer young people are replenishing the workforce as baby boomers retire. Given these trends, it's no surprise that competition for talent is now more intense than it has ever been.

Although times have changed, many companies haven't. They continue to recruit the same way they did 20 years ago — posting openings and screening out unqualified candidates. Although this process of elimination has worked reasonably well in the past, more progressive companies are realizing there are more efficient and effective ways to attract and retain talent. They've begun to harness the power of employer branding, applying the same kind of rigor and creativity that companies have long applied to winning and keeping customers.

Throughout this book, we provide detailed guidance on how to begin to build the kind of workplace and employer brand that attracts, engages, and retains the world's top talent. In this chapter, we deliver the big-picture view, so you have a conceptual framework of employer branding and an overall understanding of what it involves.

# What Is Employer Branding?

*Employer branding* is the process of creating a distinctively great place to work and then promoting it to the talent whose knowledge and skills are needed by the organization to meet its business goals and objectives. Like consumer branding, employer branding involves less push and more pull — developing the kind of positive reputation that will help attract talented individuals when and where they're needed.

In this section, we highlight the benefits of this approach and step you through the process/cycle of employer branding, so you have some idea of what you're about to get yourself into.

## Recognizing the benefits of employer branding

Some companies are reluctant to invest in employer branding, because the costs may seem steep in relation to the immediate returns. After all, to build a strong employer brand, you need to spend money on research and creative development and add to the workloads of already busy departments, including recruitment, human resources (HR), and marketing. Before you commit time, money, and other resources to employer branding, you and others in your organization naturally want to know "What's in it for us?"

To spark the passion and drive needed to build and maintain a distinctively great employer brand, you need to answer that question for yourself and for everyone else in your organization, especially for those in leadership positions. Everyone involved needs to be aware of what's at stake and the positive impact a strong employer brand can have on the success of the organization and everyone who's a part of it.

Here are just a few areas where employer branding can positively impact an organization's success:

>> **Recruitment:** Companies that have a strong employer brand attract larger numbers of qualified candidates, improving the quality of new hires while reducing the overall cost of recruitment.

>> **Engagement:** Employer branding involves creating an environment in which employees are fulfilled by their work and proud of the company they work for. Such a work environment drives engagement, and higher levels of engagement lead to higher levels of productivity and customer satisfaction.

>> **Retention:** A great workplace populated with highly talented and engaged employees is a place employees want to stay. In addition, a strong employer brand clarifies what people can expect from the organization before they apply. Companies with strong employer brands experience significantly lower attrition rates.

>> **Competitive advantage:** Employer branding enables you to build an all-star team with a roster of the most talented individuals in your industry. The collective intelligence, creativity, drive, and determination of highly qualified individuals enables you to gain and maintain a competitive advantage within your industry.

# Stepping through the employer branding process/cycle

The approach to building a strong positive employer brand can be summed up in two steps:

1. **Make your organization a distinctively great place to work.**
2. **Make sure the right talent knows how great you are.**

Of course, the process is more involved than that, and it's more cyclical than linear — a continual process of building brand momentum and making adjustments in response to an ever-changing business and workforce environment. A more detailed summation of the process/cycle looks more like this:

1. **Develop a clear understanding of your organization's business objectives and the talent needed to meet those objectives.**
2. **Evaluate your current employer brand image among potential recruits and the employer brand experience of your current employees.**

   Identify how this compares with what your key target talent groups are looking for. (See Chapter 3.)

3. **Define your *employer value proposition* (EVP), the key ingredients that will make your organization a distinctively great place to work.**

**REMEMBER**

An effective EVP describes your current reality, as well as realistic aspirations — the employer you want to be and be known as. (See the later section "Defining the give and get of the employment deal.")

4. **Build your *employer brand framework,* the creative elements that collectively capture the look and feel you want to convey and the emotion you want to evoke. (See the later section, "Establishing employer brand guidelines.")**

5. **Generate engaging, story-led content and employee experiences that bring your EVP to life in ways that resonate with the talent you're trying to attract.**

6. **Actively engage with prospects through selected channels, including your organization's career website, social channels, job boards, and *programmatic* (automated ad placement driven by analytics). (See the later section, "Spreading the Word through Various Channels.")**

7. **Measure your success to determine what's working and what's not, from your overall brand strategy down to individual recruitment marketing activities. (See the later section, "Monitoring Your Employer Branding Success.")**

8. **Adjust your employer brand strategy and individual recruitment marketing activities, as needed, to improve results.**

After you've gone through the process once, building brand momentum becomes cyclical — shampoo, rinse, repeat.

**REMEMBER**

A key step we intentionally omit from this process is getting everyone in the organization, especially leadership, involved in your employer branding efforts. Your C-level executives and managers need to embrace the importance of employer branding, encourage and facilitate collaboration, and commit resources to support your efforts. Various departments, including HR and marketing, will need to contribute their insights and expertise. Employees must help with content generation, engaging with prospects, and serving as brand advocates. Without a coordinated effort, your EVP will be DOA (dead on arrival). (See the later section, "Rallying the troops [and leaders].")

# Laying the Foundation for Your Employer Brand

In many ways, branding follows the laws of physics. In physics, vectors represent forces that act on an object to move it, like a pool cue striking a ball. Every vector has a magnitude and a direction. The more vector forces and the greater their magnitude propelling an object in the same direction, the faster and farther that object travels. Forces that act in the opposite direction slow the object, stop it, or reverse its course. Forces that strike the object from different angles move it off course.

When building an employer brand, everyone in the organization needs to push in the same direction with a force of the greatest magnitude possible. With everyone working in unison, brand momentum begins to build, and you begin to win brand advocates outside the organization who put their weight and force behind the brand, moving it ever faster forward.

Branding of any kind works best when everyone agrees and all branding activities align. To achieve this alignment, you need to build your employer brand on a firm foundation. In this section, we cover the basics of laying that foundation.

## Aligning with business goals and objectives

Just as forces within an organization advance the employer brand, the employer brand is a force that propels the organization forward by delivering the talent needed for the organization to meet its business goals and objectives. As such, it must align with other forces within the organization that share that mission. Specifically, your employer branding strategy must align with the following three strategies that drive the organization's success:

» **Business strategy:** The employer brand must support the kind of talent capabilities required for the organization to compete effectively. In addition to being fit for talent, it must also be fit for business.

» **HR and talent strategy:** Your employer brand must either reflect or shape the way HR and talent management operate within the organization to ensure promises are consistently aligned with experience.

» **Marketing strategy:** The employer brand must reflect corporate and customer brand promises to maintain a general sense of brand integrity.

For maximum impact, all strategies should align perfectly, but in the imperfect reality of a business, different functions will inevitably have their own goals and objectives. Don't be surprised if you find yourself having to actively reconcile competing agendas and conflicting perspectives among your key internal stakeholder groups.

## Fitting in with your other brands

Employer brands never exist in a vacuum; they're created in the context of the corporate and consumer brands, and, for the most part, they need to align with their corporate and consumer counterparts:

>> **Corporate brand:** The reputation your company is seeking to build based on its *purpose* (the reason for its existence, beyond making money), *vision* (what it's striving to achieve), and *values* (guiding principles)

>> **Consumer brand:** Customer perceptions of the company's products and services and the brand associations that the marketing team is trying to promote

>> **Employer brand:** The company's reputation as an employer inside and outside the organization

Aligning the employer brand with the corporate and consumer brands is complicated by the fact that corporate and consumer brands can be associated in several different ways. In some cases, such as Apple and Shell, the corporate and consumer brands are synonymous. In others, such as the Coca-Cola Company, the company shares the same name as its leading product but not the rest of its product portfolio. And in other cases, such as Unilever and P&G, the corporate brand may be only loosely associated, if at all, with its many consumer brands.

Prior to launching any employer branding initiative, you need to decide how closely and in what ways you want your employer brand to align with your existing corporate and consumer brands. When the needs of consumers diverge from those of employees, close attention needs to be paid to how the brand is communicated to each target group. For example, "Citi Never Sleeps" made perfect sense to potential CitiBank customers, but would have made a particularly poor call to action for potential CitiBank employees.

## Rallying the troops (and leaders)

If you're in charge of employer branding, part of your job is to make sure everyone's on the same page, clear about his or her responsibilities, and collectively accountable for doing his or her part. To be successful, you need the backing and support of a wide range of different stakeholders throughout your organization:

>> **Senior leadership:** For the brand to be truly authentic and fully embedded in the organization, it needs to be led by the CEO and collectively owned by the entire senior leadership team. The key to getting the leadership team onboard is to make a strong case for employer branding, as explained in the earlier section, "Recognizing the benefits of employer branding." Senior leadership needs to appreciate the crucial role employer branding plays in securing the talent the company needs to achieve its growth ambitions.

>> **Marketing and communications:** The folks in marketing and corporate communications tend to be very protective of the corporate and consumer brand and resist the notion of a separate employer brand because it can appear to threaten brand integrity. You can make them more receptive to the idea of an employer brand by showing them how it can help to build internal brand engagement and extend the appeal of the brand to external audiences who may not have otherwise considered the brand.

>> **HR:** You definitely need HR on your side. Nobody has more direct accountability for shaping people management processes and more influence over talent strategy. Initially, HR may be reluctant to take on the additional responsibilities associated with employer branding, but making a strong business case and appealing to HR's desire to keep up with best practice are generally sufficient to win its support.

>> **Line management:** Like HR, line management is likely to be reluctant, at first, to commit time and personnel to employer branding. To rally their support, tailor your presentation to their pain points and aspirations. Highlight the fact that a strong employer brand will help to deliver the kind of talent they need to meet their objectives and ensure they lose fewer key players to competitors.

# Taking an Honest Look at Your Employer Brand

Regardless of whether you've done anything to build an employer brand, you already have one. Your employer brand is written on the faces of the people you meet who ask you where you're working. It's present in the gory or glorious detail of your Glassdoor reviews. It's embedded in the energy or malaise of your everyday working environment. Your employer brand is your reputation as an employer — whether your organization's work environment is distinctively great, generically mediocre, or exceptionally bad.

Before you invest time and resources into building an employer brand, perform an honest self-assessment of the brand you have to work with. In Chapter 3, we provide detailed guidance on how to conduct an employer brand health check. Here are the four areas to examine:

>> **What you already know or perceive:** You probably have some sense of what your organization's employees and people outside your organization think of it as an employer. Add to this knowledge any additional information you may already have, such as feedback from customers and partners, recent employee surveys, or a general review of sentiment across your social media channels.

>> **Employment experience:** The employment experience and how employees perceive it contribute significantly to your organization's reputation as an employer. Conduct employee surveys and focus groups to find out what current and former employees think of you, and any gaps that may exist between what you offer and what they want. Although compensation and benefits are often ranked pretty high, they're rarely at the top of the list.

>> **External perception:** You need to figure out what people outside the organization think of you as a potential employer. How well are you known among the talent you're trying to attract? What are you known for? And how do people feel about you? In Chapter 3, we provide suggestions on how to gauge awareness, brand associations, and sentiment.

>> **Competition:** The organizations you compete with for talent are typically those within your industry from which you hire and lose the most people. Add to that list the top employers attracting the best talent from every industry to learn what they're doing better.

**WARNING**

Don't mimic what other organizations are doing to win the competition for talent. Your goal is to become *distinctively* great, and you can't accomplish that by doing what everyone else does. What other organizations do may not work for you. Find ways to capitalize on your organization's unique qualities. Use your research on other companies as a stepping stone for your own creative ideas.

# Putting the Pieces in Place

As with most strategic operations, execution of your employer branding initiative requires coordinated and persistent effort, which is best accomplished if you have everything in place prior to launch. With employer branding, "everything" consists of your EVP, brand framework, and compelling communication content. In this section, we describe the three pieces you need to have in place before initiating any employer branding operations.

# Defining the give and get of the employment deal

The purpose of employer branding is to attract people with the knowledge and skills your organization needs to meet its objectives and then convince these people to work for your organization. This purpose can be described in terms of the give and get of the employment deal — you're offering people something they value (money, recognition, opportunities to be creative or make a positive impact in the world, and so on) in exchange for something you value (knowledge, skills, passion, creativity, and so on). In employer branding, this give and get is distilled and communicated through the EVP. It consists of a *core positioning statement* (the one thing about your company that sums up how and why it is a distinctively great place to work) and three to five pillars (details that support and expand upon the *core positioning statement*).

Here's a simple example from Facebook whose EVP is shaped by its strong mission and company values, along with the key attributes identified by employees, which make working at Facebook unique.

> **Core positioning statement:** Connecting the world takes every one of us.
>
> Facebook's mission is to give people the power to share and make the world more open and connected.
>
> **EVP pillars:**
>
> - **Build social value.** Facebook was created to make the world more open and connected, not just to build a company. We expect everyone at Facebook to focus every day on how to build real value for the world in everything they do.
>
> - **Move fast.** Moving fast enables us to build more things and learn faster. We're less afraid of making mistakes than we are of losing opportunities by moving too slowly. We are a culture of builders; the power is in your hands.
>
> - **Be bold.** Building great things means taking risks. We have a saying: "The riskiest thing is to take no risks." In a world that's changing so quickly, you're guaranteed to fail if you don't take any risks. We encourage everyone to make bold decisions, even if that means being wrong some of the time.
>
> - **Be open.** We believe that a more open world is a better world because people with more information can make better decisions and have a greater impact. That goes for running our company as well. We work hard to make sure everyone at Facebook has access to as much information as possible about every part of the company so they can make the best decisions and have the greatest impact.

- **Focus on impact.** To have the biggest impact, we need to focus on solving the most important problems. It sounds simple, but most companies do this poorly and waste a lot of time. We expect everyone at Facebook to be good at finding the biggest problems to work on.

**TIP**

Here are a few suggestions for developing a solid EVP and getting stakeholders to buy into it at the same time:

» **Establish your employer brand objectives.** Decide what you're trying to achieve and your priorities (for example, attraction, engagement, retention).

» **Do your homework.** Find out how current employees and potential candidates think about your company as an employer, either from existing data or commissioning your own research.

» **Gather the right people.** Invite representatives from key stakeholder groups to participate in the employer brand development process, including representatives from HR, talent management and resourcing, marketing and communications, and where possible, line management.

» **Conduct an EVP workshop.** Run your workshops as brainstorming sessions to explore research findings, gather insights, and generate ingredients needed to formulate your employer brand's core positioning statement and pillars.

» **Clarify the give and get of the employment deal.** What does the company need from employees and what is it willing to offer employees in return? Think beyond financial compensation.

» **Balance strength and stretch.** An effective EVP reflects current strengths but also incorporates realistic future aspirations.

» **Differentiate your company from its competition.** Far too many companies take a "me too" approach to employer branding. Be distinctive by offering your employees a unique experience and then marketing that experience in a creative way.

# Establishing employer brand guidelines

A brand's impact is primarily a function of standout and consistency. Brands need to catch people's attention and maintain that attention within a crowded environment through a clear and consistent identity. Employer brand guidelines (commonly referred to as the *brand framework*) help to maintain a consistent look, feel, and overarching message that differentiate you from your competition. The brand framework commonly includes the following:

- **EVP:** The EVP establishes the key ingredients of your employment offer, particularly the elements that distinguish you from your key talent competitors.

- **Company logo(s):** These guidelines generally cover how and where the company logo is presented within typical digital and print communication formats, including websites, advertising, brochures, and presentations.

- **Design elements:** Guidelines for design elements cover graphics other than the logo, such as background texture, line style, white space, and color blocks, that must be consistent in order to reinforce brand recognition.

- **Color palette and fonts:** These guidelines establish the range of colors and fonts suitable for brand communication.

- **Photography:** These guidelines may specify a range of acceptable images to be used when communicating the brand or, more loosely define, a recommended style of photography (with illustrative on-brand and off-brand examples).

REMEMBER

Your brand must be consistent to build reliability and trust but flexible enough to adapt to different target audiences and changes in candidate and employee preferences over time. A brand framework generally accomplishes this goal by preserving the core while allowing changes around the periphery — closer to where the core meets the audience. At these touch points, the brand must flex to address the unique needs of each talent group.

## Giving your target talent a reason to tune in

When your goal is to build a strong employer brand, the worst that can happen is that the talent you're scouting for doesn't care enough to visit your company's career website, check out your list of job openings, or submit an application. You need to give them a compelling reason to tune in and engage, and that reason comes in the form of relevant content that the heads you're hunting deem valuable in some way — educational, entertaining, engaging, enlightening, or perhaps all four.

TIP

As you strive to attract and recruit the best talent for your organization, keep in mind that content is king. Here are a few content categories to stimulate your imagination:

- **Employee profiles:** The last decade has experienced a significant increase in employee-focused content, as opposed to content primarily focused on the company. A wide range of profiles are possible, including the following:

  - *Job profile:* A story in which an employee presents her unique perspective on her position within the organization, including her responsibilities and typical "day in the life" challenges

- *Culture profile:* A story that captures the attitudes, values, and behaviors that everyone in the organization shares (or ideally you would hope should share)

- *Passion profile:* A story in which an employee is given creative license to reveal his personality and outside interests and show how these resonate with his work

- *Hero profile:* A story about an employee who overcame a significant challenge with the encouragement and support of the organization

- *Team profile:* A story of how the collaborative efforts of two or more employees within the organization achieved something neither of them could have done on his own

- *Inside stories:* A backstage pass that gives prospects a behind-the-scenes look at what really goes on in the organization

>> **Facts and figures:** Cold, hard data that's relevant to the audience and can't be found anywhere else is often enough to draw the attention of the right people. For example, you could include your average annual investment per employee in training or the number of employees working outside their home countries. Infographics are often a great way to present data in a more accessible and appealing format.

>> **Photos:** Photos of employees, teams, innovations, company picnics, and so on are a simple and proven way of attracting more views and comments.

>> **Video clips:** YouTube, Snapchat, and other social channels make posting video easy. Short, captivating video clips often go viral. Deloitte pioneered the practice through its Deloitte Film Festival, encouraging employees to post short video clips in answer to the question, "What's your Deloitte?"

>> **Games:** Simple game mechanics incorporated with more traditional content can be highly effective in attracting and engaging the talent your company is looking for. This may include tests, challenges, competitions, or visuals that indicate progress through a series of steps.

TIP

The best content is often free. Posting on blogs or discussion forums often sparks active discussions in which the participants generate content for you. Consider posting questions or introducing relevant issues for discussion and allowing others to create content for you. If you own the blog or forum, be sure to monitor it closely to ensure participants treat each other respectfully.

In addition to posting content on your own online properties, consider posting in relevant forums you don't own, like Medium, Tumblr, GitHub, Facebook, and other platforms. When you're engaging with talent online, become an active member of the communities they belong to.

# Spreading the Word through Various Channels

With a compelling EVP, distinctive brand framework, and engaging content in hand, you're ready to start promoting your brand and reaching out to key target prospects. Where you choose to share your content depends on where you're likely to reach the talent you're looking for, but you have numerous options, including the following:

» **Company career website/page:** At the very minimum, you should have a company career page with job postings and a way for interested prospects to submit applications online. A step up is to have a separate company career website or a section of your company website devoted to career information and jobs at your company. (See Chapter 9 for additional guidance on building a company career website.)

» **Company career blog:** A company career blog is a great venue for sharing career information and insights, stimulating relevant conversations, and engaging with prospects. When you assign different levels of access to different users, you can set up the blog in a way that anyone and everyone in the organization can contribute content and engage with prospects. Perhaps best of all, blogs often draw the attention of search engines and earn higher-than-average search rankings.

» **Social channels:** You have plenty of options to engage with prospects on popular personal and professional social channels, including LinkedIn, Glassdoor, Facebook, Twitter, YouTube, Snapchat, and Pinterest. You can create your own company career account or page on most of these sites to establish a presence there and join various relevant groups where the targets you want to attract are active. (See Chapter 11 for more about engaging talent via social channels.)

» **Job boards:** Certain job boards automatically scrape company career websites and web pages to gather job postings. Others allow you to post jobs for free or for a fee. You have numerous job boards from which to choose, including the biggies — Monster (www.monster.com), CareerBuilder (www.careerbuilder.com), and Indeed (www.indeed.com). You can also find plenty of specialty job boards for a variety of talent, including sales, technology, and marketing.

» **Search engines:** You can leverage the power of search engine optimization (SEO) to improve your search engine rank and drive more traffic to your company career website or blog. You can also use search engine marketing (SEM) to pay for sponsored ads that appear in search results. Using the two together often creates a synergy with paid advertising improving your organic search engine rank.

>> **Programmatic:** A relatively new option, programmatic automates the process of advertising placement through analytics. Primarily used for placing online advertising, programmatic is expanding into traditional media, including TV, radio, newspapers, and magazines.

>> **Traditional channels:** Traditional channels, including newspapers, magazines, TV, radio, and even billboards, can still be effective tools in recruitment advertising and building a strong, positive employer brand, as long as they further the objectives of your employer brand strategy.

>> **College campuses and internships:** Establishing a positive physical or virtual presence on college campuses is a great way to recruit college students, graduates, and graduate student. It's so effective, in fact, that we devote an entire chapter to the topic (see Chapter 13).

REMEMBER

Companies with the strongest employer brands increasingly hire through referrals from current and former employees. As you reach out through social channels, don't lose sight of the fact that the employees you already have can be your most valuable source of high-quality applicants and new hires.

# Staying True to the Promise of Your Employer Brand

Common sense dictates that in order for promises to be of any value, they must be kept. Employees who feel as though they're working for one of the best employers in the world are more likely to refer friends, family members, and professional contacts to the organization and sing its praises on social channels, such as LinkedIn and Glassdoor. Employees who are disappointed by their employment experience may start to think that the EVP and any new employer branding initiative is an empty promise at best, and a self-serving gesture at worst.

TIP

To continue to earn employee trust and engagement, do the following:

>> **Stress to the CEO the importance of creating an exceptional employment experience.** The CEO must make it her personal mission to earn a reputation for being an employer of choice by shaping a healthy organizational culture and supporting a consistently positive employee experience. Ideally, the senior team should take the lead in launching the employer brand

(including their key future commitments) and briefing management on what is required from them to deliver on the brand promises.

» **Do more in a distinctly better way.** Strive to continually do more in a distinctly better way for employees. Your goal is to create *brand-signature experiences* — elements of your company's employment experience that make the experience unique and superior to that offered by organizations competing for the same talent. Brand-signature experiences are of value to employees and to the organization, but they also serve as constant reminders of the company's culture and values.

» **Take a customer service approach to HR processes.** Manage the employee experience as carefully as you would manage the customer experience. Strive to make every important people management interaction (or *touch point*) with employees a signature experience and every stage in an HR process a consistently positive "on-brand" experience for the employee. Follow the customer service model practiced by most airlines, in which the customer experience is managed from the time the customer starts shopping for a flight until he boards and ultimately exits the plane.

# Monitoring Your Employer Branding Success

Becoming the employer everyone wants to work for requires considerable effort, expertise, and coordination, so you want to make sure that everything you're doing is having the desired effect on your employer brand. If it's not, then you know you have to do it better, or do it in a different way. To gauge the impact of your employer branding initiative and activities, analyze both short- and long-term outcomes:

» **Short-term outcomes:** Metrics for measuring the short-term outcomes of employer branding activities relate to the level of engagement your marketing content is generating, the number and quality of the applicants you're attracting and hiring, as well as the total cost-per-hire. Use analytics software and any other tools at your disposal to track the success of your overall recruitment marketing strategy, your recruitment marketing campaigns, and specific recruitment marketing activities used in each campaign. Analyze the channels through which you recruit candidates, as well, to determine which are most fruitful for attracting the desired talent. (See Chapter 17 for details.)

**REMEMBER**

When tracking short-term outcomes, measure the success of a marketing campaign, activity, or channel in terms of the objectives for each campaign and the type of talent you're recruiting. A social channel that's very effective in engaging IT professionals, for example, may be next to useless in recruiting sales staff. Make sure you understand the difference.

» **Long-term outcomes:** Metrics for measuring long-term outcomes of your employer branding efforts are related to your brand awareness, overall attractiveness as a potential employer, and employer brand image. Internally, long-term outcomes can be measured in terms of employee pride and advocacy, employee engagement and performance, and the number and quality of referral applicants and new hires. Ideally, you should also seek to evaluate the long-term outcomes and return on investment (ROI) of your brand investment in talent, in terms of business performance measures, including productivity, customer satisfaction, and sales. (See Chapter 18 for details.)

In addition to tracking short- and long-term outcomes of your employer branding efforts, you need to look to and plan for the future. In many ways, employer branding is like trying to hit a moving target. Constant shifts in talent availability, competitive positioning and activity, your organization's goals and objectives, and evolving talent preferences all play a part in influencing what your organization must do to attract, recruit, engage, and retain the best and the brightest. To keep from falling behind, you must continually look ahead.

# Chapter **2**

# Preparing for the Journey

I f employer branding is a new concept for your organization, you have plenty of work to do to lay the groundwork that will make it a success. You need to

» Find the right fit for employer branding, so it aligns with everything else your organization is doing to achieve its goals.

» Evaluate what you're doing well and not so well in terms of attracting, engaging, and retaining employees.

» Prove the potential value of employer branding to yourself and other key stakeholders.

» Get buy-in and a commitment to support your efforts from these same stakeholders.

In this chapter, we set you on the path to building a strong employer brand by preparing yourself and other stakeholders in the organization for the difficult but rewarding work ahead.

# Finding Your Fit within the Overall Company Strategy

Employer branding success depends on coordinated action throughout the organization. An employer brand should work within the broader strategic hierarchy, as shown in Figure 2-1.

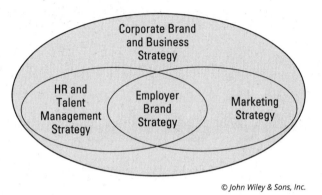

**FIGURE 2-1:** The integrated strategy model.

This illustration of corporate brand and business strategy places employer brand strategy at the intersection between human resources (HR) and talent management and marketing, because employer brand strategy is part of all three:

>> **Corporate brand:** Your employer brand must reflect the corporate and customer brand promises and ambitions of your company.

>> **HR and talent:** Your employer brand must support the kind of talent capabilities required for the organization to compete effectively, and it must align with the way HR and talent management operate within the organization.

>> **Marketing:** Marketing efforts must reinforce the corporate, customer, and employer brand while eliminating any confusion or conflict among the three.

**REMEMBER**

Ideally, line management, HR management, and marketing management are in complete alignment, but organizations operate in an imperfect world. For this reason, employer brand strategy often plays a reconciliatory role between these different stakeholder groups to help maximize the effectiveness and coherence of all three.

In the following sections, we explain how to position employer branding in the organization to optimize success.

# Aligning with the corporate brand

The term *corporate brand* is generally used to describe the overall reputation of the company, as opposed to its more specific reputation as an employer. In addition to finding your fit within the strategic hierarchy, you need to clarify your place within the brand hierarchy, as shown in Figure 2-2.

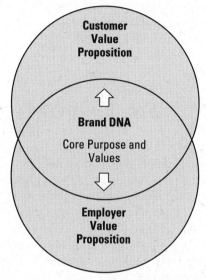

**FIGURE 2-2:** The integrated brand model.

From a management perspective, the most discernible manifestation of the corporate brand is its visual identity — the corporate logo, colors, fonts, and design elements used to present a consistent face to the world. (For more about this aspect of corporate branding, see Chapter 5.) Many companies also try to define some of the more intangible components of identity, including the following:

>> **Purpose:** The organization's reason for existence beyond making money — what the organization does. Google provides a great example of purpose: "To organize the world's information and make it universally accessible and useful."

>> **Vision:** The organization's current end goal — what the organization is striving to achieve within a given time frame, "a dream with a deadline." A powerful historical example of this is Microsoft's original company vision (when access to computers was still highly limited): "To put a computer on every desk in every home."

>> **Values:** The organization's guiding principles — how the organization does what it does. A few examples from Southwest Airlines are "Work hard," "Have FUN," and "Treat others with respect."

If your organization has a defined purpose, vision, and values, these statements provide an important starting point for defining your employment offer and employer brand strategy, with clear alignment between the company's core beliefs and the more specific proposition you're setting out for current and potential employees.

**WARNING**

Don't let the lack of a clear statement of purpose, vision, and values hold up the process of defining and promoting your employer brand. Question the leadership team on the medium- to long-term direction of the company, and their views on the kind of culture they believe the company should promote internally to achieve these longer-term goals.

## TAKING AN INSIDE-OUT APPROACH

In *Built to Last,* James Collins and Jerry Porras shared the results from their study of 18 enduringly successful companies, commonly referred to by other CEOs as "visionary," including P&G, American Express, Boeing, Walt Disney, and HP. One of the clearest characteristics they found within these companies was a very clear sense of purpose and shared values:

> Like the fundamental ideals of a great nation, core ideology in a visionary company is a set of basic precepts that plant a fixed stake in the ground: "This is who we are, this is what we stand for." Like the guiding principles embodied in the American Declaration of Independence ("We hold these truths to be self-evident . . .") and echoed 87 years later in the Gettysburg Address ("A nation conceived in Liberty and dedicated to the proposition that all men are created equal").

From a corporate brand perspective, this core ideology can also be described as the organization's core proposition. This ideally combines the organization's statement of purpose and its core values, which Collins and Porras define as follows:

> Purpose: The organization's fundamental reasons for existence beyond just making money — a perpetual guiding star on the horizon; not to be confused with specific goals or business strategies.

> Core Values: The organization's essential and enduring tenets — a small set of general guiding principles; not to be compromised for financial gain or short-term expediency.

You can find plenty of other definitions of purpose and value, but from our perspective, these are the clearest and most useful. Employer brand development should always start with a clear understanding of corporate purpose and values, because these core elements of the corporate ethos should be reflected throughout everything the organization says and does.

**REMEMBER**

Start your employer brand development with a clear understanding of the corporate brand and the parameters within which the employer brand needs to function to ensure consistency within the overall brand hierarchy. Your organization's employer value proposition (EVP) must align with the organization's core statement of beliefs — its purpose, vision, and values. See Chapter 4 for detailed guidance on how to align these core statements of belief with your EVP.

## Aligning with the customer brand

Maintaining consistency with the customer brand depends on how closely the corporate and customer brands are associated:

>> **Corporate and customer brands are identical or nearly identical.** In many organizations the corporate brand name is carried by the company's products and services, as is the case with Apple, Shell, Vodafone, and Deloitte.

>> **The corporate brand name is carried by a leading product.** In some cases, the company name is carried by the leading product or service within a wider product portfolio (for example, L'Oréal, Coca-Cola, and Ferrero).

>> **The corporate brand name is loosely, if at all, associated with products.** The corporate brand name may not be used directly in naming any of the company's products or services, as is the case with Unilever and P&G.

After recognizing the relationship between your organization's corporate and customer brands, you're ready to start thinking about how closely you want to align your employer brand with the existing brand associations.

### Aligning your employer brand with existing brand associations

When corporate and customer brands overlap to some degree, start with an understanding of how the products and services are perceived and the kind of brand associations the customer brand marketing team is trying to promote. Then decide how closely your organization's employer brand should be associated with its existing corporate and customer brand identities.

To build an employer brand that's closely associated with your organization's corporate and customer brand identities, develop a relationship with the customer brand marketing team to agree how you can support each other in building a brand reputation that works for both employees and customers.

**REMEMBER**

Your employer brand reputation inevitably reflects the customer brand. For example, L'Oréal is widely known for its female beauty products, and inevitably its employer brand is generally more attractive to women than to men. Vodafone's customer brand campaign "Power to You" inevitably shapes expectations of employee empowerment.

### Diverging from existing brand associations

If your employees have needs that differ from those of your customers, create an EVP, as explained in Chapter 4. The EVP draws focus to the attributes of your organization that are most relevant to the talent you're recruiting. Identify which brand attributes the customer and employer brands can and should share. For example, at McDonald's, certain brand associations are shared between customers and employees, while others are not:

>> **Family feel:** Shared by customers and employees

>> **Low prices:** Valued by customers, but likely to discourage candidates

>> **Future focused:** Valued by employees, but neutral for customers

**WARNING**

When envisioning an employer brand, be prepared to break away from an existing brand identity that's likely to discourage targeted applicants. For example, Citibank's advertising line "Citi Never Sleeps" was designed to appeal to customers, but it was far less appealing from the perspective of potential candidates.

### Choosing to align with a corporate or customer brand

If your organization has a corporate brand along with multiple customer brands, consider the degree to which you want to align your employer brand marketing within specific business units with the overall corporate brand or with the more immediate customer brand that those employees will be working for. For example, would candidates prefer to work for Bentley or Volkswagen (the parent company)? Would they prefer to work for Ben & Jerry's or Unilever?

Discuss the options with your organization's senior management team. A strong desire to build the corporate brand may influence you to align your employer brand more closely with the corporate brand. On the other hand, a desire to maintain the distinct character of individual brands within the portfolio (including strong employee identification with the customer brand) may encourage you to create a range of employer brands with the corporate employer brand playing a more supporting role.

**TIP**

If you choose to create a range of employer brands, consider using the corporate brand as the "management brand" for those likely to seek a wider career across the group, with the customer-facing brand playing a more dominant role in attracting and engaging local, frontline employees.

## Supporting the business strategy

*Business strategy* is the plan an organization has in place to achieve its long-term objectives; it defines where and how an organization can best compete in the marketplace. P&G CEO A.G. Lafley suggests the two key business strategy questions are: "Where should we play? And how can we win?"

Business strategy is beyond the scope of this book, but whatever your organization's strategy is, be very clear about the resources and capabilities the business requires to build and sustain competitive advantage. These resources and capabilities include the kind of talent profile(s) you focus on, the employment benefits you use to attract them, and what you expect from employees in return if they choose to join you.

## Getting the right talent onboard

Three goals of every employer branding initiative are to attract, engage, and retain the *best talent.* To accomplish these goals, you first need to figure out what "best talent" means in the context of your organization. The best talent for your organization isn't necessarily the brightest, most creative, or most highly skilled candidate. More likely, your ideal candidates possesses a unique blend of knowledge, skills, confidence, drive, imagination, integrity, and a host of other qualities that make them perfectly suited for your organization, its mission, and the positions to be filled. Employees with "the right stuff" enhance your organization's corporate culture and contribute to its diversity. They make your organization better in all the ways that make it distinctive, and they help to reinforce its competitive advantage.

**REMEMBER**

As Intel once declared, "Our rock stars aren't like your rock stars." We can't provide you with a list of attributes that make the ideal candidate for your organization, but we can provide you with the guidance to conduct such an assessment of your own. In this section, you discover how to define the talent you're targeting, so you have a clear idea of whether your current employer brand is achieving the desired results and, if it isn't, what you need to do to make sure it does.

# Determining the desired culture fit

Most organizations require a variety of different skills and competencies to meet their resourcing requirements. However, before you start segmenting your workforce into different target talent groups, identify the overall qualities you would like all your employees to share in terms of the desired culture and values. These qualities may already be clearly articulated in a statement of your company's values. If they're not, then consult with your leadership team to determine these baseline characteristics. Typically desired qualities fall into the following three categories:

>> **Collective purpose:** The ability and commitment to work with others to achieve a common goal. This category includes customer focus, teamwork, respect, honesty, integrity, and communication skills.

>> **Mental agility:** The ability to adjust one's thinking to best meet the challenges of work. This category covers innovation, imagination, learning ability, resourcefulness, and problem solving.

>> **Drive:** The dedication to completing a task or achieving a goal. This category includes personal initiative, passion, confidence, decisiveness, performance focus, and persistence.

Although all these qualities are certainly desirable, the important distinction between a generic target profile (good people) and the specific profile targeted by your employer brand (the right people) is *differentiation.* Among the generally positive qualities, which particular qualities do you emphasize? On which dimensions do you want people to overindex (outperform)? To answer this question effectively you must be clear about the culture your business most needs to achieve its strategic objectives and win in the marketplace. Here are several examples:

>> Google looks for the following qualities in its ideal employee: A desire to use technology to make the world a better place, an entrepreneurial spirit for developing and selling new ideas, and "Googliness" (a mashup of passion and drive that Google describes as hard to define but easy to spot).

>> In addition to the requisite professional and technical knowledge to join the world's most prestigious consulting firm, McKinsey also looks for the following personal characteristics: an unusual blend of passion, dedication, and energy. It looks for people who are creative and insightful problem solvers, who enjoy working in teams, who have an entrepreneurial spirit, and who are interesting people outside the office.

>> Helmut Schuster, the Executive Vice President of HR at BP, describes the combination of qualities BP looks for in prospective employees as

- Thinking ability, and the right level of experience in its field

- Social competence, emotional intelligence (EQ), and the ability to communicate with other people

- Drive, combined with commitment to the long-term interests of the company

» A.G. Lafley prioritized innovation as P&G's primary competitive weapon and engine for growth. According to Lafley, "We had to redefine our social system to get everybody in the innovation game." Although P&G continued to recruit for values, brains, accomplishment, and leadership, it shifted its determining factors for assessing cultural fit to curiosity and an entrepreneurial spirit.

**WARNING**

Don't assume that your organization's existing culture is what the leadership team deems necessary to support the organization's forward-thinking strategies. Consult the leadership team, so you're clear about its vision and about the culture its members deem most suitable for executing that vision.

## CULTURE AT THE LEGO GROUP

Effective leaders typically have a good sense of the organization's culture. Asking them to describe it in their own words can be a powerful way of clarifying to potential candidates what makes the organization tick. The following example is from the CEO at the LEGO Group:

What a strong culture is about is people know what to do without reading a little book. You have an intuitive sense of how to do things. But that doesn't mean there is only one solution to the same problem. That would be so untrue of the basic idea of LEGO Organization where we recognize there are many solutions to the same problem and you have to put your imagination and creativity to work to make the best solution.

One day I went off to work and my oldest son said, "Who are you going to spend time with today?" and I said, "I'm going to spend time with Kjeld, who is the owner of the LEGO Group," and my son's immediate reaction was, "So what are you going to build?"

The company is still very much about playing and building. We're constantly reminded of that wonderful quote: "We don't stop playing because we grow old, we grow old because we stop playing."

As you work toward developing your EVP, keep track of the employee perspective on what the corporate culture really is. This perception can shed light on changes your organization needs to make to bring the culture more in line with what leadership decides is best for the organization.

## Targeting diversity

Culture fit doesn't imply uniformity. In addition to identifying the qualities you'd like all employees to share, also consider how you can ensure your employees represent a diversity of backgrounds and perspectives. All other qualities being equal, research suggests that a diverse workforce is superior to one lacking in diversity for several reasons:

>> **Diversity makes a team less susceptible to groupthink and more open to alternative approaches.** *Groupthink* is a phenomenon that affects teams with members from similar social backgrounds. With groupthink, the desire for acceptance within the group often overrides the motivation to consider alternative courses of action.

>> **Organizations with greater racial and gender diversity tend to perform better in terms of sales, revenue, number of customers, and market share.** Research agency Catalyst found that U.S. Fortune 500 companies with the highest representation of women on their top management teams experienced a 35 percent better return on equity.

>> **Diverse organizations are more capable of evaluating and meeting the needs of a wider range of customers and clientele.** Analysis conducted by Cedric Herring (sociology professor at the University of Illinois at Chicago) among 506 U.S. organizations showed that a one-unit increase in racial diversity increased sales revenue by an average of 9 percent.

>> **A commitment to diversity expands the available candidate pool in both depth and breadth and makes the organization more attractive to a wider range of candidates.** Some highly qualified candidates may be reluctant to apply to a company where they will be a small minority.

>> **Employees working in a diverse environment are better equipped to advocate for diversity and engage candidates who come from diverse backgrounds.**

REMEMBER

Before you develop or refresh your employer branding, clarify your leadership team's diversity objectives or, alternatively, bring to their attention the need to incorporate a diversity perspective within your employer brand strategy.

## Identifying critical skills and competencies: Workforce planning

In addition to creating an overall target talent profile, you must determine the different kinds of talent your employer brand needs to appeal to. Workforce planning describes the process of ensuring the right number of people with the right skills are employed in the right place at the right time to deliver on your organization's short- and long-term goals.

Not every organization has a formal workforce planning process, but you should obtain answers to the following key questions before setting out to develop your employer brand strategy:

» How many people will the organization need to hire over the coming one to three years to replace employees who leave (based on the existing/projected level of employee attrition)?

» How many additional employees will need to be hired to deliver on the organization's growth targets?

» What kind of employees will you need to recruit?

- By function/job group (for example, production, sales, customer services)

- By level of experience (for example, graduates versus mid-career professionals)

- By location

» Which talent groups are most critical to the success of the business? (For example, relationship managers tend to be the critical target group for private banking and wealth management firms, whereas geologists and reservoir and drilling engineers are generally regarded as a highly critical talent groups to oil and gas companies.)

» Which target talent groups are likely to be the most difficult to attract (especially from the most critical groups you've identified)?

The answers to these questions will provide a key input to your employer brand strategy because they will help to determine

» The appropriate level of investment in employer branding and recruitment marketing

» The target groups your employer brand most needs to appeal to

» The degree to which you may need to position your employer brand differently to different target groups

To identify the critical skills and competencies your organization needs, obtain input from your organization's leadership team and from function/job group managers (in HR, sales, marketing, and so on). Functional/job group managers are often in the best position to determine the knowledge and expertise required to do each job. They also have a good feel for the personalities and attitudes required to excel in various positions.

## Aligning with human resources

Your organization's HR and talent priorities and plans have a significant impact on what you can credibly incorporate within your EVP, so before you start to formulate your employer brand strategy, understand the HR agenda. The focus of HR investment moving forward is of special relevance, because it may indicate how and where you can upgrade your current claims by taking into consideration forthcoming improvements. For example, the claims you make about your organization's commitment to people's personal and professional growth could certainly be up-weighted if the HR agenda includes one or more of the following:

>> Introducing a new performance and development system

>> Reimbursing employees for continuing education courses

>> Improving access to training through e-learning

>> Implementing a new career-path model

>> Promoting career mobility through open job posting

>> Increasing bench strength through more disciplined succession planning

# Building Your Business Case for Employer Branding

Some companies are reluctant to invest in employer branding, because the costs may seem steep in relation to the immediate returns. After all, to build a strong employer brand, you need to spend money on research and creative development and add to the workloads of already busy departments, including recruitment, HR, and marketing. Before you commit time, money, and other resources to employer branding, you and others in your organization naturally want to know "What's in it for us?"

Although an argument generally has to be made for investing in employer brand development over and above regular current recruitment activities, companies rarely define a formal business case. Instead, they tend to justify the investment on the basis of more general aspirations, such as improvements in reputation and attracting talent.

In this section, we help you develop a more formal business case for employer branding by pointing out specific areas where employer branding is likely to save costs and improve performance in the long run.

Building a strong business case for employer branding can help you rally stake-holders and other key players in the organization to support your cause.

## Considering cost-cutting benefits

A LinkedIn survey of 2,250 corporate recruiters in the U.S. revealed that the average cost-per-hire in organizations with a strong employer brand was two times lower than those with employer brands ranked moderate to poor. In addition, LinkedIn discovered that the employee turnover rate among companies with a strong employer brand was 28 percent lower than among companies with weaker employer brands. Given that the average cost of employee turnover, including training and lost productivity, can range from 90 percent to 200 percent of an employee's annual salary, the cost savings involved in this lower rate of attrition are clearly significant.

Cost savings derive from a number of factors, including the following:

» **Direct sourcing:** Taking a more proactive approach to employer branding helps you to bring your recruitment marketing in-house, and reducing your dependency on search firms significantly reduces your cost-per-hire.

» **Better targeting:** Employer branding focuses on targeting the right talent with the right messages through the right channels. This cuts costs in three ways:

- Focuses your recruitment marketing investment where you know you'll get the best return

- Reduces the number of applicants who fail to meet your general requirements, saving time and reducing processing costs

- Ensures you attract and hire the right candidates with a clear (and realistic) understanding of what they can expect

» **Rationalizing your creative spend:** By focusing investment on a single creative framework with a shared selection of high-quality creative assets, rather than taking a more localized and ad hoc approach, you can save a significant amount of money. This logic extends beyond global advertising campaigns to career sites and other online domains where coordinated investment in website development and recruitment marketing content generally benefits from similar cost advantages.

» **Building brand awareness and equity:** Decades of brand research have demonstrated that consistent brand messaging builds greater awareness and a stronger, more impactful brand image over time than is accomplished by more fragmented approaches. After you've established a positive brand reputation, subsequent marketing activities benefit significantly from the *brand halo effect.* In simple terms, you get more bang for your marketing buck when people feel generally familiar and favorable toward your brand than when they don't know you.

» **Enhancing your pull power:** In addition to more cost-efficient and effective push marketing, a clear employer brand image attracts (pulls) a much higher proportion of unsolicited applications from target candidates. Likewise, a positive employer brand experience encourages a higher level of advocacy and referral activity (a source of hire known for its low cost and high quality). It also provides access to a much wider pool of potential talent.

» **Hiring good people for less:** Convincing midcareer candidates to leave one organization and join another typically requires a salary increase or conversion premium. Conference Executive Board (CEB) research indicates that the average conversion premium required to attract a midcareer candidate to an organization with a strong employer brand reputation was close to half that demanded from an organization considered to have a weak employer brand reputation.

» **Reducing unwanted attrition and rehire:** If you're clear about the kind of people who will fit in and thrive within your organization, you're clear about the kind of employment deal you're offering them, and you deliver on your employer brand promises, you're likely to enjoy a significantly lower level of unwanted employee turnover. The cost savings can be significant, particularly with regard to misfit attrition within the first few months — before an employee has been able to make a meaningful contribution to performance.

# Checking out possible performance benefits

A recent study from the Boston Consulting Group and World Federation of People Management Associations ("From Capability to Profitability") involving 4,288 HR and non-HR managers in 102 countries revealed that employer branding, alongside effective recruitment, onboarding, and retention, appears to be highly correlated with strong business results. Companies that had made the Fortune 100 Best Companies to Work For list at least three times between 2001 and 2011 significantly outperformed the S&P market average during this same period, finishing 99 percentage points higher. The factors driving these differences in performance are likely the following:

» **Hiring more high performers:** The business value of getting the right people on the bus can be significant, which explains why more companies are measuring recruitment efficiency in terms of quality of hire instead of cost-per-hire. Research from McKinsey suggests that compared to average performers, top quartile performers deliver 67 percent more revenue in sales, 49 percent more profit in general management roles, and 40 percent greater productivity in operational roles. (Netflix calculated that the best performers are two times better than average and ten times better than average in creative/inventive work.) A strong employer brand enables you to attract more candidates, through building greater awareness, consideration, and preference among key target groups, providing the organization with a deeper and broader talent pool.

» **Onboarding new hires more effectively:** A strategic and systematic approach to onboarding is a necessary feature of most effective employer brand management programs. A study of nearly 200 organizations conducted by Aberdeen Group found that the 20 percent best-in-class onboarding companies retained 86 percent of their first-year employees (compared to 56 percent among the bottom third). It also found that these leading companies reported 77 percent of their employees met their first performance milestones on time, compared with only 41 percent of employees in the laggard group of companies.

» **Improving employee engagement:** More than two decades of rigorous and persuasive research shows that higher levels of employee engagement are associated with a wide range of positive business effects. In an analysis of its U.S. engagement database representing four million employees, Hewitt Associates discovered that average levels of employee engagement among companies that had delivered double-digit growth over the last five years were 20 percent higher than slower-growing companies. Comparing the median differences between top and bottom teams, Gallup recently demonstrated that high levels of employee engagement were associated with 10 percent higher customer satisfaction, 21 percent higher levels of productivity, and 22 percent higher levels of profitability.

» **Enhancing communication and change management effectiveness:** In 2013, Towers Watson included an EVP measure in its Change and Communication ROI Report for the first time. This survey drew on a global sample of 651 organizations, representing a broad range of industry sectors and headcounts. Results showed that the top third of organizations in terms of communication and change management effectiveness were significantly more likely than the bottom third to have defined a formal EVP.

» **Building brand engagement:** While the focus of employee engagement activities tends to be reactive and generic, effective brand engagement is more proactive and specific. In the latter approach, the organization chooses the brand pillars it wants employees to be engaged by and prioritizes its activities and communication accordingly. In theory, the resulting brand mix should incorporate a more balanced selection of factors driving employee engagement and factors that are more directly related to performance.

# Making Friends and Influencing People

Effective brand management is a team sport, with clear accountabilities for different groups and shared ownership of the total net brand reputation and experience. If you're leading the employer branding initiative in your organization, part of your responsibility is to rally the troops, so everyone is onboard. To be successful, you need the backing and support of key players throughout the organization, from senior management and HR to the creatives who communicate the employer brand.

**REMEMBER**

A thriving, brand-led company has no room for petty politics.

## Getting senior leadership onboard

Ultimately, for the brand to be truly authentic and fully embedded in the organization, it needs to be led by the CEO and collectively owned by the entire senior leadership team. The key to getting the leadership team members onboard is understanding their agenda and demonstrating how a stronger employer brand will help them achieve their business goals.

The most obvious area of alignment with CEO concerns is the role that employer branding plays in securing the critical talent organizations need to achieve their growth ambitions. Close to three-quarters of the CEOs surveyed by PWC in its 2015 and 2016 global leadership surveys expressed a concern over the availability of people with in-demand skills (particularly tech talent). Other key potential areas of alignment with senior leadership goals and aspirations could be

>> **Employer brand reputation:** Many leadership teams express a desire to be the employer of choice within their industries.

>> **Organizational transformation:** Securing the support of employees through periods of change is often a major leadership concern, especially given the implications this often has to the underlying employment deal. In this situation, clarifying the role that a clear EVP can have in highlighting the benefits of the new deal can be a persuasive argument for employer brand investment.

>> **Cost reduction:** The ability of employer branding to improve cost efficiency through direct sourcing and lower employee attrition is particularly relevant if cost reduction is a major focus of the leadership team.

# Convincing marketing and communications to go along with the idea

Marketing and corporate communications people tend to be very protective of the corporate/customer brand and resist the notion of a separate employer brand because it can appear to threaten brand integrity. You can take a number of steps to win their support, including the following:

>> **Swear allegiance to the brand identity.** Clarify that the rules governing the corporate brand identity will be applied to the employer brand with equal rigor and that nothing will be signed off on without their full support.

>> **Clarify the role of the EVP.** The best way to position the EVP to corporate communications is to describe its role as translating the corporate brand into the employment context, highlighting the brand benefits that are most relevant to current and potential employees (as opposed to other key stakeholder groups). Likewise, from a customer marketing perspective, the role of the EVP is to clarify to HR staffers how they need to deliver an employee experience aligned to the desired customer experience (that is, reflecting the same brand values).

>> **Request some freedom within the brand framework.** If you police brands too tightly, you inevitably squeeze the life out of them. Unless a brand adapts and flexes to the different environments in which it needs to operate, it will generally lose relevance. If you apply the same brand standards to investors looking for a safe place to invest their money and to Gen Y candidates looking for an exciting place to launch their careers, you're likely to miss the mark with at least one of these target audiences, if not both. Likewise, if you apply the same style of brand communication to both customers and employees, you're unlikely to address the needs and expectations of both as they tend to be looking for different kinds of relationship and benefits from the brand.

REMEMBER

The strongest brands apply consistent design standards to maintain a coherent frame, but constantly adapt the content of the communication and offer to stay fresh and relevant to different audiences.

In short, issues related to control of the brand identity are moot. The corporate brand and communications team can continue to focus on consistent identity standards and brand communication to high-priority corporate stakeholder groups, while HR and marketing can work together to tailor the brand to the needs of current and prospective employees.

# Getting HR comfortable with the language and thinking of brand management

To successfully tailor the corporate brand to the needs of current and prospective employees, you need to be close to your audience. You need to understand the kind of messages and content that will resonate. You also need to closely align your presentation of the brand with the brand experience you're striving to deliver. For these reasons, we believe the HR/talent management function is in the best position to tailor the kind of brand communication and experience that targets current and potential employees, while playing within the overall brand guidelines determined by the corporate brand and communications team.

At first, the HR and talent management team may be reluctant to come to the party, especially if their agenda is already overflowing with other people management initiatives. However, while they're certainly likely to take on the lion's share of the work, they're also likely to reap the lion's share of the benefits of having a strong employer brand — more engaged and productive employees, increased retention rates, and so forth. Winning the support of the HR and talent management teams may be simply a matter of citing the potential benefits, as explained in the earlier section, "Building Your Business Case for Employer Branding"; however, you may also need to take the following steps to overcome some of the more emotional barriers to adopting employer brand thinking:

>> **Take time to explain the language.** Many of those on the HR team may not be familiar with the language used in brand management and marketing. Because it's sometimes easier to resist and reject the unfamiliar rather than embrace it, take time to explain as simply as you can the basic marketing processes and terminology.

>> **Demonstrate how employer branding will help support the overall HR agenda.** Employer branding may often appear to be no more than an add-on to the existing agenda, a further drain on existing HR resources. In this respect, other members of the HR team may see employer branding as a distraction to what they're trying to achieve. To address this concern, clarify how a stronger employer brand can support a broad range of existing HR objectives.

Chapter **3**

# Conducting an Employer Brand Health Check

Before pursuing any initiative to create or revitalize your employer brand, you need to take its vital signs to determine the existing strengths as an employer that you can build on, and diagnose any failings that may need to be addressed to strengthen your future employer brand image and experience.

In this chapter, we explain how to give your employer brand a checkup to determine its effectiveness or ineffectiveness in the following three areas:

» **Employment experience:** How satisfied are your employees with their experience of working for your organization? What stands out as particularly positive or distinctive?

» **External perception:** What is your organization's reputation as an employer within and beyond the industry in which it operates? How well does this match the expectations and aspirations of your target candidates?

> » **Competition:** How does your organization stack up as an employer against other organizations competing for the same talent? What, if anything, differentiates you from your competitors?

**TIP**

After persuading your senior team that the organization needs to invest in its employer brand (see Chapter 2), resist the common temptation to fast-forward to a new employer value proposition (EVP), communication campaign, and improved results. Strong brands are built on a firm foundation of insights, and the most important of these is a clear-headed assessment of the current health of your employer brand reputation and experience.

# Taking a Look in the Mirror

Although one of the key reasons you build a strong employer brand is to attract candidates from outside your organization, external appearances should never be too far separated from internal experiences — the actual employment experience. After all, reputation is usually a reflection of reality. Before you examine how people outside your organization see you, look at how people inside your organization feel about the organization as an employer, and take an honest look at whether you're doing all you can to be a best-in-class employer.

In this section, we explain how to conduct an internal audit of your existing employer brand to reveal its strengths and weaknesses as perceived by employees within the organization.

## Finding out what you already know

Before you start conducting fresh research, check out any existing sources of data that may available to you. Digging up previous research studies can often save you from asking the same questions and investing in research that's already been done. This is especially true of large organizations where knowledge often remains trapped in local pockets.

**REMEMBER**

Send a message to your key local contacts letting them know that you're planning to create or revitalize your organization's employer brand and requesting any information they may have that could be useful. This is the first stage in most effective research projects. It can also be a useful first step in engaging local support.

Your organization may have already conducted some form of employee survey. Even though such a survey may not have been designed specifically to define your

EVP, the data may still be useful for this task, as long as it's reasonably recent (within a year or two) and no major organizational change has occurred since the survey was conducted.

If your organization has an EVP or corporate values, get hold of the research that informed these existing statements and any research conducted subsequently to determine how consistent these statements are with the employment experience. If you work for a multinational company, you may not have a global EVP, but check whether any parts of the business have developed EVPs at a more local level. Local EVPs can provide useful insights and certainly must be taken into consideration if you're ultimately trying to align everyone behind a single global EVP.

# Conducting employee surveys and focus groups

Your greatest resource for understanding the current status and future potential of your employer brand are the employees within your organization, who know what it's really like to work there. They're well aware of whether their employment experience is living up to any existing employer brand promises, and they're well placed to contribute ideas for improving the employment experience and communicating what your organization has to offer future candidates.

To obtain feedback from employees, conduct an employee engagement survey to provide a solid foundation of quantitative data and focus groups to provide more specific and qualitative insights into what your employees are thinking and feeling.

Without employee feedback, evaluating your employer brand is like marketing your consumer brand without product testing or developing your service brand without customer feedback. In short, without employee feedback, you're flying blind, which is a highly dangerous pursuit.

## Conducting an employee engagement survey

An employee engagement survey is a key component of employer brand management, because it exposes the realities of the employment experience. Most companies invite all employees to participate in this kind of survey. The most common format is a 20- to 30-minute online survey administered by an independent external agency to ensure employees feel confident that any negative opinions will not be traced back to them. Companies typically provide their employees with a two- to three-week window to complete the survey, and aim for at least a 60 percent response rate to ensure the findings are representative of the majority view.

Your survey should include questions to gather the following data:

» **Demographics:** These questions enable you to identify different types of employee, so you can identify any variations that may exist in perceptions or preferences between subgroups. This typically includes gender, age group, tenure (years working at the company), business unit/function, and location. You may also consider adding some diversity questions, such as ethnicity, disability, sexual preference, and so on if diversity and inclusion are a strong focus for the organization.

» **Perceptions of the employment experience:** These questions cover overall perceptions of the company and working experience. Questions may address

- The perceived status of the company (for example, stability, market success, and brand reputation)

- The company's vision, purpose, and strategy (are they clear, credible, and inspiring?)

- Working relationships (for example, mutual respect, level of friendliness, and quality of teamwork)

- Empowerment (for example, level of personal responsibility, degree of autonomy, ability to make a difference, flexibility, and work-life balance)

- Learning (for example, training, development, and management coaching)

- Career opportunity, including career path clarity, speed of progress, and scope for international mobility

- Performance (for example, focus on quality, results, and customer service)

- Management style, including quality of communication, support, recognition, and individual care

- Reward, including the perceived quality and fairness of employee pay and benefits

» **Employee engagement:** These questions help to identify levels of employee engagement and commitment to the organization. They commonly address motivation (willingness to go the extra mile), loyalty (intention to stay at the organization), and pride and advocacy (likelihood of recommending the organization to friends and personal/professional networks).

Results from your employee engagement survey provide you with five key pieces of analysis that reflect current perceptions, identify the credibility of your employer brand promises, and help to determine the interventions required to strengthen the employer brand experience:

>> **Engagement heat map:** With the results you've obtained, you can color-code your organization from hot (fully engaged) to cold (disengaged). Your heat map enables you to identify where your organization is performing best from an employer brand perspective, and where it needs the most remediation.

>> **Performance scorecard:** An effective employee survey reveals your organization's overall strengths and weaknesses as an employer. It also indicates the level of cultural consistency across the organization. For example, major differences in feedback from different divisions and departments may indicate the need for a more segmented approach to your EVP and employer brand messaging.

>> **Engagement drivers:** Correlation analysis enables you to identify the key factors driving employee engagement. This analysis involves mapping engagement feedback to results that reflect the perceptions of different aspects of the employment experience. If the majority of people who claim the company is good at professional development (perception) also score well on engagement, and similarly those who feel the company is poor at development score badly on engagement, then professional development is likely to be an important factor in driving engagement. In statistical analysis, the term used to describe the strength of this linkage is *correlation*.

>> **Differentiators:** If you hire an agency to conduct the survey, it should be able to provide you with external benchmarks that show how your organization stacks up against the competition. These benchmarks help you determine in which areas your organization is performing above and below the norm.

>> **Momentum:** In addition to analyzing current strengths and weaknesses of your employer brand, survey results help you monitor the direction of change in each attribute of the employment experience. An attribute's credibility is determined not only by its current status, but also by its forward or backward momentum.

## Gathering employee feedback via focus groups

An engagement survey provides you with a robust understanding of the strengths and weaknesses of the employer brand experience, as well as the needs and aspirations of your employees. However, it doesn't necessarily provide you with the rich cultural understanding that's vital in evaluating the health of your employer brand. For this you need to turn to qualitative research — focus groups.

TIP

Focus on the positives by asking questions such as "What are you most proud of?," "What's working?," "What are we like at our best?," and "What strengths can we build on?" instead of the more typical critical questions: "What are you dissatisfied with?," "What's wrong?," and "What do we need to fix?" Wording questions to elicit constructive feedback doesn't mean glossing over the difficult issues. You're still getting feedback on what needs improvement — you're just taking a more positive, constructive approach, which leads to much better results.

**TIP**

Conduct your focus groups like workshops, where employees co-create potential solutions instead of merely telling you how they feel. Try to have some fun in the process. Use projective and enabling techniques, such as personification and role playing. These techniques are fun, engaging, and immensely useful in exploring the culture and personality of the organization, which people often find difficult to express in response to more direct questions. Here are some of the questions and techniques that have proven useful in running this kind of focus group:

>> **Imagine you're an undercover reporter who's been sent to the organization to write the inside story. What would your headline be?** This is a good warm-up question to get a feel for what's going on in the part of the organization you're researching and whether the focus group participants are going to be spontaneously positive or more downbeat in their evaluation of the organization.

>> **If the organization were represented by a single person, what type of person would he or she be?** Consider starting with a few iconic examples, such as Nike or Google, to warm people up. After participants have entered the spirit of this exercise, you can ask a series of more specific question, such as "What kind of car would he drive?," "What kind of paper would he read?," or "What kind of pets would he have?"

>> **What would you put in an advertisement to present the very best of what the organization can offer?**

>> **Who would appear in the organization's hall of fame and why?**

>> **How would Disney tell the organization's story if Disney made it into a film?**

Consider conducting separate focus groups for recent joiners and longer-serving employees. Recent joiners can offer a relatively fresh perspective on the way the organization seems to work, as well as insight into the gaps between their early experience of the organization and their external expectations as candidates. Longer-serving employees bring a wider range of experience and are generally better able to differentiate between the official line ("This is what we're expected to say") and the inside story ("This is the way it really works").

Another useful line of inquiry for longer tenured employees relates to the cultural momentum of the organization. Here's an example:

>> What's on the way out?

>> What's the flavor of the moment?

>> What do you see on the horizon?

# Taking a Look from the Outside In

Employers develop a brand reputation regardless of whether they consciously set out to define one. Your organization's reputation as an employer is a fundamental component of your *employer brand equity* (the inherent value of your brand) and ultimately determines the potential size and quality of your *talent pool* (the number of candidates matching your desired target profile who would consider working for you). Understanding how your organization is perceived as a potential employer can be a complex exercise, because it's influenced by several factors, including the following:

>> How well your organization is known as an employer (in terms of both brand awareness and familiarity)

>> The organizations you're competing with for talent

>> The degree to which your organization is considered to be a potential employer and preferred to immediate rivals

>> The relative appeal of different employment attributes in determining candidates' consideration and preference for potential employers

>> The attributes you're most associated with as an employer (your employer brand image)

>> The factors that appear to be shaping your employer brand image and appeal the most, including your current employer brand marketing, the image of your products and services, and general perceptions of your industry sector

In this section, we break down the analysis of your brand reputation into the factors that contribute to defining it. What you discover in the process can help you determine whether your employer brand reputation needs improvement and, if it does, help you identify the areas you need to work on.

**REMEMBER**

Some organizations enjoy high levels of global awareness and a fairly consistent reputation, but we recommend a more focused approach to targeting your measurement of brand reputation, so results are more reflective of what the people you're targeting in your employer branding initiatives think about your organization as an employer.

## Gauging employer brand awareness, consideration, and preference

The first measure of your employer brand reputation is awareness and familiarity. What proportion of your target audience has heard of your organization and knows what it does? The next step is to assess how many of those claiming awareness of your organization would consider your company as a potential employer, and finally how many people within your target audience, if any, regard you as an ideal potential employer.

The most straightforward way to establish a bench line of external awareness and familiarity for small to medium-size companies is to establish an applicant survey. The aim of this is to determine how many of those responding to job advertising claim to have been aware of your company and how many felt reasonably familiar with your company prior to seeing your job vacancy. This method is prone to bias, because research suggests that those familiar with your company are far more likely to respond to advertising. However, the objective of this exercise is to provide a relative benchmark rather than an absolute measure. Your findings will, of course, vary depending on how and where you advertise your job vacancies, so consider these factors when analyzing the data. For example, awareness and familiarity are likely to vary geographically depending on how far the applicants are from your main company locations. Likewise, if your product and services are largely business-to-business you would expect awareness and familiarity to be higher among those currently working within your industry sector.

**TIP**

Because this survey method requires some time to deliver useful data, you may also consider a more immediate qualitative approach. Posing the same questions to your new joiners and recruiters (both internal and external) can also provide a useful indication of general awareness and familiarity among your target audiences than can feed into the overall evaluation of your current employer brand status.

An alternative method is to make use of LinkedIn's Talent Brand Index tool, which provides a useful measure of your current levels of "reach/familiarity" and "engagement/active interest" within LinkedIn's membership base, as compared with your key competitors. We provide more detail on this form of analysis in Chapter 18.

Establishing more accurate levels of brand awareness, as well as additional data reflecting consideration and preference, requires a more robust survey among the broader target population. Universum conducts annual talent surveys every year among students and young professionals, recording awareness, consideration, and preference among the top 100 to 150 employers in more than 60 countries. Survey respondents are asked which employers they're aware of, which they would consider working for (typically 15 to 20), and which 5 they would prefer to work for. Universum also conducts tailored surveys for those not currently listed as top employers, following a similar methodology. This enables employers to compare the relative strength of their employer brand with key talent competitors among both the general population and key target groups such as business students or qualified engineers.

Being known and considered as a potential employer among the general population is reassuring, but the more important measures are awareness, consideration, and preference among the target groups you most need to recruit. Bear this in mind if your company operates primarily in a business-to-business environment, rather than consumer products and services, where higher levels of general awareness and consideration are more likely to result from your consumer marketing. In a business-to-business environment, focusing more specifically on the findings within your industry and geographical locations generally makes more sense.

## Identifying your key talent competitors

Because organizations compete for talent in the same way that they compete for customers, one way to gauge the relative strength of your employer brand is to measure it against the strength of the organizations you're competing against. Theoretically speaking, you're competing with every employer on the planet, but a more practical approach is to identify a reasonably small subset of your toughest competitors. Here's how:

1. **Identify organizations from which you hire the most people and those your employees tend to leave your organization to join.**

2. **Add to this list any other employers that appear to be outcompeting you for the kind of talent your organization is trying to attract.**

When identifying the organizations you're completing against for talent, broaden or narrow your focus based on functions and critical roles. Here are some examples:

>> For front-line, volume-hire roles, such as customer service staff, your key competitors are likely to be the leading employers in your city or region.

>> For people with sector-specific skills, your key competitors are likely to be the other key players in your industry.

>> For more portable technical skills, such as information technology (IT), your key competitors are more likely to be employers from a wider range of sectors with particularly strong reputations within their chosen discipline, such as Google, Microsoft, and large banks.

You can try to collect this information yourself, but the alternative is to make use of LinkedIn's Talent Flow Analysis tool (which provides information like that shown in Figure 3-1), which provides a useful analysis of the relative current inflows and outflows of talent by company. However, be sure to supplement this insight with additional research into the talent you're targeting but not currently reaching due to candidates' lack of awareness or familiarity with your organization.

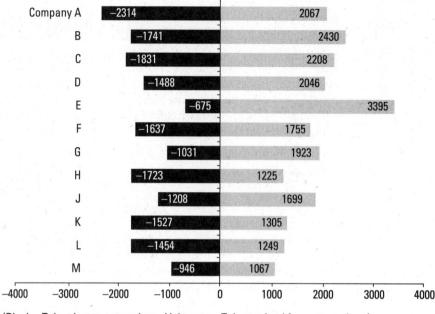

**FIGURE 3-1:**
Use this information to analyze inflows and outflows of talent.

(Black = Talent lost to competitors, Light gray = Talent gained from competitors)

## Evaluating the strength of your organization's employer brand image

*Your employer brand image* is the idea that people form in their minds when they think of your organization as an employer. Evaluating this image is important, because it will help you to understand why potential candidates consider or choose to work for your organization or one that's competing against you for that same talent. To evaluate the strength of your organization's employer brand image, you need to measure the degree to which your key target audiences associate you with the kind of attributes people generally consider important when judging the relative attractiveness of employers. As for awareness, consideration, and preference, you can include this question in an applicant survey. Or, for a more robust analysis of the wider potential target population, you can use a specialized research provider.

To provide some indication of the kind of image attributes you may wish to consider, Universum uses the following standard attribute framework for the measurement of employer brand image:

## Corporate image attributes

- Attractive/exciting products and services
- Corporate social responsibility
- Corporate transparency
- Ethical standards
- Fast-growing/entrepreneurial
- Innovation
- Inspiring leadership
- Inspiring purpose
- Market success
- Prestige

## People and culture

- A creative and dynamic work environment
- A friendly work environment
- Commitment to diversity and inclusion
- Enabling me to integrate personal interests in my schedule
- Interaction with international clients and colleagues
- Leaders who will support my development
- Recognizing performance (meritocracy)
- Recruiting only the best talent
- Respect for its people
- Support for gender equality

## Job characteristics

- Challenging work
- Customer focus
- Flexible working conditions
- High level of responsibility

- » High performance focus
- » Opportunities for international travel/relocation
- » Professional training and development
- » Secure employment
- » Team-oriented work
- » Variety of assignments

**Remuneration and advancement opportunities**

- » Clear path for advancement
- » Competitive base salary
- » Competitive benefits
- » Good reference for future career
- » High future earnings
- » Leadership opportunities
- » Overtime pay/compensation
- » Performance-related bonus
- » Rapid promotion
- » Sponsorship of future education

Results from this image survey enable you to clarify how you're perceived as a potential employer and the degree to which you're associated with attributes that are most attractive to your target audiences. The key findings to focus on are

- » **Distinctive strengths:** Where do you outperform in relation to the industry norm and key competitors? These image dimensions represent your current external brand differentiators.

- » **Comparative strengths:** Where do you perform in line with your industry and key competitors?

- » **Key weaknesses:** On which dimensions of highest appeal to your target audience do you rate poorly compared to your key competitors?

- » **Reputation versus reality:** Where do external perceptions differ most from your internal survey findings?

**REMEMBER**

Your employer brand is ultimately defined by people's perceptions. Defining an employer brand in terms of perception is useful, because it provides you with a more realistic measure of your employer brand's true status and value. It helps you recognize that your brand is ultimately shaped by what people hear about you and how they experience your organization. It keeps you honest and ensures you're clear about where you need to focus your efforts most to strengthen the value and appeal of your brand.

## Evaluating the factors that shape your organization's brand image

After you have a clear picture of what your brand image is — how people perceive your organization as a potential employer — you're better prepared to evaluate the factors that may have contributed to shaping that brand image. To conduct such an evaluation, answer the following four questions:

>> **How successful does your employer brand marketing appear to have been in shaping your image?** If you've been active in communicating your employer brand, to what degree does this appear to be reflected in your brand image findings, particularly among the targeted talent groups? Recognize that it takes time to shape your brand image, but if you've been active in communicating a number of key messages for at least 6 to 12 months, you should expect to see some impact of those efforts on your brand image. If you're seeing little or no impact despite success in creating a valuable employment experience (as determined by the last question in this list), you may need to rethink your communication strategy and tactics.

>> **To what extent does your image appear to have been shaped by your customer marketing?** If your products or services enjoy a reasonably high level of awareness through long established presence or active recent advertising, you should consider the potential effects this may have had on your employer brand image results.

For example, given L'Oréal's strong investment in female focused product advertising, the company finds it much easier to attract women than men, and communication professionals than scientists, because the type of employment opportunities are strongly influenced by what candidates can see (cosmetics and female models) versus a corresponding underestimation of what they can't see (the scientific and operational infrastructure that underpins the final product). The frequent "low price" advertising of McDonald's tends to reinforce an image of "low pay," despite the fact that its salary levels are highly competitive. Likewise, companies that sell luxury products tend to be associated with high levels of pay.

Make a list of the kind of employer you would expect based solely on your customer marketing. Compare this with your employer image results, and look for the possible crossover.

>> **To what extent does you image reflect general perceptions of your industry?** This question engages a similar thought process to the previous question but extends to business-to-business organizations. In addition to looking at your own image results, take a look at the general pattern within other employers within the same industry. Some of these are likely to be true to reality. For example, investment bankers tend to be paid well. But other general industry preconceptions may not reflect the reality of your own company. Law firms generally score low on innovation and teamwork, but this is certainly not true of every law firm. Where does it appear that your image reflects general industry expectations, despite the evidently opposite focus within your own organization?

>> **How does your image compare with reality?** In the long run, reputation generally catches up with reality, but there is often a lag. Compare your external image with your employee survey results. Where do they align and where do they differ? Big differences suggest that you've not been active enough in communicating your strengths. Hidden strengths point to future communication opportunities. Hidden weaknesses, where expectations exceed your current ability to deliver, point to potential future difficulties. Your answer to this question may highlight areas that require greater internal investment to close the gap, or a conscious focus on expectation management before you seal the deal on new hires.

**REMEMBER**

Understanding the factors influencing your employer brand image isn't always straightforward. Seldom does brand image perfectly align with employer brand marketing. You need to consider a wider range of factors and do your best to counteract these influences where necessary. You should at least try to assert some control over the factors your company can manage, including your corporate and customer advertising and communication. If you're a major player in your industry, you may even consider joining forces with others to address some of the more negative or misguided perceptions of your market sector that may be restricting your potential talent pool.

# Weighing Your Competition

In addition to understanding how your employer brand image and relative preference among target talent compares with your key competitors, you can gain valuable insight by understand how and why your competitors may be perceived as more attractive. In this section, we explain how to take a closer look at the organizations competing against you for the same talent.

# Benchmarking your competitors' media presence

Fortunately, competitors' career sites and social media pages provide an open book when it comes to most of their employer brand marketing activity. This should enable you to benchmark their activity (media, messages, and social engagement levels) in order to assess your comparative online presence, positioning, and impact.

## Checking out your competitors' career sites

Most companies have their own career sites, but the quality varies significantly. We cover career site best practices in more detail in Chapter 9, but the following provides a checklist that you can use to compare your own career site with your main competitors' and identify where you may have an edge or some ground to make up:

>> Does the home page clarify and dramatize the organization's overall employment offer rather than just direct people straight to job vacancies?

>> Does the site contain some sort of "Why join?" section that describes the potential opportunities and benefits of working for the organization?

>> Does the site provide more tailored information for different kinds of visitors (for example, graduates versus more experienced candidates)?

>> Is information provided on the different functions and roles offered by the organization (for example, sales versus research and development versus operational support)?

>> Does the site provide personal profiles of current employees?

>> Is good use made of imagery to break up the text and make the site more visually attractive?

>> Does the site include any video content — such as a company overview, personal profiles, or inside stories — to help dramatize the offer?

>> Does the site feature a user-friendly application process?

## Visiting your competitors' social media and video sites

Companies commonly supplement their main career sites with career-specific areas on LinkedIn, Facebook, Twitter, Instagram, and YouTube. In Chapter 11, we provide guidance on how to reinforce your employer brand on these and other social media and video sites. For now, use the following checklist of best practices to compare your current social footprint with that of your leading talent competitors:

>> Which social media and platforms and video sites are your competitors represented on, and on which of these do they feature career specific content?

>> Do their social and video sites feature a consistent visual brand identity?

>> Do their home pages feature consistent employer brand messaging?

>> Do these social properties maintain a reasonably steady flow of fresh, relevant content? (If the most recent content posted is more than six months old, the answer is no.)

>> Does the posted content represent a reasonable variety, not just job advertisements?

In addition to checking the type of content being posted on these sites, check out relative levels of engagement (likes, comments, shares, and followers, or the relevant platform equivalents). To gauge the relative impact of their content, weight the results to reflect the number of employees in each organization. For example, a company with a ratio of 40,000 LinkedIn followers to 10,000 employees is performing far better than a company with 50,000 followers to 100,000 employees.

## Mapping your competitors' brand positioning

In addition to assessing where and how your competitors are communicating their employer brand, you should also assess what their key messages are. In brand speak, this is described as *positioning* — how companies position themselves in the minds of potential recruits. Here's an excellent approach to mapping your competitors' brand positioning:

1. **List the taglines and headlines featured across each competitor's main career site pages (home page, "Why join?" page, or equivalent, and so forth), social home pages, and any recruitment campaign materials you can get your hands on through a Google search.**

2. **Mark which of the following positioning categories these messages fall into (some messages may fall into more than one category):**

   - *Purpose:* Company mission, customer value, social responsibility

   - *Teamwork:* Team spirit, friendliness, diversity, inclusion

   - *Empowerment:* Autonomy, making a difference, flexible working arrangements

- *Innovation:* Scope for fresh ideas, entrepreneurialism, creativity
- *Learning:* Training and development, supportive managers, expertise
- *Career:* Advancement opportunities, leadership opportunities, job mobility
- *Performance:* Results orientation, quality focus, commitment to excellence
- *Status:* Global scale, market success, attractive products and services

3. **Complete the following position grid by writing the number of messages that fall into each category for each of your competitors.**

| Positioning category | Company A | Company B | Company C |
| --- | --- | --- | --- |
| Purpose | | | |
| Teamwork | | | |
| Empowerment | | | |
| Innovation | | | |
| Learning | | | |
| Career | | | |
| Performance | | | |
| Status | | | |

4. **Highlight the primary positioning category for each employer — the key message each employer highlights above all others.**

   This may be the employer's core tagline (if it has one), the main headline on its career home page, or simply the predominant impression you get from reading its career-related copy.

# Spotting generic plays and opportunities to be different

Spotting generic plays and opportunities to be different involves identifying common patterns of communication — words, phrases, and images that crop up with noticeable frequency across your competitive set. Patterns tend to be particularly obvious within industries where companies often reach the same "route one" conclusions about what will attract target talent, with noticeable examples of companies that stand out from the crowd.

## Spotting similarities across your industry

The first place to start is spotting similar headlines. For example, global companies, particularly financial institutions, have made frequent use of the phrase *world of opportunities*. Over the course of the last five years, we've noted more than 30 leading global companies using this very same headline, making it possibly the most generic employer brand headline of all. Among tech companies with a more missionary zeal to change the world, a similarly common headline is *making a difference* or *making an impact*. Likewise, pharmaceutical companies commonly use the phrase *improving lives*.

Another approach is to pay attention to the underlying narrative structure of the brand promise, where the words used may be slightly different but the overall pattern is very similar. For example, a recent analysis of how major engineering employers in the oil, gas, and automotive industries described their employment offer revealed the following generic pattern.

| Image attribute | Examples |
|---|---|
| Committed people | **Shell:** Talent and tenacity <br><br> **ExxonMobil:** Exceptional people <br><br> **Chevron:** People with the drive to keep moving <br><br> **GE:** Dedicated people <br><br> **Rolls-Royce:** Committed to delivering <br><br> **BMW:** Passionate people |
| Creating innovation solutions | **Shell:** More innovative solutions <br><br> **ExxonMobil:** Take initiative and be innovative <br><br> **Conoco Phillips:** Innovation and excellence <br><br> **GE:** Dedicated to innovation <br><br> **Rolls-Royce:** Relentless innovation <br><br> **BMW:** Innovative ideas |
| Taking on big challenges | **Chevron:** Our team has the technology to take on big challenges <br><br> **Schlumberger:** Addressing the most challenging engineering problems on the earth <br><br> **GE:** Taking on the world's toughest challenges |
| Shaping the future | **Shell:** Shaping the future of energy <br><br> **Chevron:** Laying the groundwork for decades of progress <br><br> **E.ON:** Your energy shapes our future <br><br> **BMW:** There's no need to predict the future. You can create it. |
| Realizing their potential | **ExxonMobil:** Unlocking your potential <br><br> **Conoco Phillips:** Realize your full potential <br><br> **EDF:** Fulfill your potential |

Although these employment pitches are not necessarily weak in isolation, they represent opportunities for other companies to stand out from the crowd by deploying more distinctive and unique phrases and patterns of communication.

TIP

As you identify similarities among your talent competitors, look for opportunities to be more distinctive in addition to identifying attractive attributes that may be missing from your competitors' employer brand marketing.

## Analyzing competitors' visual positioning

Alongside your analysis of how your competitors present their EVP and tell their story, take a look at how they present themselves visually. We've found that most markets follow very similar visual codes, as in the following examples:

>> **Global financial services:** For many years, global banks have illustrated their career pages with a very similar visual. It presents a diverse group of people (generally four) representing both genders, a mix of ages (though tending toward the young), and a number of ethnic backgrounds. The people are relaxed and smiling at each other. They're dressed in what the British call "smart casual," which for the men means smart white shirts but no ties. They look like they're friends hanging out together rather than doing any serious work, except they're not in a coffee shop. They're usually pictured against a large glass window, with a clear view of sky and a hint of corporate status and ambition.

>> **High-tech companies:** This presents a far more chilled-out version of the financial visual code. The typical visual contains the same gender and ethnic mix, but the people are all young. No suits. More casual than smart casual, but definitely smart looking, super bright, and funky. These people tend to be smiling at each other rather than at the camera. The setting looks more like a trendy bar or social club than an office.

>> **Pharmaceutical companies:** Companies in this sector also put the emphasis on people, but more on the people outside the work setting — consumers rather than employees. The core message is health and vitality. You see people running on the beach, mountain biking, or simply playing with their children.

>> **Engineering companies:** This one doesn't take long to guess. The key image is men in hard hats standing in front of impressive examples of large-scale engineering projects.

These images all make sense in the context of their industry sectors. However, from a communications perspective, they give little indication of the individual character of the organizations they represent. As for the narrative positioning, when you understand the visual codes of the market you're in, you can consciously decide to follow the code or find a way to present your company that stands out from the crowd and highlights what makes you special. In the financial services market, Deutsche Bank decided on a visual presentation that made it a clear outlier from a visual point of view. Instead of the classic "rule of four" diversity team photo, Deutsche Bank's global career page featured bright splashes of color and a row of clothes hooks. This communicated a similar diversity message to many of its global competitors, but in a far more expressive and imaginative way. The employer brand tagline was "agile thinking," and use of this alternative image neatly demonstrated that claim.

WARNING

One note of caution in exploring visual presentation is to bear in mind current levels of familiarity with your employer brand and your existing brand image. If your brand isn't particularly well known, you may need to stick closer to the standard (expected) visual codes in the marketplace to establish what marketers refer to as your *category membership*.

# 2

# Developing an Effective Employer Brand Strategy

Chapter **4**

# Defining Your Employer Value Proposition

An *employer value proposition* (EVP) defines the qualities you'd most like to be associated with as an employer. It provides current and future employees with clear reasons to choose and stay with an employer. It conveys what employees can expect from an employer and what is expected of them in return. Employers that manage their EVPs effectively attract more people to their potential talent pool and enjoy higher levels of employee engagement and retention.

Effective customer and consumer brands are founded on a *proposition* that defines the key benefits customers and consumers will derive from their relationship with the brand. The EVP helps to provide a similarly consistent point of reference for everything you say and do to promote a positive employer brand reputation and experience.

In this chapter, we describe how effective EVPs are structured and step you through the process of developing an effective EVP for your organization.

**REMEMBER**

Strong brands are founded on positive associations built through consistent and persistent brand communication and experience. To build a strong brand, you must be crystal clear about what your brand stands for and the benefits your brand promises and delivers.

# Setting Your Sights on the Goal: A Sample Employer Value Proposition

EVPs appear in a number of different formats, and the language used to describe the different parts of the proposition varies. However, the EVP format most commonly favored by leading employers comprises a clear and concise brand statement supported by three to five supporting qualities, often referred to as *pillars* (see Figure 4-1). The brand statement serves as an umbrella, summarizing the overall employment deal or focusing on one predominant aspect of the employment deal. This statement conveys the brand essence or *core positioning* — the one thing you most want to be famous for as an employer. The pillars support and delineate the brand statement or employment deal.

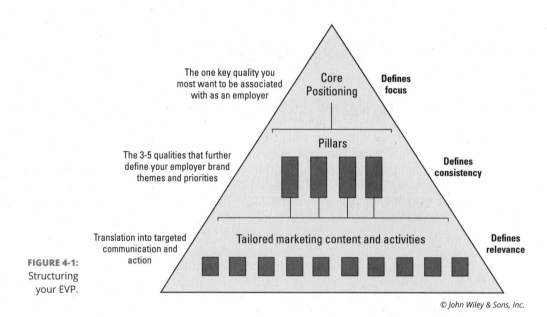

The one key quality you most want to be associated with as an employer

Core Positioning

**Defines focus**

Pillars

The 3-5 qualities that further define your employer brand themes and priorities

**Defines consistency**

Translation into targeted communication and action

Tailored marketing content and activities

**Defines relevance**

**FIGURE 4-1:** Structuring your EVP.

© *John Wiley & Sons, Inc.*

For example, the EVP for Adidas is defined as follows:

**Brand essence/core positioning:** Shape the future of sport

**Pillars:**

1. **Through sport, we have the power to change lives:**

   Sport matters. It gets people off the couch and into the gym. It fights disease, deepens friendships, and improves lives. It strengthens muscles, increases self-confidence, and teaches lessons that last a lifetime. Through sport, we have the power to change lives.

2. **The future runs on diverse and fresh perspectives:**

   Adi Dassler looked at factory workers and saw athletes. He picked up army surplus canvas and saw track spikes. It's the people who see the world a little differently than the rest who create the breakthroughs that inspire us all. The more diverse perspectives and life experiences we support and encourage, the more often those breakthroughs will happen. At adidas Group, we seek people with different perspectives and life experiences and allow them to bring their true self to work every day. This isn't just a nicety. It's a business necessity.

3. **Careers without borders:**

   Exposing your talents to as many different cultures, languages, life experiences, and points of view as possible is the fastest way to grow.

4. **Pioneering the future of work:**

   Imagination, teamwork, and the courage to share your ideas all need the right environment to thrive. Which is why we're focused on being at the epicenter of global culture and pioneering a future workplace that facilitates faster decision-making, creative solutions, and more opportunities for spontaneous collaboration.

5. **Sport needs a space:**

   Sport needs a healthier, stronger, more sustainable, and more socially responsible world. Changing the way an industry does business isn't quick or easy. It's a marathon, not a sprint. Which is why we've made this a core priority for the entire adidas Group.

6. **Collaborating with those that inspire us:**

   We invite anyone and everyone whose curiosity and creativity inspires us to be part of our brands. We open our doors to collaborators from all walks of life, open our ears to their points of view, and are generous with our own insights and experience, so that we can all co-create the future together.

Likewise, the EVP for SUEZ reads as follows:

**Brand essence/core positioning:** Join the resource revolution

**Pillars:**

1. By working at SUEZ, you can contribute to the sustainable development of our societies. By working at SUEZ, you can contribute to the resource revolution.

2. By working at SUEZ, you will help to create new jobs for the future, ensuring the transition from a linear economy (extract, build, consume, throw away) to a circular economy (save, reuse, recycle).

3. By working at SUEZ, you will benefit from working closely with others to solve major resources challenges.

4. By working at SUEZ, you can have a career that is full of variety.

5. Working at SUEZ means joining a group of dedicated people who are encouraged to be themselves in a safe, caring, and respectful environment.

# Brainstorming to Generate Ideas and Content

Prior to writing your EVP, brainstorm with individuals from a wide range of locations and departments within your organization to gather information, insights, ideas, and content that will drive EVP development in the right direction. In the following sections, we offer guidance on how to select the right people and how to conduct productive EVP development workshops.

REMEMBER

EVP development generally works best as a collective exercise for two key reasons:

>> Strong EVPs need to balance a number of different perspectives, which you can do more effectively with a diverse range of people than from a narrow functional perspective, such as human resources (HR) or marketing.

>> The ultimate success of employer branding relies on the understanding and commitment of a wide range of different stakeholders. Because brand development is something that few people outside the marketing department may have been involved in, it's very beneficial for key stakeholders from a number of different functions and positions to be directly involved in creating the EVP. Involving stakeholders helps them reach a far better understanding of the employer brand development process, and, as co-creators of the EVP, they're far more likely to champion the end result.

## SANTANDER, PEPSICO, AND LAFARGE

Santander's recent global EVP development project was jointly led by managers from three of the countries within the group: Spain, Brazil, and Argentina. This collaboration reflected both the importance of these markets in terms of employee numbers and the leadership each of these respective countries had already demonstrated in people management and communication.

PepsiCo chose to run EVP development workshops in several key regions and then consolidate its findings in a global workshop. It ran a workshop in Asia with participants from its key emerging markets — India, China, and Russia; a workshop in London, bringing together a number of its key European managers; and a workshop in the United States to pull everything together.

Lafarge, the French building materials giant, adopted a similar approach, conducting workshops in its key emerging markets of China, India, and Egypt before running a final global workshop in Paris with representation from a much wider range of markets.

## Gathering the right people

Invite representatives from key stakeholder groups to participate in an EVP development workshop, including representatives from HR, talent management and resourcing, marketing and communications, and where possible, line management. For global EVPs, include representatives from various regions to ensure global relevance and local management acceptance. Another option for global organizations is to conduct a workshop for each region and then bring all the findings together in a final global EVP development workshop.

## Drawing insights from your data

Developing a strong EVP is partly a creative exercise informed by fresh ideas, but it should also be based on the kind of solid research presented in Chapter 2. After you've collected your data, identify the key insights and translate them into a format that's easy for other people in your organization to digest. The following outline is useful for performing this high-level review:

### Employer brand objectives

- What are we trying to achieve?
- What are the corporate brand parameters that we need to work within?
- What are our priorities (attraction, engagement, retention, and so on)?

### Organization capability needs

- What key capabilities does the organization need to reinforce and build?

- What other aspirations does leadership have for our employer brand?

### Key target audiences

- Whom do we most need our employer brand to appeal to?

- How much variation do we need to account for among our target groups?

### Current external reputation

- How familiar are people with our organization?

- How are we currently seen in terms of image and reputation?

- How accurate are these perceptions?

- What is our relative position to key talent competitors?

- How, if at all, are we perceived to be different?

### Current employee experience

- What are our current levels of employee engagement and advocacy?

- How are we rated as an employer by our current employees?

- How do our scores compare with relevant industry and high-performance benchmarks?

- How much variation is there between different parts of the business?

### Attraction and engagement drivers

- What most attracts our target audience to a new employer?

- What are the key factors driving employee engagement and retention?

Answers to these questions enable you to formulate your *insight platform* — a summary of the data analysis you conducted and deem relevant to EVP development. Your insight platform provides everyone involved in the EVP development process with the information and insights needed to stimulate his or her own thinking and creativity.

# Conducting a productive employer value proposition development workshop

**TIP**

Conduct your EVP development workshops as brainstorming sessions, exploring the research findings, gathering insights, and generating potential ingredients to include in your EVP. Set a goal of reaching an 80 percent solution rather than a complete and final conclusion to leave room for creative modifications and to give decision makers some flexibility in making final choices. Ideally, by the end of the workshop, you should have the following:

» A short list of potential EVP ingredients supported by key insights (see the later section "Brainstorming employer value proposition ingredients")

» The give and the get of the employment deal — what your organization promises to deliver and expects in return from its employees (see the later section "Clarifying the give and get of the employment deal")

» Key areas of current strength and future stretch (see the later section "Weighing current strengths and future aspirations")

» Similarities and differences between your organization and your leading talent competitors in terms of what you offer to and expect from employees (see the later section "Differentiating Your Organization from the Competition")

» Your desired brand personality (see the later section "Defining your brand personality")

» A number of potential core positioning options (see the later section "Choosing Your Core Positioning")

Here, we provide guidance on how to conduct a productive EVP development workshop.

**TIP**

Don't drown participants in data. Make the information you're presenting accessible and encourage engagement and creativity. Here are a few suggestions for conducting a successful EVP development workshop:

» Highlight the key insights and challenges and make your presentation as visual as possible.

» Provide rich descriptions of your typical target talent groups to bring them to life. (See Chapter 2 for more about identifying the right talent for your organization.)

» Cite quotations from the research to illustrate key points.

» Show how your competitors advertise themselves.

- » Ask participants to share their stories and personal perspectives.

- » Alternate the presentation of data with exercises and discussions to ensure participants have an opportunity to ask questions and digest what's been presented.

- » Make sure people are jotting down thoughts and ideas.

If you're doing it right, your EVP development workshop should take the "work" out of "workshop."

## Delivering your employer brand briefing

Before you launch into your brainstorming session, deliver an employer brand briefing to make sure everyone is on the same page. Your employer brand briefing should touch on the following items:

- » **The reason why:** The challenges you're seeking to address and the ultimate benefits you're seeking to deliver to the business through defining your EVP and strengthening your employer brand

- » **Terminology:** Definitions of key terms and distinctions between key concepts — for example, the difference between an *employer brand* (reputation or how you're perceived) and the EVP (your promise to employees or how you want to be perceived), as well as core positioning EVP and pillars

- » **Clarity on the brand hierarchy:** An explanation, preferably accompanied by one or more illustrations, to show the relationship between the corporate, customer, and employer brand and, if relevant, between the global and local employer brands

- » **Employer brand implementation:** The scope of likely activity required after the EVP has been defined, including creative development, validation, internal and external communication, and internal initiatives potentially required to deliver on the promise

**REMEMBER**

You can deliver much of this material in advance, as a pre-briefing, but a top-line run through near the beginning of the workshop is useful to make sure everyone is on the same page and to give participants the opportunity to ask questions and have any of their concerns or reservations addressed.

## Presenting the insight platform

After delivering your employer brand briefing, present the insight platform you created earlier in the section "Drawing insights from your data." The insight platform typically includes the following:

>> The business context, including desired capabilities and ultimate performance objectives

>> The core target profile and key talent segments to be considered

>> External reputation and attraction drivers, including key perception gaps

>> Employee engagement and retention drivers, including external benchmarks

>> Competitive analysis

TIP

Keep an open mind. Pause for questions and comments during your presentation of the insight platform to give participants a chance to ask questions and share their insights. Participants may have different and valuable perspectives that may require adjustments to the insight platform. Collaboration is key at this point, because subsequent workshop activities rely on the accuracy of the insight platform.

## Brainstorming employer value proposition ingredients

EVP ingredients are the key qualities that make your organization an attractive place to work. One of your goals for the workshop is to identify a range of potential ingredients to inform and inspire your final EVP. To structure this exercise, consider providing a framework into which the ingredients can be posted, like those highlighted in the positioning wheel in Figure 4-2, which divides Universum's employer brand attribute framework into nine common positioning "territories." The value of this framework is that it encourages people to think beyond the more obviously generic categories like purpose, innovation, and career progression to consider the more specific ingredients that will differentiate an EVP from others. The attributes presented here are designed to provide a starting point, not a definitive list of your potential options.

## Paring down employer value proposition ingredients to a short list

Like most brainstorming sessions, the EVP development workshop is likely to provide you with far more ingredients than necessary or reasonable to include in your EVP. Spend some time during the workshop prioritizing items on the list. In the later section "Balancing Competing Perspectives," we present a few methods that will help you pare down to a short list of final ingredients.

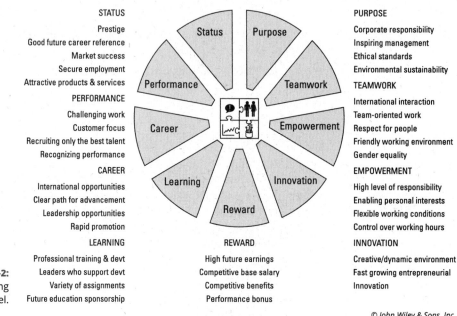

STATUS
Prestige
Good future career reference
Market success
Secure employment
Attractive products & services

PERFORMANCE
Challenging work
Customer focus
Recruiting only the best talent
Recognizing performance

CAREER
International opportunities
Clear path for advancement
Leadership opportunities
Rapid promotion

LEARNING
Professional training & devt
Leaders who support devt
Variety of assignments
Future education sponsorship

REWARD
High future earnings
Competitive base salary
Competitive benefits
Performance bonus

PURPOSE
Corporate responsibility
Inspiring management
Ethical standards
Environmental sustainability

TEAMWORK
International interaction
Team-oriented work
Respect for people
Friendly working environment
Gender equality

EMPOWERMENT
High level of responsibility
Enabling personal interests
Flexible working conditions
Control over working hours

INNOVATION
Creative/dynamic environment
Fast growing entrepreneurial
Innovation

**FIGURE 4-2:**
The positioning
wheel.

© John Wiley & Sons, Inc.

## Defining your brand personality

Your *brand personality* embodies the human characteristics or traits you'd like to be attributed to your brand. The EVP ingredients or pillars determine *what* you want to communicate, and the brand personality determines *how* it is communicated. Brand personality in the corporate context is sometimes geared to what investors and regulators may be looking for in a brand — competence rather than excitement. If this is the case with your organization, you may need to mix in a little more emotion to ensure that the organization doesn't come across as too corporate or stuffy, particularly among millennial talent. Jennifer Aaker's brand personality map (see Figure 4-3) serves as a useful starting point to stimulate discussion.

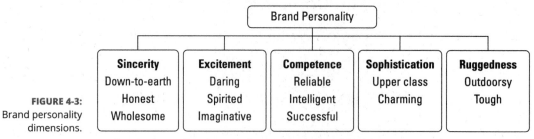

**FIGURE 4-3:**
Brand personality
dimensions.

Illustration courtesy of Jennifer L. Aaker (from "Dimensions of Brand Personality," https://faculty-gsb.stanford.edu/aaker/PDF/Dimensions_of_Brand_Personality.pdf)

# Balancing Competing Perspectives

When developing your organization's EVP, keep in mind that it must address competing perspectives or needs, such as the needs of the employer versus those of the employee, what your organization offers now as compared to what it hopes to offer in the future, and how your EVP is likely to play to different audiences (for example, how well your global EVP will appeal to a local workforce or how effective it will be for staffing specific departments).

In the following sections, we describe key competing perspectives to consider and provide guidance on how to balance these perspectives.

## Clarifying the give and get of the employment deal

The most effective EVPs clarify the *give and get* of the employment deal — what the employer promises and delivers to the employee and what the employer expects in return. Clarifying the give and get of the employment deal helps to ground the EVP in the reality of the business and working experience. If the priority for the organization is quality, customer focus, or enterprise-wide collaboration, for example, then reflecting these desired capabilities in the EVP mix is as important as addressing the perceived needs and aspirations of potential candidates.

**TIP**

Approach this particular balancing challenge as a mix-and-match exercise. Create a two-column table with the "gives" in one column and the "gets" in the other. Here's an example followed by an explanation of why each item appears in the column it does:

| Gives | Gets |
| --- | --- |
| Work-life balance | Engagement and retention |
| Enabling people to perform at their best | High performance |
| Empowerment | Initiative, innovation, and accountability |

Here's why each item appears in the column it does:

>> Work-life balance tends to be more "give" than "get" from an organizational perspective. It should be seen as an important means of achieving more sustainable levels of performance, but in practice it's often deemed a necessary cost to engage and retain employees.

>> High performance tends to be more "get" than "give" as it rarely appears among leading employee attraction and engagement drivers. However, it can be a prominent feature within the employment deal. The balancing benefit from the employer should be giving employees the support they need to perform at their best.

>> Empowerment tends to be a more evenly balanced deal. The organization gives the employee greater scope for personal initiative (which most employees regard as an attractive benefit), while expecting employees (in return) to take more personal accountability for delivering on their objectives.

TIP

When striking the balance between give and get, consider adjusting the balance based on workforce supply and demand. Where the supply of talent exceeds demand, as it often does during an economic downturn, you can afford to up-weight the "get" side of the deal. On the other hand, if the demand for talent outstrips the supply, you'll need to up-weight what your organization is willing to give to attract and retain personnel.

## Weighing current strengths and future aspirations

When developing your EVP, combine credible here-and-now strengths solidly grounded in the current employment experience with more future focused stretch aspirations underpinned by tangible leadership commitments and planned investment. Playing to current strengths builds credibility and trust, which provides the essential underpinning to any brand. Playing to future aspirations builds vitality, which is also critical in maintaining a brand's forward momentum and competitive edge. Stretch areas tend to include those aspects of the employment deal that require significant investment from employers to meet employee expectations, such as training and development, career progression, and flexible working.

If your company is investing in a significant program of organizational transformation, then you can probably afford to put more weight on the stretch side of your EVP (as long as these aspirations align with the direction of change). If the commitment to change is weak, focus more on current strengths, including only a select few stretch elements that you feel can be delivered without expending significant resources. Likewise, if the desire for change is strong but the change will take a long time to implement, then plan to add stretch to your EVP as you make progress rather than overload your EVP with too much aspiration.

WARNING

Don't rely solely on current strengths. Aspire to deliver a better experience to current and future employees. Adidas recently suggested that "an EVP should be uncovered not created," but few organizations can afford to simply celebrate existing strengths. For most organizations, the EVP is a future focused statement of intent, grounded in a robust leadership commitment to build on existing strengths.

# CASE STUDY: A DRINKS COMPANY

When a leading drinks company developed its first company-wide EVP a number of years ago, it recognized that two elements within the proposition — teamwork and empowerment — were credibly strong, but the opportunity for employees to develop within the company was weak. To address this existing weakness, the company decided to incorporate a promise to improve into the EVP, because it recognized how critical employee development was to attracting the right candidates, engaging current employees, and optimizing future business performance. When this EVP was recommended to the board, it came with a qualification: Development should be included in the proposition only if the company would make a step-change in investment; otherwise, the promise would be seen as nothing but wishful thinking and undermine, rather than build, the brand.

The leadership team made the commitment. The company began to invest more consistently in front-line training across the 27 countries in which it was then operating, established clearer career paths, and improved talent mobility. The reward was a 9 percent increase in development-related employee favorability scores over the following two years, a similarly high 9 percent increase in employee advocacy, and a top-ten place in Great Place to Work's European-wide rankings. This external recognition came with a special prize for "employee development and progress."

# Balancing global and local considerations

To build an effective EVP and messaging platform, balance global consistency with local relevance. *Global* means expressing and delivering elements within your proposition consistently throughout your organization. *Local* may refer to a country or a region, a division within the company, a business unit, a specific target group, or a job function. To maintain brand integrity, your core EVP pillars should work everywhere, but they may be expressed or delivered in a slightly different way at the local level.

You can accomplish EVP localization in the following three ways:

>> **Choose which of the EVP pillars you're going to play up and play down at the local level.** The EVP can be thought of as a brand "chord," with each pillar representing a separate note that can be played louder or softer, and more or less frequently, depending on its local importance. For example, if your EVP incorporates both empowerment and development, your local research and experience may indicate which of these two elements is stronger or more attractive within the local context, in which case you should make this element more prominent in your local communication mix.

>> **Increase local representation by incorporating local faces, locations, and stories in communications.** Even if your core message is *Global Opportunities,* showing someone local in an international context is better than simply falling back on standard global imagery or photos of your head office.

>> **Supplement your global EVP themes with additional ingredients that you know to be particularly important to local target groups.** For example, a leading energy company found that "flexible working conditions" were of very low importance to the majority of employees in its conventional nuclear- and carbon-generated power plants, and it was not included within the company's global EVP. However, within the company's renewable energy division, where the average age was at least 15 years younger than the rest of the company, and the working patterns very different, flexibility was one of the most important elements within the employment deal; as a result, it was included within a localized adaptation of the EVP.

**REMEMBER**

Deciding on the right balance between global consistency and local tailoring largely depends on your starting position. If you're starting with an unmanaged mess where everyone is doing his or her own thing and the general level of employer brand understanding at the local level is limited, emphasize global consistency. This approach makes your new employer branding easier to understand, easier to police, and more likely to succeed in establishing more disciplined brand management processes and habits. If reasonably consistent employer brand management processes already exist in recruitment and HR, and the local level of understanding and application is reasonably high, then you can probably afford to provide more freedom within your overall brand framework to adapt, experiment, and tune the global employer brand to ensure maximum relevance and engagement at the local level.

# Differentiating Your Organization from the Competition

For many years, the number-one objective of most employer brand development projects was consistency. At the time, fragmented regional and local recruitment communication had failed to build marketing synergy and brand equity. The game has moved on, and the more pressing challenge for those who have now achieved sufficient employer brand consistency is *differentiation* — setting your organization apart from your competitors. This requires more creativity, more courage, and more stakeholder management to ensure everyone feels comfortable with a more distinctive and potentially disruptive EVP and employer brand.

As stated earlier in the chapter, nine dominant themes tend to crop up in most employer brand propositions: status, purpose, teamwork, empowerment, innovation, learning, career progression, performance, and reward. The problem is that many employers don't think beyond the most generic description of these positioning territories. Consequently, many global career sites use the same headline phrase *World of Opportunities*. It's also why so many employers are "Shaping the Future," "Winning Together," "Making a Difference," or "Realizing People's Potential."

To differentiate your EVP, think beyond the general territory you're occupying and identify the distinctive way in which you deliver this characteristic. Take innovation, for example. Ironically, many companies describe themselves as innovative in a very similar way. *Innovation is in our DNA* has recently become a common phrase. However, the truly innovative companies tend to go a step further and describe their approach to innovation in more unique terms. Disney, IKEA, and Facebook all position themselves as innovative places to work, but each has found its own distinctive way of expressing this quality. Disney describes its approach to innovation as "Imagineering," IKEA defines its brand of innovation in terms of "democratic design," and Facebook talks about driving innovation through "moving fast and breaking things." These slogans are not simply creative turns of phrase; they're deeply rooted in each company's ethos (character) and way of working.

**WARNING**

Never settle for sameness. Be bold. Dare to be different, and talent will beat a path to your door. To make your employer brand stand out from the crowd, dig deep into the distinctive qualities that make your company special. And if you can't find any qualities that differentiate your organization from your competitors, work harder to establish the points of difference that every company requires to compete effectively both for talent and for business.

# Choosing Your Core Positioning

The purpose of *core positioning* is to highlight one overall characteristic that you most want people to associate with your organization as an employer. This single-mindedness is valuable from a brand communication perspective. Establishing one major brand association in everyone's mind is generally easier than establishing many smaller ones. You can still communicate a range of different messages to different target audiences, but try to incorporate these more specific and localized messages into one overall theme that provides a more consistent global umbrella.

Start with your corporate brand. If the corporate positioning translates well into the employment space, maintaining the same positioning in your employer brand marketing makes a lot of sense. For example, for many years the heart of

Microsoft's corporate brand was the core purpose: "To help people and businesses throughout the world realize their full potential." This core positioning also worked well from the perspective of its employer brand positioning. Note, however, that you're not locked into a single statement. Microsoft used a number of different campaign headlines to convey its core positioning. On Microsoft's career sites it used the line "Come as you are, do what you love," which sums up the message that whatever experiences, skills, and passions you bring to the company, you can take them further with the resources of Microsoft behind you. In a recent UK graduate campaign, Microsoft conveyed a similar notion through the line "What makes you, makes Microsoft." Other good examples include GE's "Imagination at Work," EY's "Building a Better Working World," Ericsson's "Taking You Forwards," and Grant Thornton's "An Instinct for Growth."

Alternatively, you may find that your corporate positioning provides a good starting point, but you need to refine and sharpen the positioning to make it more relevant and compelling to current and potential employees. Deutsche Bank provides a good example of this approach. The corporate positioning, "Passion to Perform" clearly set the tone for the employer brand, but the core positioning the bank chose for the employer brand was "Agile Minds," delivering a more specific message about *how* Deutsche Bank performs — through the mental agility and quick thinking of its people. P&G's longstanding employer brand focus on serving up a rich flow of stimulating challenges ("A New Challenge Everyday") played a similar role in bringing greater personal relevance to P&G's overall corporate positioning, "Touching Lives, Improving Life."

You may also decide that a core positioning is unnecessary. Some companies, such as McDonald's, attribute their EVP to a number of equally weighted pillars, without highlighting one overall characteristic. This approach provides their operations in different countries more flexibility in choosing how to position themselves in local markets, which fits the devolved and franchised nature of the business.

**TIP**

Given your organizational context, your approach to core positioning may be pretty clear. If it's not, then short-list a number of potential options and test them alongside the EVP pillars among your target audiences, as explained next, before making a final decision.

# Writing Your Employer Value Proposition

Many people should be involved in identifying the right ingredients for your EVP, but the task of writing a compelling proposition is likely to be better performed by an individual, or a Lennon and McCartney duo, than a management committee. It's important to recognize that your EVP is primarily designed to provide a clear foundation for the employment deal and credible marketing communication. For this reason, clarity should take precedence over creative expression. If there's more sizzle than steak — it sounds good but lacks substance — then it's not going to provide a very effective employer brand platform. On the other hand, an EVP description seldom works effectively as a plain list of factual claims. If your EVP is too dry to convey the spirit of the organization, it's equally unlikely to inspire. You need to transform what makes sense from a rational point of view into what feels right — something that captures the essence and not just the dimensions of the employment offer.

After compiling your EVP findings, pass them along to your creatives — your Lennon and McCartney duo — to see what they can come up with. Be prepared to kick your EVP back and forth several times between your creatives and your critics to produce a satisfactory draft. With draft in hand, you're prepared to move on to the next step: testing.

# Sense Checking and Stress Testing

You may be able to conduct an initial assessment of the relative strength and stretch of your core positioning and EVP pillars, but you should conduct a more rigorous evaluation after you've established a short list. Your employee survey data may have helped you to identify what employees feel is most positive about the employment experience and what most needs to be improved, but this kind of data seldom provides the tangible proof points you may need to underline your claims externally. As a secondary stress-test exercise it's important to list the facts and figures necessary to clarify and support your pillars.

In the following sections, we explain how to evaluate your core positioning and EVP pillars by identifying tangible claims and proof points and by testing your EVP with local target groups.

## Identifying tangible claims and proof points

Developing a pie-in-the-sky EVP to attract talent without paying due care and attention to your organization's ability to deliver on your promises is seldom a good idea. False promises destroy credibility and trust and undermine your employer brand. Prior to finalizing your EVP, clarify your claims and put some facts and figures behind them. We suggest you do this in two steps, as follows:

1. **Translate your draft pillar description into a series of more specific claims.**
2. **Test whether the evidence/facts support these claims.**

For example, if one of your potential pillars focuses on "a strong sense of community" within your organization, break it down, as follows, into specific claims and then subject each claim to a series of proof-point test questions:

When we say we offer a "strong sense of community" we mean:

**Claim 1:** We are a closely interconnected global company where you're likely to work alongside people from many different parts of the world.

**Proof-point test questions:**

- What's the average diversity by country of origin across our business units?

- What proportion of our employee population have worked in, visited, or communicated with business units outside their home country?

**Claim 2:** We encourage people to develop a wide personal network within the organization.

**Proof-point test questions:**

- What's the average number of LinkedIn and Facebook connections people have with other employees in the company?

- What proportion of these connections is outside the employees' immediate business unit?

**Claim 3:** We are a relatively informal company with an open and accessible approach to management.

**Proof-point test questions:**

- What proportion of managers sit in an open office environment?

- How often do front-line employees get an opportunity to ask questions directly to members of the leadership team?

**REMEMBER**

You can find the answers to some of these questions by analyzing existing data, but you may need to conduct additional research to answer others. What's important is that the answers are based on tangible evidence and not wishful thinking, policy statements (which may or may not reflect reality), or isolated examples (which may or may not reflect common experience).

## Field-testing your draft employer value proposition

In addition to establishing whether the facts exist to support your EVP claims and promises, check the credibility and appeal of the EVP with your key target groups before you finalize your employer brand platform. In this section, we offer guidance on how to field-test the EVP you've drafted.

## Knowing what you're looking for: Appeal and credibility

The aim of field-testing your draft EVP is to discover the following:

>> How attractive/compelling people find each EVP pillar (and core positioning option)

>> The perceived relevance/importance of each EVP pillar to each target group

>> How credible these pillars would be in describing the current employment experience (both every day and in relation to the company at its best)

>> What more needs to be done for the EVP to credibly describe the organization

>> What, if anything, people feel is missing from the proposition

## Assembling target groups

The three key groups we suggest you conduct this research with are

>> **Current employees:** Surveying current employees is the least expensive and most convenient option. Conduct focus groups with a range of your most important talent segments, separating out each target group so you're clearer about any significant differences that may exist in terms of their needs and perceptions.

>> **Local functional teams and key stakeholders:** In addition to checking out the EVP with employees, consult and elicit feedback from local functional teams, including HR, marketing, and communications, and from key senior stakeholders. Involving functional teams and key stakeholders helps to win the engagement and support of these key players in addition to obtaining their insights and resources for fine-tuning your EVP.

>> **Prospective candidates:** Using focus groups to check your EVP externally tends to be very expensive (you may need to pay handsome incentives to get the right people to participate). The alternative is to run an online survey using a variety of sources to identify and attract the right participants; for example, existing contacts from your Applicant Tracking System (ATS), search agency contacts, LinkedIn invites, and employee referrals. The last option requires a greater communication effort but is generally the most cost-efficient and

effective if your ATS falls short. You can ask the same appeal and credibility questions as you would with managers and employees, but it generally pays to mask the name of your company when checking out the appeal of different attributes and describe the kind of business you're in when checking credibility.

## Identifying reasons to believe

**TIP**

As you conduct target group sessions, try to collect additional *proof points* (tangible reasons for employees and candidates to believe the EVP), and gather related stories that may be used to support your future marketing. If EVP attributes appear to reflect people's current experience of the organization, then ask, "Could you give me a specific example of this?" or "How does this work in practice?" Likewise, if the EVP attributes don't appear to reflect current experience, ask, "What would you need to see happening for this to be more credible?"

## Evaluating target group feedback

After you've gathered the data and insights from your consultations and validation exercises, refine your draft EVP to reflect your key findings. This review places you in a strong position to make a final recommendation to your senior team. Outline your rationale for choosing each of the key ingredients of the EVP with supporting evidence from your initial research, EVP development workshop, and field testing. In addition to clarifying the elements within your recommended EVP and pillars that reflect current reality, point out where the claims you wish to make are more aspirational (your wish list) and require the senior team's commitment and support to deliver.

**REMEMBER**

Your research findings will show whether your core positioning and pillars align with what your organization actually delivers. If the results indicate a discrepancy between what's promised and what's delivered, you have two options:

>> Change your EVP to align with the facts.

>> Change the facts to align with your EVP.

You can use your research to support the case for your final EVP, but leadership judgment is also critical. Experience suggests that the more you involve key stakeholders in the decision-making process, the more likely they are to understand, sign off on, and commit to ensuring your recommendations are supported and delivered.

Chapter **5**

# Building Your Employer Brand Framework

A key feature of strong brands is consistency, and it seldom if ever happens naturally. It requires the disciplined application of a clear *brand framework* (guidelines) that typically incorporates your *brand propositions* (defining the core qualities you'd like your brand to be associated with), as well as the core creative ideas and aspects of visual design that serve to inform and frame the way you bring your brand to life through marketing.

**REMEMBER**

Your brand must be reliably constant to build familiarity and trust, but it also must constantly adapt to maintain its relevance and competitive edge. To accomplish this goal, a brand framework generally preserves the core while allowing change around the periphery — closer to where the core meets the stakeholders. At these touch points, the brand must flex to address the unique needs of each stakeholder group.

In this chapter, we describe how to work within the wider corporate brand framework, align with the customer brand (where appropriate), and tailor your recruitment marketing to different target groups without undermining the overall integrity of your employer brand.

# Aligning Your Employer Branding with Your Corporate and Customer Branding

The employer brand forms one branch of the overall brand tree. The trunk of this tree is the corporate brand, which includes those elements (including core values and identity guidelines) that should ideally be reflected in every branch of brand communication (to current and future employees, customers, investors, business partners, and other key stakeholder groups). Likewise, the employer brand defines the core elements that should be reflected in some form across every branch of recruitment marketing and employee communication. This overall framework, branching outward from the corporate center, is often referred to as the *brand hierarchy*. (See Chapter 2 for more about the brand hierarchy and the relationship between brand identity and employer propositions.)

In this section, we explain the key factors to consider when deciding how closely to align your employer brand with your corporate and customer brand. In the process, we introduce you to the three main types of brand framework that you may need to work within.

## Working with a monolithic brand

The *monolithic* or *branded house framework* describes organizations that work with a single overarching brand, such as Amazon, Apple, IBM, and LEGO. The LEGO Group offers up a great example of a branded house framework that is both consistent and adaptive. Although its early branding focused narrowly on LEGO products and customers, the company recognized the value of tailoring the brand to different stakeholder groups. The result was the LEGO brand framework (see Figure 5-1).

In the LEGO Group's case, the Mission, Vision, Spirit, and Values define the core, and the four promises define their tailored propositions to the company's four main stakeholder groups: customers (the Play Promise), partners (the Partner Promise), employees (the People Promise), and community (the Planet Promise).

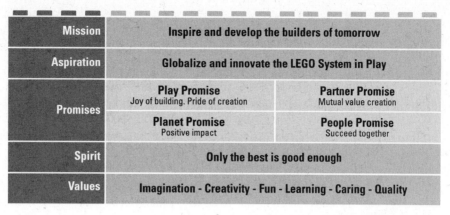

| Mission | Inspire and develop the builders of tomorrow | |
|---|---|---|
| Aspiration | Globalize and innovate the LEGO System in Play | |
| Promises | **Play Promise** Joy of building. Pride of creation | **Partner Promise** Mutual value creation |
| | **Planet Promise** Positive impact | **People Promise** Succeed together |
| Spirit | Only the best is good enough | |
| Values | Imagination - Creativity - Fun - Learning - Caring - Quality | |

**FIGURE 5-1:**
The LEGO brand framework.

Brand Framework 2015

*Reproduced with the permission of the LEGO Group*

In the context of a monolithic brand, which is probably the most common, you need to be particularly aware of the relationship between the employer brand and the customer brand, because the associations built through customer brand marketing and experience are most likely to influence people's expectations of your employer brand. As pointed out in Chapter 3, you must consider the influence of the customer brand and experience when reviewing your current employer brand image. Likewise, your customer brand affects where and how you build bridges between your customer and employer value propositions and marketing strategy. Generally speaking, building bridges wherever possible is to your advantage, but you need to pay attention both to the potential resonance and to the potential dissonance between customer brand benefits and the employment offer:

>> **Potential resonance:** Look for aspects of your customer brand that may be highly relevant to your employer brand. The most obvious aspects tend to be higher-order associations with the following:

- *Purpose:* The value the customer brand brings to individuals and society.

- *Teamwork:* For example, the customer marketing of McDonald's, which focuses on family and friends, translates well into the "family feel" McDonald's promises employees working in its restaurants.

- *Empowerment:* For example, many tech brand promises such as Vodafone's "Power to You" focus on empowering and enabling qualities that translate extremely well to the work context.

- *Innovation:* Because employers place a high value on innovation, building a clear bridge between innovation in the customer brand and the employment offer makes sense, as long as the degree of participation in innovation is sufficient to make it a working reality.

- *Performance:* Customer claims, such as Avis's famous line "We try harder," can set a positive tone and expectation for the employment experience, but this needs to be handled with care, as explained next.

>> **Potential dissonance:** Some customer brand promises don't translate as well into employer brand promises. For example, given the widespread desire of people to achieve some form of work/life balance in their careers, Citibank's previous tagline "Citi never sleeps" may have played very well with customers but not necessarily as well with potential employees.

If you're working within a branded house framework, carefully assess potentially positive overlaps between the employer and customer brand. Also, address any potential conflicts.

# Navigating within a house of brands

An alternative to the branded house framework is the *house of brands framework,* commonly found within consumer goods companies — companies with a single corporate brand but many different product brands. Examples include P&G, Unilever, and Diageo. With the integrated branded house framework, you have one employer brand but a more diverse range of consumer value propositions.

A key objective within the branded house framework is to educate prospective employees on the relationships between the company and its product portfolio. For example, Unilever smells sweeter when prospective candidates realize it owns the leading global brands Axe and Dove. Such communication helps potential candidates to better understand the full reach of the company's footprint and the potential scope of opportunity available.

If your company's name is identical to the name of one of your leading products, as in the case with Bacardi, Ferrero, Pepsico, and the Coca-Cola Company, high levels of product awareness may work both in your favor and against you. Having such a popular product in its line certainly makes the Coca-Cola Company well known to talented individuals around the world. However, the Coca-Cola Company and its similarly named bottling companies are often assumed to sell only Coke, which can appear very limited to potential candidates. In this situation, it's even more important to promote the wider portfolio of brands that the company owns to ensure that potential candidates don't underestimate the full scope and diversity of the company.

# Optimizing the parent-subsidiary house of brands framework

A common variation on the house of brands framework involves a group or parent company acting as an umbrella brand for a number of subsidiaries. In this situation, you may need to consider two levels of employer brand — the group/parent brand and the subsidiary brand, as in the following examples:

| Group/Parent Brand | Subsidiary Brand |
|---|---|
| Intercontinental Hotels Group (IHG) | Holiday Inn |
| PepsiCo | Frito-Lay |
| The Walt Disney Company | ESPN |

The group brand generally sets the parameters within which the subsidiary brands operate. These parameters differ significantly from group to group and vary depending on which end of the spectrum the group operates:

>> **Loose (weak) group brand:** In some holding companies, the relationship between the group and its subsidiaries is purely financial, with very few restrictions on the subsidiary branding or management style. At this end of the spectrum, it makes sense for each subsidiary to develop its own EVP and employer brand to best reflect its organizational style, culture, and customer brand positioning.

>> **Tight (strong) group brand:** At this end of the spectrum the only difference between subsidiaries within the group is the company name, with every other aspect of management consistent across the group. Here it makes sense for the company subsidiaries to operate under one group-level EVP and employer brand identity.

Between these two extremes is a range of possibilities where branding is more a question of balancing the roles of group and subsidiary employer brands. To strike the right balance in this middle ground, place greater emphasis on the group EVP and employer brand identity when

>> The group brand carries significant equity, adding appeal to any subsidiary brand it is attached to — for example, Volkswagen (Group) and Skoda (subsidiary).

>> The primary group-level objective is to leverage synergies and efficiencies of scale.

>> The organization wants to promote shared values and culture across the group.

>> Emphasis is placed on creating a group-wide leadership cadre through a shared leadership development scheme and promotion of career mobility around the group.

>> Overall engagement with the group is more relevant or desirable than maximizing frontline engagement with the product or service brand that the subsidiary delivers.

Shift the emphasis to subsidiary EVPs and employer brand identities when

>> The group brand carries low or negative equity in relation to a subsidiary — for example, Volkswagen group in relation to Bentley and Porsche (subsidiaries).

>> The primary group-level objective is to maximize the distinctive brand personality, autonomy, and agility of its subsidiaries.

>> The group espouses a diverse, multicultural organizational ethos, where each subsidiary is allowed to operate within its own value system within the limits of a basic code of ethics.

>> The organization places a greater emphasis on leadership loyalty and specialism within subsidiary companies than on talent mobility across the group.

>> The group wants subsidiaries to maximize frontline engagement with its product and service brand.

**TIP**

You can also choose to operate a sliding scale of group/subsidiary brand identification, depending on the role and seniority of employees. With this model, the group employer brand operates as a management and shared services brand, with the subsidiary employer brand taking the lead in the process of hiring and engaging frontline employees.

**WARNING**

Don't treat the relationship between the corporate brand and employer brand as a one-way street, with the corporate brand dominating the higher ground and dictating all the moves. Recent research from Edelman suggests that developing a strong employer brand has become a highly critical component in driving the overall corporate brand reputation.

# Creating a Visual Brand Identity with Impact

Both what you say and how you say it (your body language) are important factors in making a strong positive impression on people. In branding, think of your visual brand identity as the body language of your brand. Use the corporate brand identity described in your EVP as the starting point for any decisions relating to how you present your employer brand from a visual perspective. In most leading companies, corporate brand identity guidelines are designed to cover every form of brand communication, but you may find that your existing brand guidelines are more limited. Ideally, your corporate brand identity guidelines should contain guidance for the following visual elements:

>> **Company logo(s):** These guidelines generally cover how and where the company logo is presented within typical digital and print communication formats, including web pages, advertising, brochures, and presentations.

>> **Design elements:** Guidelines for design elements cover graphics other than the logo, such as background texture, line style, white space, and color blocks, that must be consistent in order to reinforce brand recognition.

>> **Color palette and fonts:** These guidelines establish the range of colors and fonts suitable for brand communication.

>> **Photography:** These guidelines may specify a range of acceptable images to be used when communicating the brand or more loosely define a recommended style of photography (with illustrative on-brand and off-brand examples).

The corporate brand guidelines should provide a general set of parameters for your employer brand identity, but it's common practice to adapt the "look and feel" deployed in recruitment marketing and employee communication to the specific needs and preferences of the target audience. This practice tends to follow a regular pattern in the following respects:

>> Corporate branding tends to favor a relative narrow, muted, and conservative range of colors (more generally suited to investors). Employer branding tends to be more effective where a broader, richer, more expressive range of colors is deployed, because it generally suggests a more welcoming, personal (less corporate), and diverse working environment.

>> Corporate branding tends to favor relatively formal design schemes (expressing solidity), whereas the design elements deployed by successful employer brands tend to feature more vibrant and flowing design elements (expressing human energy and creativity).

>> Corporate and customer branding often put greater emphasis on presenting the product and other more tangible manifestations of the company, such as buildings. Employer branding tends to be more effective where it places much greater emphasis on images of people.

In practice, this approach generally results in a separate set of employer brand guidelines carefully balancing alignment with the overall corporate and customer brand guidelines, but also adapted to the more human context of employment.

TIP

Pay close attention to the "look and feel" of your talent competitors' employer brand, so you can consciously choose colors, visual design elements, and photographic styles that clearly help people recognize your brand and differentiate your company from others within the same industry or talent pool. If you're employing a creative agency, be sure an analysis of your talent competitors' branding is incorporated in the creative brief and ask the agency to demonstrate how its creative solutions help you to stand out from the crowd.

REMEMBER

After establishing your visual brand identity, apply it consistently across all your digital career domains, so that prospective candidates clicking between one domain and another, as they commonly do, immediately recognize the overall integrity and unique flavor of the brand.

# Developing Overarching Recruitment Campaigns

Five to ten years ago, leading employers often translated their EVPs into *overarching recruitment advertising campaigns* — marketing dominated by single-minded investments in high profile, tagline-driven, creative concepts delivered across multiple media platforms from digital advertising to career site home pages, on-campus presentations, and career fairs. This kind of "big-bet" advertising-led campaign still has a place in recruitment, but it comes with a warning: Intrusive digital advertising has suffered from the growing use of ad-blocking software and a significant decline in click-through engagement.

Still, deploying a consistent, overarching campaign message has some potential benefits. If you're trying to build awareness, it can deliver greater impact than a more varied content marketing approach. It could also help you stand out from your competitors if you have a distinctively single-minded point of differentiation to communicate. If this sounds like you, then keep reading for guidance on how to launch a compelling and effective overarching recruitment advertising campaign.

## Setting campaign objectives

The first step in developing a recruitment advertising campaign is to jot down your primary objectives. These objectives will guide your decisions as you move forward and provide a benchmark for measuring your campaign's success.

**TIP**

Listing campaign objectives is easier if you break them down into two categories. List the primary objectives from an external image perspective and a recruitment perspective. Use the following example as a guide, but don't limit yourself to the campaign objectives presented here.

Objectives from an external image perspective

- Build brand awareness and familiarity either overall or among a specific target group.

- Create a new image (perhaps by countering misconceptions or introducing new brand associations).

- Reinforce existing brand perceptions.

Objectives from a recruitment perspective

- Drive immediate hiring volume.

- Improve the quality of new hires.

- Build a longer-term talent pool.

## Writing a creative creative brief

After establishing your recruitment advertising campaign's primary objectives, combine this with your desired EVP and an informative and stimulating package of research insights, compelling proof points, and stories to formulate your creative brief. The *creative brief* serves as a recipe for preparing and executing your campaign. Your creative brief may delineate your creative approach to the employer brand as a whole or to a single, targeted recruitment campaign. The creative brief can be as distinctive as you're willing and able to make it, but at the bare minimum it should address the following critical elements:

>> **Brand identity parameters:** Corporate colors, fonts, design elements, and photographic style. As explained in the earlier "Creating a Visual Brand Identity with Impact" section, regard these parameters as a starting point not a straightjacket.

>> **Target audience:** Your target audience obviously consists of job candidates, but try to dig deeper by listing the qualities of the ideal candidate(s) for the position(s) you're trying to fill.

>> **Your campaign's objectives:** One objective of every recruitment advertising campaign is to communicate your EVP, but you may have additional objectives, as explained in the previous section.

>> **The intended media channels:** Media channels may include your organization's website, social media such as LinkedIn, and specific trade publications. (See the chapters in Part 3 for complete coverage of media channels.)

>> **Budget:** In addition to reining in spending, the amount budgeted for a campaign helps to guide your decisions in a way that gives you the most bang for your buck.

>> **Time frame:** Although employer branding overall has an open time frame, you may have a specific date by which hiring decisions need to be made (for example, when hiring people from a graduate training program).

## Choosing the right creatives to work with

Planning, developing, and executing a recruitment advertising campaign is a specialized task that should ideally involve people with previous advertising or marketing experience. Some companies have the in-house resources and expertise to develop their own recruitment campaigns, but most companies brief a number of external agencies and choose the agency that's most likely to develop an imaginative and cost-effective solution. In this section, we provide guidance on how to choose a top-notch agency.

REMEMBER

Even if you believe that you could develop your recruitment campaign in-house, hiring expertise outside your organization is often a good move for the following two reasons:

>> **An outside firm may have expertise and experience that's unavailable internally.** This expertise and experience can help to avoid dangerous or costly pitfalls, adopt best practices, and support and train managers involved in the project.

>> **Outsourcing some or all of the workload provides a short-term boost when the organization must maintain business as usual.**

### Managing the pitch process

The standard process for selecting an agency is to issue an outline of your brief and invite a number of providers to participate. Participants may include

>> Agencies that are already providing related advertising services to your customer marketing team.

>> Larger, well-established, "full-service" recruitment advertising agencies.

>> Smaller, often more recently established agencies that are developing a reputation for break-through creative work. (These agencies may or may not be specialists in employer branding or recruitment marketing but may provide more "outside the box" creative routes for you to consider.)

If you're inviting more than four agencies that you haven't worked with before, issue an initial *request for information* (RFI) to obtain details about the agency's size, scope, capabilities, and experience. The RFI may be useful in limiting the number of agencies you ask to prepare a full and more specific response to your creative brief, often referred to as a *request for proposal* (RFP).

**TIP**

When issuing an RFP, provide agencies the opportunity to ask questions and request any further information that they think may better enable them to provide an effective response.

Most companies ask potential agencies to provide a written response to the proposal first, before the company selects a smaller number of agencies to pitch their recommendations and ideas face to face to a gathering of key decision makers and stakeholders. The proposal and pitch should ideally include

>> The agency's creative methodology and approach

>> The agency's thoughts on the desired communication objectives

>> The agency's insights on the competitive context and target audiences

>> Relevant examples of similar work the agency has conducted for other clients

>> The agency's initial creative ideas

## Selecting the best agency

Selecting the best agency to meet your campaign brief is not as straightforward as it may seem. You may be tempted to award the project to the agency that comes up with the most creative ideas, but consider these additional key factors:

>> **Creative agility:** The ability of the agency to propose big creative ideas that meet the brief in an impactful and imaginative way are clearly important, but be sure to broaden your judgment to consider the agency's creative agility:

• Has the agency demonstrated the ability to adapt advertising ideas to the needs of different target groups and communication channels?

• Does the agency have the ability to translate core creative ideas beyond conventional advertising into other kinds of content that may be required for social media?

- Beyond the agency's ability to combine catchy taglines with impactful images, can it demonstrate a much broader range of practical, creative skills in bringing its ideas to life?

>> **Capability:** During a pitch the most obvious capability on display is an agency's ability to win pitches, which generally involves a heavy dose of showmanship. To select the best agency, broaden your assessment to incorporate a number of other capabilities that are key to longer-term success:

- How well has the agency explained the thought process behind developing and selecting its creative ideas?

- Do the agency's ideas reflect a good understanding of your EVP, the competitive context, and your target audiences?

- How strong does the agency's project and relationship management appear to be?

- Does the agency have the capability to service your business in the necessary geographies?

- Does the agency have the required skills and experience to deliver the goods?

>> **Existing knowledge and connections:** Selecting an agency that's already working with your corporate communications or customer marketing teams may be advantageous, because it's already familiar with your culture and corporate/customer brand. The agency may also help to build a stronger bridge between the HR/talent/resourcing team and the marketing/communications team.

**TIP**

The experience and expertise required for effective employer branding and recruitment marketing is often quite different from that required for corporate and customer branding. If an existing agency is geared more toward advertising to consumers and investors, you may be better off selecting an agency that's better at attracting and engaging talent.

>> **Commitment:** Find out whether the people involved in the pitch are the people who will be developing and servicing the campaign. Some agencies send in their best pitch team to win the work, but then assign the delivery to less-able or less-experienced people in the agency. Make sure you meet the people the agency is going to commit to the work.

Also, determine how this work relates to the agency's other ongoing client commitments. A big agency may be attractive when considering its capabilities and experience, but be careful not to become the poor cousin to the agency's larger and more lucrative client accounts. Likewise, be careful to assess whether a smaller agency may be too under-resourced and over-stretched to service your business effectively.

>> **Chemistry:** The main focus in selecting an agency is to evaluate the information and materials presented by the agency, but you should also assess the people you'll be working with. Your preference may be more of a gut feeling, but having a productive working relationship is essential to success. Ask yourself the following questions:

- Do you feel you can trust the people you've met?

- Would you be happy to put them in front of your leadership team?

- Do they feel like they would be a good fit with your company culture?

- Do they appear to be good listeners?

- Very simply, do you like them?

TIP

Choose carefully the people in your company you invite to hear and evaluate agency pitches. The more people you invite to cast their vote, the more likely you'll end up with a decision based on immediate creative impact and showmanship instead of the broader range of factors in this section. Be sure to invite the people whose support for the agency decision will be important in executing the final campaign.

# Testing Creative Solutions

Your brand framework comprises a number of potential *creative solutions* — ideas and presentations that support your employer branding and help you achieve your brand-building and recruitment objectives. To maximize your success, test any creative solutions you develop with target audiences and key stakeholders to ensure they work before you commit to rolling them out. In the following sections, we explain how to test your creative solutions and choose the most effective solutions.

TIP

Involve key stakeholders and other influential individuals throughout your organization in the testing and selection process. You'll not only reap the benefits of having additional input, but you'll also win the support of personnel who are key to executing those solutions.

## Checking whether a creative solution works across different target groups

To test whether a creative solution works effectively across different target audiences, we suggest taking a similar approach to those recommended for validating your EVP using focus groups and/or online quantitative surveys to evaluate people's responses (see Chapter 4). In this section, we provide guidance on how to present your creative concepts and how to gather and interpret feedback.

## Testing creative concepts in focus groups

To test the appeal of different creative ideas and presentational styles, use stimulus boards or mocked-up advertising layouts (sometimes described as *adcepts,* short for *advertising concepts*). Concept boards present the creative idea in a relatively loose way with a tagline, key phrases, or a description of the creative idea, surrounded by images portraying a specific visual style. In some cases, the same words can be presented with different visuals (for example, black and white versus full color or photography versus illustrations) in order to test which is the most impactful and appealing. Adcepts are designed to look more like fully finished adverts.

**REMEMBER**

The benefit of using focus groups to test creative work is that selecting the most appealing individual elements from the complete range of stimulus materials is easier than simply evaluating overall preference between different concepts. For example, people may like the tagline but not the visual style in one concept board or adcept. They may like some aspects of the visual style but not others. Separating out these individual elements makes it easier to reach conclusions about the ideal creative mix.

Start by evaluating spontaneous general reactions to each concept board or adcept, using the following questions:

>> What's your initial response to this?

>> How impactful is it? Do you think this would catch your eye?

>> What does it make you think and feel?

>> Is the overall message clear to you?

>> How appealing is this? How credible?

Next ask more specific questions about the different elements:

>> Which aspects of this (if any) do you find most appealing?

>> What do you think about the creative idea?

>> How strong is the verbal expression of this idea?

>> How appealing are the visuals? What do you like most/least?

As for the testing of your draft EVP, you can ask your creative agency or an independent research agency to conduct this research, or you can conduct it internally (in focus groups with your own employees).

## Testing creative concepts using online surveys

The alternative to using focus groups is to test creative concepts through an online survey. This method is generally more advantageous when you're seeking to make a final choice between two or three different creative routes in adcept format. It also offers the potential benefit of broadening the scope of your evaluation to a much larger number of people.

You may be able to administer this kind of survey through an interviewer, but most companies opt for self-completion, because it enables you to collect most of the necessary information to make a choice between different concepts at a much lower cost per respondent. Unless you have access to a good database of the kind of candidates you're targeting, you need to seek the support of an agency to set up this kind of survey externally.

For each creative concept, we suggest you ask the following questions (on a seven-point scale ranging from "Very" to "Not at all"):

>> How well do you think this advert would catch your attention?

>> How attractive do you find the central claim in this advert?

>> How credible do you find the central claim in this advert?

After presenting a pair of creative concepts, ask the following questions:

>> Which of these creative ideas do you like best? (Have participants rank them in order of preference.)

>> Why did you prefer this creative idea over the others?

**TIP**

When using a self-completion survey, try to keep the advertising as simple as possible — for example, a tagline and a picture — because you're largely seeking to evaluate people's immediate responses, and most people won't take the time to read the copy.

## Choosing the best creative solutions

When choosing the best creative solutions, the first order of business is to ensure that the decision makers are well informed of the overall strategy and not merely making a judgment based on their own personal response to the creative work. Everyone claims some expertise in judging creative ideas, because advertising is so pervasive and everyone is experienced in passing judgment as a consumer. However, those involved in choosing creative solutions need to be as objective as possible and evaluate options based on how appealing they're likely to be to the targeted talent.

WARNING

Caution decision makers about the dangers of judging creative solutions from their own perspective rather than from the perspective of the target audience. Instruct them to look at each creative solution through the eyes of the target audience for the following reasons:

>> **The efficacy of the creative work is measured by how well it appeals to the target audience and not by how well it appeals to internal stakeholders.** A senor HR manager may have a completely different sensibility than that of a graduate trainee.

>> **As consumers, people tend to judge creative communication on the immediate impact of one or two instances, without considering the sustainability of the creative idea over time or its adaptability to different audiences.** What appears to have a big immediate impact may have a relatively small impact in terms of its wider applicability.

>> **People tend to expect ideas to be presented in a familiar format (typically, a headline and an image), while in employer brand marketing this format is seldom the dominant means of expression.** As a result, those called on to judge a creative concept may have a significant limitation to the thinking required to develop (and accept) an idea that needs to work across a wide range of different media and formats.

Another important consideration is the number and diversity of people involved. The boldest creative decisions tend to be made by relatively small teams or an individual. However, bold isn't always effective, especially when targeting a diverse audience. At the other extreme, large committees tend to default to the safest option, which is easy for the decision-making body to agree to and equally easy for target audiences to ignore.

TIP

Generally, to achieve the right balance between bold and broad, cast a wide net to obtain feedback and insight on the potential creative direction while letting a smaller, more qualified team make the final decision.

In decentralized organizations, where signing off may be more democratic, beware of rounding down to a creative solution that sacrifices bold for broad and is unlikely to inspire or excite interest. A better option is to provide a broader scope that facilitates and encourages local adaptations; this approach stimulates local creativity within certain boundaries.

**REMEMBER**

When seeking feedback from those involved in the creative decision-making process, give everyone a copy of the creative brief, including the overall communication objectives, and clarify the following key points:

» **The need to distinguish feedback relating to the overall creative idea and the way it's expressed through individual executions:** For example, you may like the idea of focusing your employer brand communication on career progression, but not the use of a ladder to represent this idea, as you may feel this visual metaphor is too generic or outmoded.

» **The degree of consistency required, as well as the adaptations necessary to meet local needs:** For example, determine whether the creative idea is designed to appeal to a relatively narrow target audience (female engineers in California) or a much more diverse range of audiences (business and engineering students across a range of different countries).

» **Their role in the process:** For example, are they decision makers giving the thumbs up or thumbs down, or are they providing feedback for others to consider when making a final decision?

# Chapter **6**

# Generating Engaging Content

C reating engaging content is crucial to winning the attention and interest of your target audiences and building the long-term reputation of your employer brand. Advertising can play an important role in grabbing people's attention, but it's seldom enough to maintain brand engagement. In the new social mobile media environment the game has moved on, with growing demand for a more authentic and continuous flow of people-focused, story-led content.

Ideally, you do such a good job of engaging your target audiences that they share your content with others. Content generation begins to take on a life of its own, and a vibrant community emerges populated by individuals who genuinely enjoy interacting with one another. Over time, that energy and excitement begin to draw top talent from around the world, who want to join your organization and contribute to its success.

In this chapter, we offer guidance on how to generate content that ignites and feeds the flames of engagement.

# Grasping the Need to Go Beyond Recruitment Advertising

Traditionally, the kind of recruitment advertising campaign described in Chapter 5 was the primary means by which organizations built their employer brands, but this approach is quickly becoming less effective as demand for a richer, more diverse range of marketing content grows. If you're looking for reasons to ditch old-school recruitment advertising to free up resources for generating more engaging content, you'll find plenty. Here are five good reasons to replace recruitment advertising with more engaging content marketing:

>> **People are experiencing advertising overload.** Over the last 15 years, most recruitment advertising has moved online. When first introduced, online advertising was a comparative novelty, and the proportion of people clicking on advertisements was reasonably high. In 2004, the average click-through rate for banner advertising was 4 percent. However, as the volume of advertising increased, click-through rates sharply declined. By 2008, the click-through rate dropped to 1 percent, and it now stands at around 0.1 percent.

>> **Use of ad-blocking software is on the rise.** The last few years have experienced a sharp rise in the use of ad-blocking software. Research conducted in 2016 and published in the *PageFair Mobile Ad Blocking Report* estimates that more than 400 million people use some form of ad-blocking software worldwide, and adoption is growing fast. This means that regardless of how enticing your recruitment advertising happens to be, fewer and fewer people will see it, especially the young, tech-savvy talent most employers want to recruit.

>> **Audiences want the inside scoop, not marketing hype.** Social media channels have given employees a stronger voice. Most people have always been somewhat skeptical of recruitment advertising. They understand that advertising is designed by communication professionals to catch people's attention and interest. It's always "sunny-side up." Advertising seldom if ever provides a fully rounded picture of what the company is really like to work for. Advertising still has a place in drawing attention to your employer brand, but research suggests that people now have a much stronger preference to hear about your company from employees, not advertisers.

>> **Showing trumps telling.** The growing influence of social media also appears to have affected the type of content people are looking for. They're much more interested in getting a feel for what the employer is like through authentic personal stories and realistic illustrations of life at work than highly polished and prepackaged advertising claims.

>> **Audiences demand variety and relevance.** People are also demanding greater variety and content that is more aligned with their specific needs and interests. Repeating the same headlines in the same advertising formats may be good for brand consistency, but it's unlikely to deliver brand engagement. This trend is particularly strong in social channels where a rich and varied flow of fresh, up-to-date content is required to capture people's attention and build a following. The same is true of career-site content. People are now more used to getting location, function, and job-specific content in addition to general company overviews.

Target audiences are no longer passive recipients of push marketing. You need to do more to earn their time, attention, and engagement.

# Mastering the Principles of Content Marketing

The five trends presented in the previous section have sparked a revolution in marketing, as Rebecca Lieb explains in her book *Content Marketing*:

> Companies have been creating and distributing content for many years, both to attract new business and to retain existing customers. However, here's the point of differentiation from more traditional forms of marketing and advertising: . . . It isn't push marketing, in which messages are sprayed out at groups of consumers. Rather, it's a pull strategy. . . . It's being there when consumers need you and seek you out with relevant, educational, helpful, compelling, engaging, and sometimes entertaining information.

Several other points differentiate content marketing from the traditional push marketing used in recruitment advertising:

>> **Content marketing looks "native" to the media in which it appears.** Although advertising is designed to stand out from the rest of the content on the page you're viewing, content marketing is designed to blend in. This is especially true in the social media context where it should look and feel more like a personal post from a friend than a corporate announcement.

>> **Content marketing lets people draw their own conclusions.** The brand communication tends to be implicit, by association, rather than explicit, by proclamation. It's a demonstration of what you are rather than a presentation of what you claim to be. If you want people to think you're cool, you don't tell them you're cool, you do cool things. If you want people to think you're funny, you don't tell them you're funny, you make them laugh.

>> **Content marketing opens up paths to the brand.** In many cases, consumers or candidates aren't seeking out your brand or business. What they're searching for is content that's relevant to their needs. They're looking for relevant information and fascinating stories. Only after they find the desired content do they discover your brand.

>> **The best content marketing is naturally contagious.** It's not just about creating content that people seek out, it's about content that finds them, because it's perceived to be relevant and compelling enough for their social and professional connections to share.

With this in mind, another way to define content marketing is

> The generation of a rich flow of engaging and shareable content that matches a wide variety of target audience needs and interests, while simultaneously building desired associations with the brand.

To achieve the objectives stated in this definition, you must master and practice the principles of content marketing as presented in the following sections.

## Balancing immediate engagement with long-term brand building

Building desired brand associations is crucial. You stand to benefit whenever you succeed in associating your brand with content that engages people's attention and leaves them feeling informed, entertained, or inspired (hopefully all three). Whenever you're able to make people feel better than they did prior to engaging with your content and brand, you reinforce your organization's brand presence, especially if the audience chooses to comment on or share that content.

However, the longer-term goal of brand management is not just to leave people with a warm glow, but to implant specific and distinctive associations that differentiate you from your competitors and impel people to buy, join, or recommend your brand. To strike the right balance between immediate engagement and long-term brand building, here's what you need to do:

1.  **Start with your employer value proposition (EVP), which provides a thematic structure.**

    Always be on the lookout for stories and other content that demonstrate and support your employer brand promises. If you're positioning yourself as an employer with a strong focus on development, for example, try to feature a strong mix of content related to employees learning new skills and progressing in their careers. (For more about developing an EVP, see Chapter 4.)

2. **Supplement your EVP with local communication objectives and engagement drivers.**

In addition to consistently building your overall employer brand, be sensitive to the local context. Local communication objectives could include building basic awareness and familiarity with what the company does. Likewise, local engagement drivers include communication themes that may not be touched on in the global EVP but are highly relevant and attractive at the local level.

From a publishing perspective, your value proposition and communication objectives provide you with the equivalent of editorial guidelines.

## Local engagement hooks

As we explain in Chapter 4, balancing global brand consistency with local color is important to maintaining core brand integrity while appealing to specific audiences. To deliver content that captures the attention and interest of specific target groups, look for opportunities to add content that matches attraction drivers specific to the countries, functions, and job types you're targeting. Here are a few examples of localized content:

>> Specific work locations and how employees make the most of where they live

>> Fresh perspectives from experts on subjects relevant to their chosen disciplines

>> "Day in the life" stories or career profiles

>> Passions and pastimes employees are pursuing outside working hours

>> Stories about how employees maintain a healthy work-life balance

# Exploring Different Ways to Pitch Your Story

The colossal challenge of content marketing is that you must deliver a steady stream of fresh, relevant, and compelling content to draw an audience and maintain engagement. Most individuals and even organizations don't have the creativity and endurance to meet this challenge. They run out of topics to cover or they just lose interest.

Although we can't serve as your personal muse or cheer you on when you get discouraged, we can help you explore content possibilities. In this section, we describe a number of content categories and formats that are likely to spark the creative imagination — yours and others' in your organization.

# Showcasing existing talent: Employee profiles and stories

The last decade has experienced a significant increase in employee-focused content, as opposed to content primarily focused on the company. This development appears to have been driven by a number of parallel trends, including a growing mistrust of corporations (and their advertising claims), the rise of social media as a dominant means of communication, and the desire of many corporations to present a more personal face to the world in order to become more attractive to Generation Y. Employee profiles have become a staple content category on career sites, a common feature of social posts, and an increasingly common focus of "inside story" recruitment campaigns. Profile types are plentiful, so they provide fertile ground for developing engaging content. In the following sections, we describe numerous profile types to keep in mind as you develop ideas of your own.

**TIP**

Look for opportunities to distribute or even outsource the burden of generating content like employee profiles. The more quality content you can encourage your own employees to provide, the less pressure there is on your marketing people to create everything from scratch. However, you may need to provide some guidance and guidelines. While you can't necessarily control exactly what your employees post and share, you can provide guardrails and direction regarding content or what's prohibited. This sort of oversight is particularly important in regulated industries.

## The job profile

In the *job profile*, the employees present their unique perspectives on their positions within the organization, including their responsibilities and typical "day in the life" challenges. The following provides a typical example:

> Over the last 20 years, I've worked in many departments, including manufacturing systems, manufacturing technology, and even purchasing and marketing. Throughout all this work, I've been motivated to find solutions that will make a difference for drivers. I believe that if you can keep finding ways to help improve people's lives, the commercial applications will follow.
>
> As IT Lead at our Research and Innovation Center, I led a project to collect and analyze data from the corporate car fleet of one of our leading customers. I'm excited about all the potential applications for this data. If organizations can

develop a better understanding of drivers, they can develop better ways of utilizing their fleet and making sure their employees are able to get where they need to be as easily as possible. And with connected cars, the possibilities are even greater. I can envision a future in which cars communicate with one another to reduce congestion and create cleaner cities.

## The culture profile

The *culture profile* puts less emphasis on the employee's role in the organization and more on her personal experience of the organization's *culture* — the attitudes, values, and behaviors that everyone in the organization shares (or is supposed to share). For example, certain companies are better than others at encouraging employees to share ideas or take the initiative in making decisions, while others are great at fostering a fun and creative workplace. The culture profile enables employees who've actually experienced the organization's culture to substantiate the organization's claims about its culture. An example of this kind of profile from the LEGO Group is provided in Chapter 2. Here's another typical example:

> In the four and a half years I've been here, I've learned the three things that will help you succeed: good communications (with customers and with each other), top-quality customer service (because that's the cornerstone of everything we do here), and remembering to have fun with customers and colleagues. We're all people in the end, and while it's good to be serious about what you do, it's also important to have a bit of fun along the way. If you put your mind to something, you'll find you can probably achieve it here, because that's how the culture of the company works. It's that sense of ownership that gets me out of bed in the morning, knowing that everything I do really counts toward the company's success and to furthering my own career.

## The passion profile

The *passion profile* gives employees the creative license to showcase their personality and outside interests and reveal how these resonate with their work within the organization. In addition to casting employees as real people and not just cogs in the wheels of the organization, the passion profile demonstrates that the organization values its employees; that it provides the time, resources, and encouragement for them to pursue their outside interests; and that it's staffed by intriguing individuals who will be fun to work with. Here is a typical example:

> Ever since I can remember I have loved to travel, whether for a week, a weekend, or a day here or there. I love meeting new people and learning about other countries. I was born in Mexico and went to school there, but soon after leaving college I moved to Europe and joined the company's international graduate program. The company encouraged me to build my personal network, making new friends all

over the world. I now work in a global role supporting some of our major engineering projects, which means I get to travel for work on a regular basis, and the company is very understanding when I want to take a day or two extra to get to know places better. I think my curiosity to learn how people in different cultures approach things has really helped me build bridges between the corporate center and the other parts of the world in which we work. I can't think of a better job for someone with my passion for travel.

## The hero profile

The *hero profile* takes a more story-driven approach, typically recounting a challenge the employee has undertaken and overcome with the encouragement and support of the organization. In addition to acknowledging and celebrating an employee's dedication and accomplishment, the hero profile demonstrates the organization's commitment to community and to doing what's right. Here's an example in which a company sings the praises of one of its employees who took the initiative to help others in their time of need:

> When hard economic times hit Michelle's town, she made a commitment to helping local businesses reduce their costs. Collaborating with one of the company's print services partners, Michelle and her team assessed each company's printing habits and offered each business a customized solution and a free eco-friendly printer. The results? Not only did Michelle help local businesses cut their printing costs by an average of 40 percent, but she also helped them to significantly reduce their paper and energy consumption.
>
> Finding smart solutions to tough challenges is just one of the qualities that make our company a great place to work, and it provides a typical example of our belief in "doing well by doing good."

Take note of that last sentence, which does an excellent job of associating the employee's excellent work with one of the company's employer brand promises.

## The paired/team profile

The *paired/team profile* highlights the collaborative efforts and accomplishments of two or more people within the organization. It underscores the organization's commitment to teamwork and the cooperative nature of its employees, casting the organization as a place where employees respect one another. Unlike the other employee profiles covered in this section, the paired/team profile requires input from more than one employee, making this particular profile type more challenging to source and compile.

Despite the common desire for employers to communicate a strong team ethic within their organizations, it's rarer to find profiles focusing on relationships or teams rather than individuals, largely due to the difficulty in collecting and stitching together stories. Here's a great example of a paired/team profile:

> I can always ask others for help. Communication between departments is very good here. I've recently been involved in developing a training program for our trade marketing team. When I asked Anca for help, she was brilliant at helping me co-create a really effective solution.
>
> — Paulo, Training and Development Specialist

> I'm always happy to share my expertise with colleagues like Paulo. The help I gave him to formulate the training program helped to ensure that it was in line with our trade marketing objectives and ways of working. It made his job easier and it helped deliver a much better solution for us.
>
> — Anca, Marketing Specialist

> We believe in growing together. This means we look for every opportunity to share our expertise and experience across teams, departments, functions, and countries. This not only provides rich learning experiences for our people but also promotes the growth of the business.

**TIP**

Show *and* tell. Although we stress the importance of *showing* (demonstrating) the attributes that make your organization an attractive target for talent, you can also *tell* your audience the point of the stories to clarify and reinforce the message while creating a valuable association between the stories and your brand. Telling is especially important if the point you're trying to convey isn't crystal clear in the stories; telling leaves no doubt.

## Inside stories

*Inside stories* are like exposés; they take the reader behind the scenes to show what really goes on in an organization behind closed doors. This genre delivers a wide-angle version of the employee profile, featuring content that throws light on the many different activities going on within the organization that may be of interest to current and potential employees. In many respects, the inside story replicates what good company magazines have been doing for many years. Some in-house publications, such as the *John Lewis Gazette* and the BBC's *Ariel*, have been published for more than 60 years and have become distinctive signatures within the culture of each organization. Oddly, much of the content produced for most in-house magazines never seems to be published externally, but given the increasing demand for inside stories and perspectives, the knowledge and network of contacts developed for this kind of publishing activity can provide organizations with a rich source of employer brand content.

## THE DELOITTE FILM FESTIVAL

Deloitte pioneered the practice of encouraging and facilitating employee-generated content for inside stories. Its external image was too conservative to attract the full spectrum of talent the company was looking for, so management invited everyone working for Deloitte in the United States to make short videos that answered the question "What's your Deloitte?"

To encourage maximum participation, the company offered film production kits, including a high-resolution Panasonic video camera, to the first 250 registrants. To the pleasant surprise of the organizers, the initiative captured the imagination of their employees to such an extent that more than 2,000 participants ended up submitting 372 short films!

The submitted films were posted on an internal YouTube-like intranet where they were viewed and rated by Deloitte employees. Winners of that competition were then launched on an external festival site attracting nearly 410,000 hits in just 22 days! These videos were fun and full of life, and they opened people's eyes to a side of Deloitte few outsiders had ever seen.

The idea soon spread around the Deloitte network, and since the initiative's debut, we've seen a number of examples in different parts of the world, including three exceptionally creative and well produced films from Deloitte employees in China.

**WARNING**

When composing inside stories, carefully avoid the tendency to deliver content with a corporate feel. One way to shed your company uniform is to pretend you're a newspaper journalist writing the inside story for your readers. Another way to accomplish this same goal is to involve your employees in the content generation, as Deloitte did with its imaginative Deloitte Film Festival campaign, as described in the nearby sidebar.

## Be bold: Cutting through the corporate speak

Too often, large organizations start to take themselves too seriously. Perhaps it's the suits. Or maybe neckties and tight-fitting collars cut off circulation to the brain, dulling the imagination of the organization's leaders. Whatever the case, your organization needs to get real. It needs to drop the boring corporate speak and learn a new language that resonates with and inspires today's workforce. Here are four ways to breathe life into your content:

>> **Get real.** Authenticity is often most evident in your organization's imperfections, so don't try to hide or excuse those imperfections. Admit challenges and failures.

>> **Be bold.** As Goethe once wrote, "Be bold, and mighty forces will come to your aid." Messages have the greatest impact when they're bold and daring. Take chances. Dare to go too far. Stop taking yourself and your organization so seriously. Of course, you need to be careful not to offend or to take an overly cavalier attitude toward the products and services you provide, but push the limits.

>> **Have fun with it.** Whether you're writing content, building slide shows, or creating videos, have fun, be playful, and be creative. Joy and passion are contagious, and they have a way of showing through whether the content is funny or serious.

>> **"Speak" in plain English.** Formal language is stuffy and boring. Be more conversational. Phrase statements to engage and entertain your audience, not to put them to sleep.

See the nearby sidebar for a perfect example of how Netflix stimulated engagement by making some bold and very "get real" statements in plain English, and how it apparently had fun in the process.

TIP

If you're striving to create a distinctively strong training and development offer, then share your challenges and your successes. If you're brave and confident enough, share your failures, too. Transparency helps potential candidates realize that your approach to training and development is more than just a question of policy and process; it's a mission.

The same goes for high performance, teamwork, talent mobility, and innovation. Share your challenges, insights, and perspective. If you have something important to say and do, then people will sit up and take notice. You don't need to generate all the insights and opinions within your organization. Consider sponsoring external content that aligns with your target market interests while building your desired brand associations. For example, if you believe in innovation, then share content relating to the latest innovations in your field. Whether the innovations are your company's or another company's, sharing them reinforces perceptions that you're committed to innovation within your industry.

This diversified content stream ensures you're meeting rule number one of social: Provide value. If your content stream is all job and company updates, you'll have a hard time attracting and engaging an audience that isn't already in the fan/familiar zone. Providing updates beyond your organization is a great way to command the attention of an audience that may not know you . . . yet.

The kind of conventional policy statements you find on most career sites differ vastly from the cultural manifesto that Netflix posted on LinkedIn SlideShare (`www.slideshare.net/reed2001/culture-1798664`). The Netflix PowerPoint deck, which lays out the company's approach to talent and culture, has been viewed more than five million times, has been widely shared and discussed, and was featured in the *Harvard Business Review*.

The 126-slide Netflix deck is delivered in a straightforward presentation, but it expresses a strong, insightful, and distinctive point of view. As Netflix founder and CEO Reed Hastings states: "It's our version of *Letters to a Young Poet* for budding entrepreneurs. It's what we wish we had understood when we started." In other words, it wasn't designed to be self-serving; instead, it's a more altruistically driven attempt to help others.

When Patty McCleod claims "we had no idea it would go viral," you believe her, because it simply doesn't come across as traditional marketing. Here's a small sample of the Netflix bullet point wisdom to give you a taste:

> We're like a pro sports team not a kid's recreational team.

> Netflix leaders hire, develop, and cut smartly, so we have stars in every position.

> There is no Netflix Vacation Policy and Tracking. There is also no clothing policy at Netflix, but no one comes to work naked.

As you can see, these statements clearly communicate the Netflix culture without getting bogged down with the drudgery of corporate, legally correct language.

You have many similar opportunities to promote your organization's insights, perspectives, beliefs, values, and expertise through SlideShare and white papers and by associating your organization with external thought leaders whose work reflects and perhaps influences your organization's culture.

**REMEMBER**

Although presentation is important, keep in mind that content is king. Seek to inform, enrich, and transform your audience with information and insights your organization and its people are uniquely qualified to deliver. If you can do that with passion and clarity, you have the secret formula for success.

## Delivering facts, figures, and infographics

People crave quantification and clarity, especially if you can deliver them in the form of a picture, such as a graph or infographic. Chances are, your organization has plenty of facts, figures, and other data that are likely to attract and impress prospects and perhaps convince them to seek employment with your organization. For example, illustrating your organization's success and growth in its industry can make your organization an attractive target for talented individuals seeking an opportunity with a company that's on the rise. This will provide potential candidates with confidence in the organization's ability to offer plentiful opportunities for career advancement. If you want to reinforce your claim to be an innovative company, such data may include the number of new products your company has launched or the number of patents it has sought. Likewise if you're focusing on development and career opportunities, you could include your average annual investment per employee in training or the number of employees working outside their home country.

**TIP**

Whenever applicable and possible, include an infographic or visual that shows rather than tells the point you're trying to convey or the process you're trying to describe. Over the last few years, infographics have become a highly popular format for sharing information, and they easily can be adapted to employer brand marketing.

## Making the most of video

Portrait photos and text remain the most common (and cost-efficient) media format, but video will dominate in the future for several reasons:

» Video ranks more highly on Google and other search engines.

» Potential candidates are increasingly relying on YouTube as their preferred search engine.

» Because body language is such an important indicator of personality and authenticity, videos deliver a much stronger impact.

» The entry fee for a novice video producer is next to nothing. What took a five-person camera crew to shoot and edit only a few years ago, many people can now put together themselves for a fraction of the cost using an iPad or comparable device.

The take-away lesson is that an increasing amount of the content you use in your content marketing campaigns should be in the form of video. Consider the following possibilities:

» A short (one- to two-minute) company overview told from the perspective of current employees (ideal for your LinkedIn home page)

» Video job profiles featuring some of your most sparky and intriguing employees explaining a typical day in the life at their jobs

>> Video career profiles with employees describing the career moves they've made within the company

>> Employees volunteering in the community or pursuing their passions outside the workplace

## Gaming your system

Interactive and immersive game content is likely to become a more common feature of future career sites as the technology involved becomes cheaper and more pervasive. However, you don't need to create something on the scale of Grand Theft Auto to capitalize on the power and influence of gamification. You can incorporate simple game mechanics into a wide variety of content applications, such as the following:

>> Tests and challenges broken into bite-size chunks of activity

>> Visible progress through the game (including incremental successes)

>> Continuous feedback, results, and rewards (such as moving up a level)

>> Competition (beating previous scores and/or moving up a leaderboard)

Of course, gaming your system requires some specialized expertise. If you have a web development team, it may have one or two people on its roster who are familiar with gaming and can implement it for your organization. If not, you'll need to hire an outside firm.

REMEMBER

The same principles applied to Candy Crush can be applied to an exploration of your company's employment offer, whether helping people match themselves to different job opportunities, role-playing how they might respond to different job-based scenarios, or simply testing their knowledge and mental agility. Your game may not necessarily raise a market valuation of $5 billion, but there's a high probability that it will raise your level of target market engagement.

# Promoting Employee-Generated Content

One of the most exciting aspects of mobile personal technology, such as smartphones and tablets, is that they facilitate the sharing of content. Whenever convenient and applicable, employees can post content (text, photos, videos, and so on) and engage with others inside and outside the organization. This presents organizations with the opportunity to amplify employee participation in a positive engagement cycle, by stimulating, curating, and sharing employee generated content (EGC), such as images, videos, and insights. In addition to supporting internal engagement, EGC also has the potential to provide the rich flow of authentic, social content that has become increasingly vital to external recruitment marketing.

Content generation and engagement, traditionally relegated to marketing, sales, and customer service, are increasingly being distributed throughout organizations via services and technologies such as social customer relationship management (social CRM) — a sort of Facebook for business. (For more about social CRM, check out *Social CRM For Dummies*, by Kyle Lacy, Stephanie Diamond, and John Ferrara [Wiley].)

## EGC AT P&G

P&G personnel are planning to introduce more employee-generated content in their employer brand communication. They see it as a valuable counterpoint to the more tightly prescribed advertising templates and digital design styles that will continue to frame their employer brand marketing.

As Scott Read, P&G's Associate Director, Global Talent Supply, explains:

> We made a conscious choice to create a framework in place to drive a consistent look and feel and a consistent voice everywhere in the world, but we've always recognized the need to retain a degree of local flexibility. We've conducted a lot of local country visits recently and what we've heard from students directly is they want to see what it's like to work here through their own eyes. They don't want us to tell them. They want to discover it for themselves, and this is where social media plays a big role. The tone has to change; it can't be us saying this is the way it is, it has to be "come see for yourself." The big shift we're starting to embrace is to be as real-time and authentic in our communications as we can be, and really get the full engagement of the everyday P&G employee. With this participation we're going to get the authenticity through whatever the employees are saying about their workday. This is also where the flexibility will come in and where the localization will take place.

Significant challenges stand in the way of initiating and sustaining this level of active engagement. Organizations must provide the technology to facilitate content sharing and engagement, address potential legal issues, and convince senior managers that the benefits outweigh the potential risks. Nevertheless a clear external demand for this kind of authentic real-time communication is growing. Smartphones and smart internal communication apps are making content generation and sharing easier than ever before. And most important of all, employees are increasingly happy to create and share their views on the world of work. Where the likes of P&G are going, many are sure to follow.

In the future, you can expect social media and social networking to play an ever-increasing role in branding as the walls separating organizations from customers, employees, job candidates, and others begin to come down. In the following sections, we guide you in the steps you need to take to facilitate and promote EGC and engagement.

## Facilitating employee-generated content with the right technology

Organizations can approach EGC in any number of ways, from structured approaches with tools that make specific content recommendations to employees, to unstructured ways where employees are sharing "in the wild." Tools such as QueSocial (www.quesocial.com) allow you to share preselected content with employees for them to share as they see fit. They often have a gamification layer to incentivize sharing. The other end of the spectrum, giving employees creative license, requires no tools but can lead to challenges identifying and amplifying content, not to mention potential legal and exposure concerns.

The sweet spot varies depending on factors including industry, regulation, and social adoption, but it's typically somewhere between the two extremes. If you over-engineer EGC, the end result will feel like corporate speak and miss the mark on the candidates you're trying to influence. Adding "guard rails" around sharing so employees know where they can't go is usually the best approach.

TIP

One of the more common practices in EGC is to have employees use a common hashtag (such as #HootsuiteLife). Employees can then share content however they'd like, using whatever platform they'd like, and still be easily found and amplified by the employer brand team. Tagboard (www.tagboard.com) is a great tool that can aggregate hashtag-based content on a unified page. This then becomes an asset you can use to *show* candidates what it's like to work there, not just *tell* them.

## Developing policies to prevent misbehavior and mishaps

Having a social media policy is an important component of EGC. Without one, you risk losing control of your employer brand or potentially finding yourself in litigation. An ideal social media policy should look like the guard rails mentioned in the previous section. Assume common sense and good intent, but be clear about any behaviors or actions that are strictly prohibited.

Companies that are successful with EGC generally provide training, guidance, and tools to help their employees understand social media platforms, video editing, blogging, and so on. Several workshops can pay massive dividends if you're equipping your employees to develop compelling content for you.

# Managing Your Content

When it comes to content marketing, the most valuable asset you have — second only to the people in your organization who generate content and drive engagement — is the content itself. Properly managing your content is crucial for knowing what you have and how to make the most of it.

In the following sections, we guide you through the process of assembling an effective content management and marketing team, and we highlight its key responsibilities.

## Assembling a content marketing and management team

Although you're no doubt eager to dive into content marketing, we recommend wading in the shallow end first and making sure you have a competent team in place to do it right. Having a content marketing and management team in place before you get started is a crucial first step, because, if your organization is like most, it hasn't collected and curated its content in any consistent or effective manner. A skilled and experienced team can manage the content in a way that ensures optimal impact.

An all-star content marketing and management team should contain people in the following roles:

>> **Employer brand specialists:** These team members typically create your EVP and brand promises either in-house or with the support of external communication agencies. They should understand your strengths as an employer and be able to tap into the HR and employee communications network to dig out strong advocates and good employment-related stories. They should also be well versed in social channels, segmentation, and community engagement.

>> **Content managers:** Content managers are in charge of storing, protecting, cataloging, and indexing both internally and externally generated content. In a large organization this may already be a specialist role, but in most companies it will be an enthusiastic communications manager or personal assistant.

>> **Subject matter experts (SMEs):** SMEs are the linchpin to any content marketing effort, because they have the knowledge to generate relevant, informative, and compelling content, and they're best suited to evaluate what the target audiences crave. SMEs include most members of the senior team, functional heads, and specialists in a range of fields that combine both the interest and the ability to provide content of interest to your target talent groups. Because this is unlikely to be written into their current job description, you'll need to explain the benefit of devoting some time to content creation, and plenty of encouragement to help them get into the habit.

## Conducting a content audit

One of the first steps in content marketing and management is to figure out what you already have in stock — existing content. Such content can save you considerable time and effort in getting your content marketing off the ground. To find out how much and what kind of relevant content already exists, perform a content audit. The aim of the content audit is to identify the following:

>> **Content you've already published that could be rechanneled:** Examples include video content on your career site that could be republished on your YouTube channel, or stories that appeared in your in-house magazine that could be rechanneled to LinkedIn or Facebook.

>> **Content you have immediately available to publish:** This might include existing photo archives.

>> **Content that may exist locally or in other functions:** For example, you might have marketing content that could be edited and repurposed for employer brand marketing.

>> **Areas of expertise that align with target audience interests that you haven't yet tapped into.**

In addition to providing a detailed record of the content and sources you have on hand, your content audit serves as a valuable tool for identifying gaps that need to be filled.

**TIP**

If you have a large quantity of existing content and want to conduct a more comprehensive audit, check out *Content Strategy for the Web*, 2nd Edition, by Kristina Halvorson and Melissa Rach (New Riders), which provides an excellent framework for this kind of assessment.

# Tagging and categorizing content to facilitate indexing and raise its search engine ranking

Whether you're taking inventory of existing content or generating fresh content, you need to categorize and tag it for indexing. Categories and tags serve as *metadata* (data that describes data), and metadata serves two very important purposes:

>> It makes content easier for you and others to search and find later.

>> Search engines rely on metadata to properly index content and deliver relevant search results to users. More important for your purposes, proper indexing can raise your content's ranking in search results.

TIP

Metadata is especially important for photos, videos, and audio clips. Search engines have a more difficult time indexing these items, because this content type contains no text that the search engines can identify. When publishing such content, try to include it on a page with descriptive text, place the item in a section with a descriptive heading, add a caption (if possible), and use HTML tags to add alt text and other descriptors that search engines can use to identify and index the content.

For the kind of employer brand content you're indexing, you should ideally add four kinds of tags to each element:

>> **Content theme:** For example, development, innovation, flexibility (depending on your EVP pillars), and other regular topics

>> **Content source:** For example, subject expert, employee generated, or third party

>> **Content type:** For example, advertising, story, or profile

>> **Content substance:** For example, employee, engineering, training, London

TIP

Whatever tags you use, make them as consistent, descriptive, and intuitive as possible.

# Building a content marketing editorial calendar

A *content marketing editorial calendar* is a tool that keeps your content marketing program on track and ensures a consistent, continuous flow of fresh content. It also facilitates the process of assigning and scheduling content development with SMEs and others in charge of generating content. You use a Microsoft Excel spreadsheet, project planning software, or advanced content management system (CMS) to create and manage your editorial calendar.

From a communication and content publishing perspective, consider scheduling your content marketing tasks based on the likely cycle time of each major element:

>> **Long cycle (limited change over 12 months):** These elements represent the hub of your brand communication efforts and typically include your career website home page along with your professional and social media profile pages. In most cases, the majority of this content should be closely aligned with your EVP.

>> **Medium cycle (3 to 12 months):** These elements include anything you can reasonably plan for in advance, including the graduate recruiting season, insight, and opinion pieces; Q&A sessions; and employee stories and profiles.

REMEMBER

Your editorial calendar comes in handy particularly for these medium-cycle tasks. Your calendar may serve as a master content plan covering all your content sourcing, curation, and distribution activities and their target dates. In addition, your calendar should identify the channel in which each content piece is to be published.

>> **Short cycle (real time):** Short-cycle tasks include the majority of job postings and the more opportunistic real-time posting and response to social media content.

An important subset of this overall content calendar is your social media calendar, which is covered in greater detail in Chapter 11.

Chapter **7**

# Rolling Out Your Employer Brand Strategy

I n previous chapters, you lay the groundwork for your employer brand. You defined your employer value proposition (EVP) and constructed the framework for your employer brand. You also started to plan the content needed to populate your career site and social domains. Now, it's show time — time to roll out your employer brand strategy and guidelines to the rest of the organization to rally their support.

In this chapter, we explain how to manage the rollout effectively, so everyone in your organization strives in unison to maintain global consistency with the employer brand while spicing it up with his or her own local flavor. Here, we explain how to assemble employer brand toolkits, complete with brand guidelines, to make your job easier and how to navigate the rollout to get everyone in your organization onboard.

## Winning Internal Hearts and Minds

If external recruitment marketing focuses on the promise, internal brand communication should largely focus on purpose and forward momentum. As such, internal engagement is a function of leadership, pure and simple. Internally, the organization must answer questions, such as:

>> What is the organization trying to achieve and why?

>> How do our recruitment goals support our overall goals?

>> What steps are being taken to enhance the employment experience so quality hires become engaged performers?

In many organizations, employer brand marketing is seen primarily as an external activity, building reputation and recruiting talent. However, you stand to gain significant advantages by extending your employer brand communication internally in a way that engages your organization's leadership and existing employees. This internal expansion helps to ensure that

>> The management teams involved in shaping the employment experience understand and commit to delivering on the organization's employer brand promises.

>> New employees discover that the organization truly delivers on the promises it communicates externally.

>> Current employees are clear about what makes the employer special, qualities that nurture employee engagement, retention, advocacy, and referral.

The major difference between external recruitment marketing and internal engagement marketing is that the former generally takes place with people who have limited experience of the organization, whereas the audience for internal communication experience the reality of the company every day. (Figure 7-1 illustrates the relationship between internal and external employer brand communications.) For this reason, alignment of external and internal communication doesn't constitute running the same kind of recruitment marketing internally. Although the overall communication themes should remain largely consistent, the way in which you communicate them needs to be different. Internally, you must place a far greater focus on content and substance than on attention-grabbing headlines.

Keep this distinction between external marketing and internal engagement in mind as you find out, in the following sections, how to build internal engagement. Here, we stress the importance of briefing managers before engaging employees, explain how to win the hearts and minds of key stakeholders, and reveal how to appeal to the emotions of everyone in the organization.

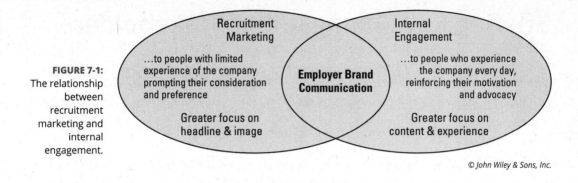

**FIGURE 7-1:**
The relationship between recruitment marketing and internal engagement.

Recruitment Marketing

...to people with limited experience of the company prompting their consideration and preference

Greater focus on headline & image

**Employer Brand Communication**

Internal Engagement

...to people who experience the company every day, reinforcing their motivation and advocacy

Greater focus on content & experience

# Briefing Managers before Engaging Employees

When a company is about to introduce a new product or service, it prepares carefully and thoroughly for the launch to ensure that everything aligns with the company's corporate and consumer brand promises. The company must check and recheck product quality, make sure the supply chain is ready to respond to demand, and nail down commitments with key partners involved in delivering the new product or service to market.

Launching a new employer brand promise is no different. Carefully lay the foundation for success prior to rolling out your new or revised EVP and employer branding strategy. The most effective approach is to divide the launch into two clear stages:

>> **Management rollout:** Conduct management briefings and action planning prior to any direct communication with employees. To fully engage employee interest and commitment, the top brass must champion the initiative. You need the backing of your senior leadership team, the HR and talent management community, and frontline managers throughout the organization. (See the following sections for more about getting the various stakeholder groups involved in EVP rollout.)

>> **Employee rollout:** After you conduct your management briefings and your organization's leaders know the roles they play in the EVP rollout, leaders need to work together to introduce the EVP to the rest of the organization.

# Briefing Key Management Stakeholders

As with any communication plan, start by setting your overall objectives, segmenting your audiences, and identifying their needs and preferences. Pitching the EVP to internal management benefits from a deal-making, give-get approach, highlighting the specific advantages of the EVP initiative to each target group and clarifying what you need from that group in return.

Table 7-1 represents a starting point for establishing objectives based on many years of experience (getting it right and wrong).

**TABLE 7-1**    ## Key EVP Questions for Internal Engagement

| Stakeholder Group | Framing EVP Benefits | Clarifying Expectations |
|---|---|---|
| Leadership team | How will the EVP help to drive organizational performance? | What do leaders need to focus on in terms of communication and behavior? |
| HR/talent community | How will the EVP support the overall HR and talent agenda? | What may need greater attention or investment to align with the EVP? |
| Corporate/internal communications | How will the EVP support the corporate communications agenda? | Which areas of communication may need to be realigned to the EVP? |
| Recruitment community | How will the EVP help to enhance employer reputation and drive attraction? | What employer branding disciplines do you expect from recruiters? |
| Line managers | How will the EVP help to enhance team engagement and performance? | What do leaders need to focus on in terms of communication and behavior? |

## Engaging leadership

The key to leadership engagement is getting in front of them early and keeping them involved through the often lengthy period of time required to develop a new EVP and employer brand. Here are several ways to start the conversation and begin to engage leadership in your employer branding initiative:

>> Present the business case for employer branding (see Chapter 2 for details).

>> Conduct leadership interviews encouraging leaders to share their perspectives and employer brand aspirations.

>> Share top-line results from the employer brand health check we describe in Chapter 3.

>> Present the draft EVP and creative options and request feedback, so leaders develop a sense of ownership.

>> Present the final employer brand platform (with local validation and confirmation).

You may not have the opportunity to use all five of these tactics with each stakeholder individual or group, but using even two or three should ensure a reasonable degree of familiarity with your employer branding initiative when you get to the activation briefing stage. All you're trying to do early on is warm up the stakeholders and start nurturing a sense of ownership in the project, so they'll be more receptive later.

TIP

The key to the final briefing is to reclarify how building a stronger employer brand will help to support performance through attracting and retaining the talent the organization needs to achieve its business goals. It's also essential for leaders to understand the role they need to play in reinforcing the employer brand promise through their communication, their personal behaviors, and their investment in a positive employment experience that delivers on the promise. For more about improving the employment experience, see Chapter 14.

## Pitching your plan to the HR/talent community

If the scope of your employer branding activities is limited to recruitment marketing, you may only need to provide a top-line briefing to the rest of the HR/talent team. However, a more integrated approach to employer brand management generally requires a more significant intervention. Keeping the key senior stakeholders within the HR and talent community up to speed through your employer brand research and development is important.

In your launch briefing, it's also important for you to explain how the EVP and employer brand strategy will support the overall HR and talent agenda. Don't assume that you'll get immediate support for employer brand activities, especially in larger organizations where HR departments may be competing for leadership focus and investment. You're more likely to receive support if you demonstrate how the employer brand will help to reinforce the success of different HR team agendas. Here are a few suggestions:

>> Point out to your compensation and benefits colleagues how the EVP will help to support their "total reward" strategy by helping to clarify the role of the non-remuneration components, like training, within the reward package.

>> Explain how the EVP will help to reinforce the importance of "learning and development" (L&D), communicating what the L&D team offers to current and

>> potential employees and reminding the leadership team why maintaining investment in this area is important.

>> Address other important EVP focus areas that may reflect key objectives for the wider HR/talent team, which may include diversity, empowerment, flexible working, identification of high-potential talent, career pathing, and succession planning.

The key to the final briefing is to ensure the wider members of the HR and talent community understand that the EVP and employer branding are not simply communication tools within the resourcing function, but have direct and important relevance to every aspect of HR and talent management. To succeed, you also need to clarify the kind of support you may need from different HR functions to review and align certain aspects of people management to ensure that they align with the company's desired employer brand promises. We cover the alignment process in more detail in Chapter 14.

**TIP**

Consider turning your employer branding initiative inside-out. Traditionally, employer branding was outside-in, with external marketing (the recruitment campaign) taking precedence over the employment experience. Some organizations have begun to switch the emphasis from communication to experience management. For example, Cisco's employer brand guidelines put the primary focus on the EVP's role in supporting the organization's global people strategy. Its brand philosophy is inside-out, with the employment experience as the top priority. The recruitment campaign guidelines and templates are positioned as playing a supporting rather than lead role in strengthening the employer brand.

## Ensuring alignment with corporate communications and marketing

As discussed in Chapter 5, it's vital that you establish a clear role and position for the employer brand within the overall corporate brand hierarchy as early as possible within the development process. If you've done this successfully, the rollout briefing should focus on how best to coordinate your communication planning rather than more fundamental questions relating to the purpose of the employer brand.

Ideally, at this stage, you should try to establish the following:

>> **The kind of process (if any) required to ensure that new recruitment campaigns and executional elements meet the necessary corporate brand identity standards.**

>> **How often you meet to share your communication objectives and media plans:** A monthly catchup is fairly typical, with a more formal meeting every quarter.

>> **The party that will take the lead on sourcing and developing different kinds of content:** The marketing and communications team often have greater resources at their disposal, so they may be chosen to take the lead when it comes to high-production video and photographic content, while the employer brand team focuses on more informal story gathering and personal profiles.

>> **The kind of content mix that will work effectively for both parties through shared social channels such as LinkedIn, Facebook, and Twitter:** Larger companies may have sufficient resources to create separate career-specific pages for each channel. Smaller companies may have only enough resources and content for a single-channel approach. With a single-channel approach, you can use hashtags to distinguish between different types of content (see Chapter 11 for details).

# Briefing Your Recruitment Teams

Although every manager within the organization should ideally understand the EVP and the important role he or she plays in building the employer brand, some groups of people, such as those involved in talent acquisition, clearly need more detailed and practical guidance on how the EVP and employer brand strategy should be implemented.

Documentation is a key component. In this section, you find out how to equip your recruitment team with an employer brand toolkit and content playbook and establish guidelines for adapting the employer brand to local recruiting needs. We also provide guidance on how to get your line managers onboard.

## Developing your employer brand toolkit

An *employer brand toolkit* is a collection of documents that provide specifications and guidelines to ensure consistent presentation of the employer brand identity by everyone in the organization involved in recruiting, engaging with, and messaging prospects. To assemble your employer brand toolkit, gather the following items:

>> **A detailed description of the EVP**

>> **Employer brand identity guidelines and design elements:** Logo usage, typography, colors, graphic elements, photography, and so on

>> **Guidelines for conveying brand personality and tone of voice**

>> **Umbrella campaign elements:** Headline structure, copy guidelines, and templates

REMEMBER

Depending on the degree of change involved in the process of recruiting and hiring candidates, the recruitment team's current level of sophistication, and its previous involvement in the development process, you may need to conduct briefing or training sessions in addition to distributing your employer brand toolkit.

TIP

Instead of distributing your employer brand toolkit via email or in the form of paper documents, consider making it centrally available online. Leading employers, including BP and P&G, are increasingly migrating their guidelines online. Smart employer brand management portals such as Papirfly (www. papirflyemployerbrand.com) facilitate the process of transforming your employer brand design and messaging framework into an online production and distribution system. Technology such as this enables you to mandate the brand elements you want to keep consistent while simultaneously empowering your local communications teams with a powerful tool for selecting, tailoring, producing, and distributing high-quality marketing content that meets their specific needs and is in their local language when required. The upfront investment may be higher for those adopting this approach, but the longer-term cost benefits, time savings, and additional brand building value involved in migrating to this kind of system are significant.

Your employer brand toolkit should contain two additional items to offer guidance on implementing an effective and efficient content marketing program: content playbooks and local playbooks, which we describe in greater detail in the next two sections.

## Creating content playbooks

Employer brand toolkits tend to focus on the more formal aspects of branding such as brand identity and advertising templates, but content playbooks provide guidance on the sourcing, generation, and formatting of the different types of marketing content described in Chapter 6. As a minimum we suggest that this includes guidance on creating

>> Employee profiles

>> Employee-related new stories

>> Infographics

>> Local posts for LinkedIn, Facebook, Twitter, and Instagram

>> Local video material for YouTube

# Providing guidance on localization

As explained in Chapter 4, organizations that operate in multiple locations face a challenge in maintaining global brand consistency while making the brand promises relevant to local populations. For example, if your EVP stresses both team spirit and career mobility, your local research and experience may indicate which of these two elements is more relevant and attractive within the local context, in which case the local business unit should make that element more prominent in its employer branding efforts.

The EVP can be thought of as a distinctive "brand chord," with each brand pillar representing a separate note that can be played louder or softer, and more or less frequently, depending on its relative local importance (see Chapter 4). As David Henderson, executive vice president for HR at MetLife, puts it:

> The umbrella brand should be sufficiently broad to capture all employees from top leadership talent to frontline employees, but the accents we place on certain aspects of the offering will differ. It's a bit like the controls on an expensive music system: The music that is playing is the same and all the variables that impact the sound quality are in play, but the dials can be changed according to the preferences of the listener. What motivates one segment of our audience might not be right for another, so if you land on an EVP, that level of agility needs to be part of the design.

The feedback you received from different parts of the organization while developing your EVP should have provided some initial indications of the degree to which different attributes and messages may need to be "tuned" up or down to match local employment conditions and target group preferences; however, we recommend that you avoid being over-prescriptive from the center. A more effective approach is to ensure that local business units are very clear about the non-negotiables contained in the employer brand toolkit (logo usage, typography, advertising templates, and so on), but also aware of their freedom within the brand framework to do the following:

>> Tune up EVP pillars and attributes that are more credible and attractive to local target audiences.

>> Tune down EVP pillars and attributes that are less relevant to local target groups.

>> Add a few additional attributes of particular local importance (as long as they aren't discordant with the global brand).

>> Supplement global advertising with local campaigns (within the agreed templates).

>> Supplement advertising with other forms of local content marketing.

Local managers are likely to tell you that a global solution will never work, because their market is different. To some degree, they're right; local business units will always have at least a few important points of difference. In practice, however, you're likely to find that global similarities far outweigh local differences. If you offer local recruitment managers the opportunity to decide for themselves which elements in the EVP are more or less relevant to local audiences, they'll likely conclude for themselves that the global EVP provides most of the right areas of focus with only limited local tuning required. However, because they've decided this for themselves, they're far more likely to feel they've been heard and to take greater ownership of the global framework.

TIP

Prior to deciding how best to tailor the global EVP to local needs, business units should obtain answers to the following questions:

>> Which local are we targeting?

>> What are they most likely to be interested in?

>> What do we most want them to know about us in terms of the EVP and core employer branding messages?

>> Where are the strongest matches between the audience and our brand?

>> What media do they use and prefer?

>> What's the best content mix to both engage the audience and inform it about our employer brand?

Here's an example of a situation in which a division of a company added a brand pillar: During EVP development at a major power company, research showed that the majority of employees in the company's conventional nuclear and carbon fuel generated power plants rated "flexible working conditions" of very low importance, so the company omitted it from the EVP. However, within the company's renewable energy division, where the average employee was at least 15 years younger than the rest of the company and the working patterns were very different, flexible working conditions was one of the most important elements in the employment deal. The renewable energy division was able to add flexible working conditions to its local rendition of the EVP.

## Getting team managers onboard

Winning the support of your senior leaders, HR, corporate communication, marketing, and resourcing colleagues represents an essential first step in implementing a new EVP and employer branding strategy, but ultimately the most important audience to win over consists of the team managers across the organization.

However well aligned your leadership team and people management processes are, the everyday behavior of local team managers probably represents the most important factor in shaping a positive, on-brand employment experience for most employees. We're surprised by how many organizations fail to conduct a full briefing of local team managers when rolling out their EVP. Even fewer organizations set up the kind of ongoing frontline leadership training (described in Chapter 14) generally necessary to fully embed the management behaviors required to deliver employer brand promises consistently at the local team level.

## SIEMENS'S INTERNAL EMPLOYER BRAND ACTIVATION

When Siemens's Talent Team redeveloped the company's global EVP, they embarked on a significant program of internal engagement. Rosa Riera, Global Head of Employer Branding and Social Innovation, commented, "Putting up posters or handing out cards with quotes of the EVP does not work. Our idea was to engage with our employees by sparking meaningful conversations based on our EVP through all relevant channels." This started with an analysis of the different communication needs and preferences of the employee population. For example, while most employees were reachable through Siemens's own dedicated internal social network, factory-based employees required a more offline approach. When the most effective channels had been established, the company identified an initial group of 30 employee brand ambassadors, whose task was to take the lead in communicating the EVP within their local areas of business. To ensure that the respective messages and tactics were relevant locally, the Siemens team put a lot of effort into establishing a culture of co-creation with the regions and businesses. The goal was to develop a global strategy that gave a lot of room for local adaptation. Part of the ambassador program involved identifying employee stories that would help to bring the EVP to life in an authentically powerful way. These employer brand ambassadors received training in how to gather and write compelling story content, and the most effective way to format and publish this content on Siemens Social Network to maximize engagement. Reflecting on Siemens's overall approach to internal activation, Christoph Knorn, the manager responsible for employer branding, concludes: "The employer brand belongs to the employees. This is why all employer branding has to start with your own people. The success of any employer branding program depends on the internal buy-in and engagement with the EVP."

Not only are team managers essential in the long-term delivery of the right employer brand experience, but they can also play a key role in communicating a new EVP to existing employees. Because team managers play such a key role, include them in your employer brand briefings and do the following:

» **Stress the potential benefits of building a strong employer brand.** Let them know that it will help in attracting more talented and motivated employees, which in turn helps team leaders build stronger teams for improved performance.

» **Reinforce the importance of local managers in helping the organization live up to external brand promises.** This way, you can avoid unnecessary disengagement and attrition.

» **Clarify what the leadership team and HR will be doing to support them.** Explain how you'll provide the necessary resources, training, processes, and central support of local managers.

# Engaging Employees

If your employer brand management efforts are focused primarily on recruitment marketing, engaging employees may be limited to a news update. However, if you're taking a more integrated approach that involves recruitment marketing and overhauling the employment experience, then some form of proactive engagement is valuable. Motivating employee engagement relies a great deal on timing and how substantial and genuine are the proposed improvements to the employment experience. Introducing a new employer brand promise often falls flat unless it's accompanied by real improvement in the workplace. Simply being reminded that they're working for a great employer isn't likely to engage employees. People are more interested in what's coming next to freshen things up and make things better.

For people to "buy" the employer brand, they first need to understand the context in which it's being introduced. In the backs of their minds, they're asking, "Why is it being launched now?," "How does it connect with the wider purpose and goals of the organization?," and "What's in it for me?" In our experience, employer brands need a strong business context to justify a major launch. What you need to do to engage employees depends on the situation:

» **An external brand re-launch requires employee behavior change.** The best way to motivate employees to change their behaviors is to ensure managers take the lead in modeling these desired behaviors. For example, if you want employees to be more responsive to customers' needs, then you need to ensure that managers are more responsive to employees' needs. If new "brand" behaviors conflict with their employer brand experience, they're far more likely to deem the initiative superficial, "a show put on for customers" rather than a natural extension of a deeply rooted brand ethos.

>> **Organization change initiatives are in the works.** If the organization is restructuring, reengineering, downsizing, right-sizing, centralizing, decentralizing, or undergoing some other major overhaul, explain the beneficial consequences of the change to employees, including potential adjustments to the overall employment deal. When employees are apprised of such changes, they're more likely to accept them and make the necessary adjustments and accommodations.

>> **The organization is experiencing a merger or acquisition.** In situations such as these, the role of the employer brand is to help establish a sense of shared purpose and identity. For the employees in the acquired organization, this represents a key moment of truth. To dispel any fears about changes that may negatively affect the employment experience, sensitively redefine both the components of the employment deal, as well as the more emotional, underlying psychological contract between employer and employee.

>> **The employee engagement survey results are in.** The employee engagement survey plays an important role in giving voice to what employees feel is important to them, but employees may perceive the local management response to be overly reactive (why did they wait until now?), disjointed (what's the overall plan?), and overly focused on failings (addressing problems rather than building on strengths). Presenting the survey findings in the context of your EVP reminds employees that longer-term leadership commitments are in place, a structured global approach to people management is being implemented, improvements are on the horizon, and the organization is committed to ongoing improvement of the employment experience.

**WARNING**

Choose and plan your major initiatives carefully. Employees tend to be cynical about the latest "big initiative," because they tend to have seen many such initiatives come and go without resulting in any major improvement. In large organizations, many internal initiatives may be running concurrently, each with its own call to action, launch pack, and instruction guide. In many cases, initiatives aren't carefully aligned and sometimes conflict. As a result, employees in big organizations tend to feel overwhelmed by information and decidedly underwhelmed in terms of inspiration and engagement.

Brand-focused engagement campaigns are particularly prone to cynicism. Whether they come in the form of internal "living the brand" marketing exercises, CEO-endorsed vision and values, or "culture change," they're often enveloped in an aura of unreality. They tend to paint a compelling picture of the future but seldom feel rooted in the current, day-to-day realities of the business. They promise much, but generally underdeliver.

You may have heard such initiatives described as "sheep dip"; the variant for brand engagement is the "brandwash."

Bearing these caveats in mind, launching an employer brand can be fraught with difficulties unless it's carefully planned and executed. One way of approaching this is to plan out your internal campaign with three important questions in mind:

>> What do we want people to think?

>> How do we want people to feel?

>> What do we want people to do?

As we explain in the following sections, launch campaigns need to address all three with equal rigor to achieve anything of lasting value.

## Think: Taking a rational, measured approach

In your enthusiasm over your new employer brand initiative, you may be tempted to go all out by launching a major internal marketing campaign complete with an all-you-need-to-know packet of information informing employees of their exciting new employer branding responsibilities. Resist the temptation. Think carefully how you're going to roll out your employer brand strategy to employees, and follow these suggestions to take a measured approach:

>> **Think twice about conducting a major launch to employees.** Unless your initiative involves changes that significantly impact employees, a more effective approach is to conduct a targeted management briefing and team up with management to improve aspects of the employment experience that support the underlying employer brand proposition, instead of talking up your new employer brand promises.

>> **Keep it simple.** Employees are a captive audience, but they're just as susceptible as consumers to suffer from information overload. Make your employer brand messages equally simple and direct. Be absolutely clear about the two or three core messages you want employees to consistently associate with the employer brand, and put 90 percent of your attention into

getting these core messages across. This may mean sacrificing some of the more detailed information you would ultimately like to communicate to employees, but if you take the longer-term view, you should have plenty of time to build this up gradually.

>> **Communicate in plain English.** Just as you would never use brand jargon to communicate the benefits of your brand to customers, don't use it with employees. A plain-speaking approach makes your branding initiative more relevant and meaningful to employees and their everyday working lives. It also tends to focus the mind on the substance of the brand offering rather than on the "wrapping."

# Feel: Nurturing emotional engagement

It doesn't really matter if employees understand your message if they don't care in the first place. Just as customer branding infuses products with positive emotions, your employer brand should ideally engender feelings of pride and commitment in employees. When employees are fully engaged, they go the extra mile, and in a highly competitive world, it's the extra mile that makes all the difference. To motivate employees to engage on a deeper level, you have to make them not only understand but also feel.

**TIP**

Here are a few suggestions for appealing to employees on a more emotional level:

>> **Stress to the CEO the importance leading from the front.** The first principle of active engagement is that it requires active leadership. Nothing is more engaging than personal contact with someone who is already highly engaged, particularly if that person has the power to shape the course of the organization. The CEO must make it her personal mission to enroll the commitment of the wider management team, and ensure they play their part in both communicating and living up to the company's employer brand promises.

>> **Create a spectacle.** As the 1960s media guru Marshall McLuhan once said, "The medium is the message." He meant that the channel through which something is delivered often communicates as much as or more than the content of the message itself. To increase the impact of your internal employer brand messaging, here's what to do:

- Stage events off-premises to signal the importance of your employer branding initiative and to inspire presenters to stir emotions. On stage, presenters typically deliver their messages with greater impact than they do in small briefing sessions.

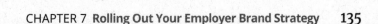

- Gather diverse groups to demonstrate leadership's commitment to bringing people together and to convey the expectation that everyone *will* work together to make the employer branding initiative a success.

- Pack the seats. People respond differently in large groups. Just think of the difference between watching a major sporting event alone on TV compared to watching it in a stadium packed with fans. As long as the home team's performance is up to snuff, you experience a quantum leap in enthusiasm.

» **Produce a film.** A well-constructed dramatization of the brand messages on film can be highly engaging. The talking heads formula, in which senior managers provide context and pledge commitment to the cause on video, tends to lack emotive impact. As an alternative (or in addition) you can often achieve greater impact by getting midlevel managers and employees representing the bulk of the audience to carry the message.

**TIP**

» **Plant the seeds.** Some of the most powerful engagement techniques involve relatively simple exercises that can be conducted in relatively small briefing sessions. As any experienced facilitator can tell you, the trick in getting people to both think and engage is not to provide all the answers but to ask the right questions. As Nicholas Ind puts it in his book *Living the Brand,* "The real challenge here is to change a manager's mind-set away from an approach that focuses on selling an idea to others in the organization to a more organic method, which following the planting of a seed of an idea, grows through the involvement and enthusiasm of others."

## Do: Inspiring employee commitment and behavior change

At the risk of sounding trite, we must say that the most crucial principle in winning employee engagement is encapsulated in the age-old maxim "Actions speak louder than words." Short-term engagement can be bought with brand promises, but longer-term commitment and behavior change can only be earned by delivering on those promises. People will only believe the brand messages, and begin to change their behaviors, when they begin to see tangible evidence from the top that the brand proposition and values are being hard-wired into the fabric of the organization, changing the way in which processes are run and important decisions are made. (See Part 4 for more about delivering on employer brand promises.)

# Maintaining consistency and continuity

Substantiation of brand promises plays a key role in earning employee engagement, but consistency, continuity, and relevance also play their parts:

>> **Consistency in internal brand messaging:** From the employee's perspective, all internal communication has the potential to reinforce or undermine how they feel about the organization. To build trust and credibility in your employer brand, be sure that all internal brand messaging is consistent. Don't fall into the all-too-common trap of treating your internal brand engagement program as a separate entity, discrete and disconnected from other subjects and sources of management information.

>> **Consistency between internal and external communications:** Keep in mind that your external communication (including both recruitment and consumer advertising) can also send powerful messages to your employees about the kind of organization you are or claim to be. Make sure your employees feel that these external promises are credible before you over-promise to current employees or new recruits. Integrity is key.

>> **Relevance and freshness:** Keeping your employer branding messages relevant and fresh while maintaining consistency and continuity is a major challenge. Brand communication requires constant creative attention to find new ways to dramatize brand messages. You must maintain the core messages while finding fresh ways to express them and build the story through your content marketing and other forms of more experiential engagement.

TIP

Maintaining continuity while keeping your employer brand messaging relevant and fresh is more like creating a TV series than producing a movie. If you launch your employer brand like it's a movie, with lots of fanfare and a big event, the audience may feel as though all the excitement is over as soon as they leave the theater. "Well, I've seen that movie; what's next?" If you think of it more like a TV series, the dynamics are different. You establish the dramatic context, introduce key characters, develop some interest, and then build from there. Over time, the audience becomes more and more engaged, and excitement builds.

REMEMBER

Instead of thinking of the internal communication of your employer brand as a launch initiative, approach it as a cycle of engagement (see Figure 7-2) that builds involvement and momentum over time.

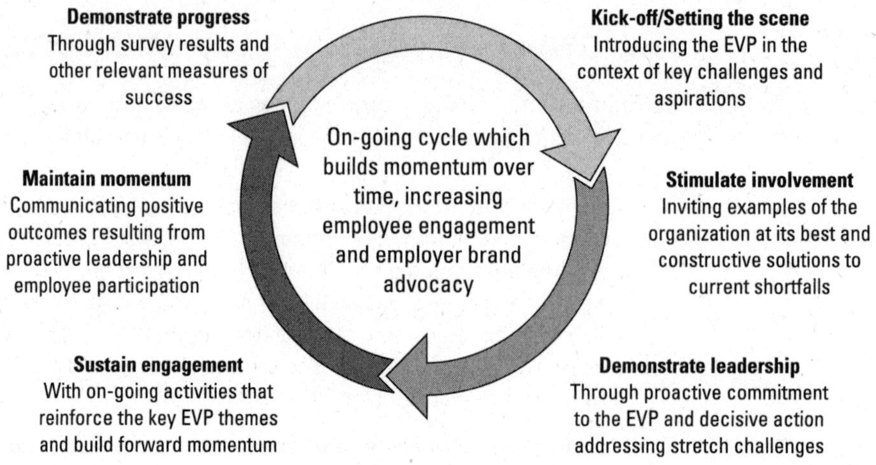

**Demonstrate progress**
Through survey results and other relevant measures of success

**Kick-off/Setting the scene**
Introducing the EVP in the context of key challenges and aspirations

**Maintain momentum**
Communicating positive outcomes resulting from proactive leadership and employee participation

On-going cycle which builds momentum over time, increasing employee engagement and employer brand advocacy

**Stimulate involvement**
Inviting examples of the organization at its best and constructive solutions to current shortfalls

**Sustain engagement**
With on-going activities that reinforce the key EVP themes and build forward momentum

**Demonstrate leadership**
Through proactive commitment to the EVP and decisive action addressing stretch challenges

**FIGURE 7-2:**
Cycle of engagement.

© John Wiley & Sons, Inc.

# 3
# Reaching Out through the Right Channels

Formulate a recruitment marketing plan that identifies your target audience's media preferences, achieves your recruitment objectives, and fits your budget.

Build an attractive and engaging career website and job microsites that showcase your employer brand and appeal to your organization's target talent groups.

Establish a network of current and past employees who will advocate for your employer brand and refer highly qualified candidates.

Harness the power of social media outlets — including LinkedIn, Glassdoor, Facebook, Twitter, and Snapchat — to spread the word about what your organization offers employees.

Launch recruitment advertising campaigns to reap the benefits of search engine marketing, paid media channels, job boards, and more.

Turn your focus to college campuses, target the right schools, market to college grads, leverage the power of college career services and student media, and spend valuable face time with prospects.

# Chapter 8

# Constructing Your Recruitment Marketing Plan

Recruitment marketing is all about attracting and engaging the type of people you want working for your company and then convincing them to come aboard. To market effectively, you need to know the people you're trying to attract and engage — whether they're college students looking for internship opportunities, recent college graduates who have a clear career path in mind, or experienced workers who feel as though they've reached a dead end at their current jobs. You need to know their media preferences — whether they prefer to read, watch video, or tap into social media. You need to examine what they want most in exchange for their time, effort, and expertise — money, flex time, creative freedom, the opportunity to make a difference in the world, and so on.

After sizing up your audience, you have what you need to develop a targeted recruitment marketing plan that defines your objectives, aligns media preferences with your targeted talent groups, coordinates attraction and engagement, and accounts for the needs and desires of the different talent groups you're recruiting. And you need to budget for the resources to execute that plan.

In this chapter, we lead you through the process of developing a recruitment marketing plan tailored to your company's talent needs. With this plan in place, you'll be well equipped to execute a recruitment marketing program that attracts and engages the best and the brightest.

# Sizing Up Your Audience

To communicate effectively, you need to think about the other person at least as much as the message you want to convey and the desired response. This principle holds true when you're trying to convince talented prospects to come and work for your company. Before you give any consideration to the messaging you want to use in your recruitment advertising campaigns or the media to use to reach out to prospects, you need to size up your audience to determine *their* preferences and what *they* are likely to find appealing.

In this section, we show you how to segment your audience, prioritize audience segments, and develop talent personas to more effectively connect with and appeal to the talent you're trying to attract and engage.

**TIP**

Approach recruitment marketing as you do consumer marketing. Just as in consumer advertising, where you need to present products and solutions in a way that aligns with customer needs, in recruitment marketing, you must present your company and the positions you need to fill in ways that align with the candidate's needs and aspirations. In both cases, a deeper understanding of the audience improves success.

## Segmenting your audience

Segmenting your audience involves differentiating between candidates you're trying to attract and convert. You can segment your audience using various criteria — for example, by experience (entry level, management, and executive), by position (software developers, human resources [HR], sales, accounting, and so forth), and by geographical area (locations where you need to ramp up your employer branding and recruiting efforts).

To segment your audience, look for categories that will help you more effectively target individuals in each category. For example, one segment may include college students and graduates, in which case your recruitment efforts are likely to focus on developing an internship program and increasing your on-campus recruiting efforts. Segmentation by position can help you determine which media to use to connect with certain segments, such as advertising in a magazine that's popular with game developers.

**REMEMBER**

When developing your recruitment marketing plan, consider the people you're recruiting. The creative and content of a campaign you'll use to attract software sales reps in APAC will differ from that used to attract software sales reps in the United States. Developing talent personas for the different candidate groups you're recruiting allows you to better understand their motivations and drivers, enabling you to build targeted recruitment marketing campaigns that speak directly to them. (See the later section "Creating talent personas" for details.)

## Prioritizing your audience segments

Hiring needs vary across companies, ranging from more generic talent (such as that needed to work the phones in call centers) to more specialized talent (such as data scientists who analyze big data to produce valuable business intelligence). Hiring needs may also vary according to location; for example, you may need to hire numerous candidates with a wide range of talent to run operations at a new distribution facility or hire highly specialized talent for several divisions of your company located in different countries.

As you evaluate your company's hiring needs, prioritize those needs, so you can allocate resources and gauge your recruiting efforts accordingly. As you prioritize hiring needs, consider the following factors:

>> **Current openings:** A high priority is filling current openings, so that the company has the personnel required to conduct daily operations.

>> **Positions that are key to strategy and revenue production:** Although all employees play a role in a company's success, some are key players in developing strategy and creating and identifying revenue-generating opportunities. These employees have a higher priority, because they create the opportunities that give everyone else in the company a job.

>> **Management:** People who can manage people and get them to work together to achieve common goals that contribute to the success of the company are high-priority hires. Those in charge of strategy and revenue production serve as the company's visionaries, but management provides the direction and coordination to execute those visions and innovations.

>> **Technical expertise:** Technology plays a key role in the success of most businesses. To optimize its potential benefits, you need people who know how to harness its power.

>> **Seniority:** You probably want to create a healthy mix of more and less experienced employees, so you have a skilled current and future workforce.

After prioritizing your hiring needs, use these priorities to inform your decisions on allocating your recruitment marketing budget and your marketing efforts.

**REMEMBER**

Hiring needs and priorities change. Monitor hiring needs closely and be prepared to reprioritize as conditions change.

## Creating talent personas

A *talent persona* is a fictional character that exhibits all the qualities you want the ideal candidate to possess. More specifically, a talent persona is

>> A fictional representation of the ideal job candidate

>> A compilation of criteria gathered from actual profiles of candidates who would likely be a good fit for your company and for the specific position along with input from others within the company who have insight into the type of person needed

>> A professional/personal portrait that's the product of well-informed speculation about the ideal candidate's professional and personal aspirations, motivations, interests, values, hobbies, lifestyle, and so on

>> A marketing tool to guide and validate the content strategy of your employer branding activities, rather than a recruiting tool to assess candidates

A talent persona features the following potential benefits:

>> It builds empathy toward target talent in a way that reports of qualitative and quantitative data alone can't accomplish.

>> It makes assumptions and knowledge about talent explicit, thereby giving the employer branding team a common language to use to talk meaningfully about targeted talent.

>> It moves the employer branding team from standard ways of categorizing talents to embodiments of key traits that are built around interests, needs, motivations, preferences, and goals.

To create a talent persona, gather the following details based on the audience segment you're going to pursue:

>> **Demographics:** Age/career level, marital status, education, career path, geographic preferences, income level

>> **Job information:** Title and similar titles, whether the position requires or provides supervision, skills required, goals of roles, career progression of role, what a typical day looks like, and so forth

>> **Challenges:** Professional and personal challenges, challenges within the industry

>> **Media preferences:** Social/digital networks used, blogs read, media preferences, professional associations (see the later section, "Evaluating Target Talent Media Preferences")

>> **Interests:** Hobbies, pastimes, passion projects, travel, and so on

## TRACING THE DEVELOPMENT OF TALENT PERSONAS

According to Ph.Creative, the concept of talent personas originated in consumer marketing in the mid-1990s with "consumer pen portraits," which were created to help develop a customer relationship management strategy. The concept was then adopted and made famous by advertising agency OgilvyOne and used by Apple to help inform the design of its user interface in 1999. Today, advertising giants use the concept with clients to develop employer brand campaigns that are deeply rooted in marketing.

The social media landscape that has enthralled us has also fragmented audiences across different channels, at different times and with different messages. Personas allow us to refocus and fine-tune our messaging so that it resonates with the people we want relationships with.

You want to be able to understand their wants and needs from their point of view, and how this information affects their buying decisions. Developing personas will allow you to identify core audience segments, understand their goals, and tailor content and products to match.

# Evaluating Target Talent Media Preferences

To connect with your target talent, your messaging needs to reach them where they hang out. Just as billboards target drivers, TV ads target couch potatoes, and pay-per-click (PPC) advertising targets people who spend time online, your recruitment advertising needs to target your talent where they spend most of their time or at least where they spend most of their time looking for jobs.

In this section, we lay out your media options, provide guidance on how to connect with the growing numbers of job candidates who consume media on the go, and provide suggestions on the different ways to approach candidates who are and aren't necessarily looking for a job — active and passive job seekers.

## Mapping out your media options

Newspaper advert? Radio ad? Podcast sponsorship? Targeted social ads? Today's world of recruitment media provides more options than ever before, but all these options dilute the impact and reach of any one option. To optimize the return on your recruitment advertising expenditures, you need to be tactical in your choice of which media options to use. Options range from traditional (including newspapers, magazines, radio, TV, billboard, and event advertising) to digital (such as search engines, websites, blogs, social networks, search engine marketing, podcasts, job boards, and email). For more about deciding on a media mix, see Chapter 12.

Assuming you created talent personas in the previous section, you should have a pretty clear idea of your targeted talent's media preferences, including what they read and what social networks they use. Mapping your media options is then just a matter of matching options to target personas.

**TIP**

To map media options to talent personas, you have the following three options:

>> **Do it yourself.** Small to midsize companies typically choose media options themselves, using options that worked for them in the past or following their intuition.

>> **Buy programmatic media.** Programmatic media buying involves using technology and optimized algorithms to purchase media across different channels. Work through a media broker, such as Rocket Fuel (www.rocket fuel.com) to determine which media options will be most effective. (For more about programmatic media, see Chapter 12.)

>> **Work with a recruitment advertising agency.** Team up with a recruitment advertising agency, such as TMP (www.tmp.com) or HireClix (www.hireclix.com), to help you set up your recruitment marketing ads and decide on optimum ad placement. This option is often preferred by large companies with ample budgets.

**REMEMBER**

Certain channels are cost-effective standards that all or most companies invest in, including social networking sites such as LinkedIn and Glassdoor. Investing in your own career website is also essential.

## Reaching people on the move (mobile)

Today's media is designed for a mobile-first world, and modern recruitment advertising must take this fact into consideration. Just look at the numbers:

>> **A majority of the people you're likely to be recruiting plan to use their mobile devices as they search for jobs.** Here's a breakdown of U.S. mobile usage for job search by age group from Indeed (http://blog.indeed.com/2014/09/18/78-of-candidates-would-apply-to-jobs-from-mobile):

- **Ages 16 to 34:** 77 percent

- **Ages 35 to 44:** 72 percent

- **Ages 45 to 54:** 54 percent

- **Ages 55 and over:** 35 percent

>> **Nine out of ten job seekers will use their mobile devices during the job search process in the next 12 months, as reported by Glassdoor.**

>> **Ninety-three percent of the consumers in emerging markets and 78 percent in developed markets look at their phones within an hour or less of waking up, as reported by Deloitte.**

No matter where you recruit in the world, mobile must be a key focus of your recruitment marketing campaigns. That means video must be shorter (no one wants to watch a 4-minute or longer recruiting video on a mobile device), and copy must be shorter and to the point. This goes for career sites, job descriptions, creative campaigns, and ad copy, too.

**TIP**

Here are a few suggestions on how to tailor your recruitment marketing for mobile users:

» **Keep copy minimal and to the point.** You don't want to make readers scroll more than necessary.

» **Pick visuals that aren't overly detailed.** If the images are too detailed, the fidelity and impact will be lost on a small screen.

» **If you use video in your recruitment marketing campaign, limit each clip to less than a minute.** That way, users on a mobile device can view on the go.

» **When developing your career website and other online properties, use a responsive design.** With responsive design, the content looks good and is accessible regardless of the size of the screen it's viewed on (desktop, laptop, tablet, smartphone, and so on). Responsive design also helps with search engine optimization (SEO); see Chapter 12 for details.

## Connecting with active and passive job seekers

Recruiters get enamored with the passive job seeker, as if there is an automatic assumption that actively looking for a job makes for a less desirable hire. This assumption is becoming less valid, as the following evidence suggests:

» **Passive job seekers are open to discussing opportunities.** According to LinkedIn, 75 percent of over 18,000 fully employed survey respondents from 26 countries consider themselves passive job seekers. When you dig deeper into how they respond to questions about being approached for new opportunities, 85 percent would be open to a conversation.

» **Passivity fluctuations with the changing job market.** As the market conditions decline, workers prefer stability and may be less inclined to leave their companies (providing they feel a sense of security there). As the economy strengthens, employees feel more confident about taking risks and changing jobs. This shifts the active/passive paradigm in a cyclical, somewhat predictable, way.

» **Passive can change to active in the blink of a social message.** In the age of social media, everyone is a prospect. Truly passive candidates, including the 15 percent from the LinkedIn study, may have no reason to visit a job board or your career site, but that doesn't prevent them from stumbling across one of your employer branded videos on Twitter or Snapchat. If they find that content compelling and interesting, and happen to see it on their way out of a rough meeting with their manager, they may be compelled to click that Apply button. That's passive to active at the speed of social.

Most candidates, whether active or not, are accessible in today's connected world. They're on Facebook. They use Snapchat. They listen to podcasts. All these outlets present opportunities to get your jobs and your employer brand in front of a receptive audience. If you approach employer branding as an opportunity to increase brand reach and exposure, whether prospects are active or passive doesn't really matter. After all, the more compelling, interesting, valuable, and relevant your employer branding efforts are, the more likely you are to convert *any* candidate.

**TIP**

Approach employer branding with the mind-set of convincing passive candidates to jump ship and join your organization. Presumably, you have to work harder to convince passive candidates to consider your opportunities because of their "passive" status. If your branding efforts are strong enough to convert that audience, they should be strong enough to convince "active" candidates as well. This approach can help simplify your branding efforts.

# Setting Out Your Plan

When you have a clear idea of your audience and your media options for reaching and engaging that audience, you're ready to formulate your recruitment marketing plan. The details of every recruitment marketing plan are different, so we can't possibly tell you specifically what to include in your plan, but here's an outline of the key points your plan should address:

>> **Audience traits:** Consult your target talent persona and list the top five to seven traits that characterize the ideal candidate.

>> **Audience motivation:** What about your employer value proposition (EVP) is likely to motivate most of the people you're recruiting? Is it your fun, creative work environment? Opportunities for advancement? Your company's commitment to the environment? (See Chapter 4 for more about developing and using an EVP.)

>> **Preferred media/communication channels:** Which communication channels and media are likely to be best for reaching and engaging with the targeted talent? LinkedIn, Glassdoor, Instagram, Snapchat, specific websites, or magazines?

>> **Connection back to EVP:** How is your recruitment marketing plan influenced by the EVP, and how does it further your employer branding efforts? Which EVP pillars does your plan emphasize?

REMEMBER

Your recruitment marketing plan may emphasize different pillars in your EVP depending on your audience, but it should be consistent with your EVP in order to reinforce your overall employer branding efforts.

# Balancing inbound and outbound marketing activities

As you develop your recruitment marketing campaign and choose preferred communications channels and media, include a plan for balancing inbound and outbound marketing activities:

>> **Outbound marketing activities** are *push actions* — traditional advertising that interrupts users and attempts to control their behavior in some way. These actions are targeted efforts to try to illicit a call to action (such as visiting your career site or applying for a job). Outbound activities include running recruitment ads, sending LinkedIn InMails, making cold calls, and displaying pop-ups or banners. Outbound activities are often ignored, but they're often necessary for reaching people who wouldn't otherwise be aware of what your company has to offer.

>> **Inbound marketing activities** are *pull actions* — typically something of value that draws the audience. Inbound marketing is designed to generate interest and earn trust. It may ultimately lead to a call to action, but the focus is more on giving the audience something of value than asking the audience to do something for you. Inbound is a longer play effort, often taking numerous engagements to develop a trusted relationship.

REMEMBER

The balance of outbound and inbound marketing activities can vary due to certain factors, including the following:

>> **Budget:** Outbound and inbound marketing activities can both be expensive — outbound in terms of advertising dollars and inbound in terms of internal time and effort in producing content. You'll need to make tradeoffs as you decide where to allocate resources.

>> **Talent persona priorities:** Your talent personas guide you in determining the advertising activities that are likely to deliver the best return on your investment. These may tilt the balance in favor of outbound or inbound advertising activities.

>> **Access to creative resources:** If your ability to execute creative recruiting initiatives is restricted, the balance may shift to more outbound advertising. If creative resources are plentiful internally, inbound marketing activities may be more effective and less costly.

>> **Where you are in your campaign:** For example, you may want to increase your outbound marketing activities at the beginning of a campaign to gain traction and shift the balance to more inbound marketing activities later to maintain momentum. Or you may decide to focus on inbound activities first, and then use outbound marketing to drive traffic to your internal content.

>> **Brand/local recognition:** If your company is well known or has a strong consumer brand, you'll likely need to spend less time telling your "who we are" story, and more time telling your "why you should work here" story. The bigger brand recognition means you can likely focus more on inbound. Lesser-known brands, or brands with bad consumer brands, must invest more time in proactively telling their stories through outbound efforts.

>> **Urgency:** Inbound tends to be a more time-consuming marketing activity because it's a longer-play effort aimed at shaping perceptions. Results may not occur quickly enough for a deadline-driven hiring initiative. So if you're building that new call center in Bangalore that must be fully operational in four months, you'll likely lean more (though not exclusively) toward outbound efforts.

# Putting a recruitment marketing system in place

In many ways, effective recruitment marketing is like trying to hit a moving target; the needs and preferences of the talent you target tend to change in response to changes in the economy, the popularity of certain social channels and media types, and shifts in interests and values. To improve your chances of connecting with and engaging the right people, put a recruitment marketing system in place that's designed to adapt to changes. Here's the six-step cycle we recommend:

1. **Evaluate your audience.**

   Identify and profile your target audience so you understand what channels they use, what their motivations are, and so on.

2. **Select media channels.**

   Determine the best channels to reach your target audience based on the results of your profiling efforts.

3. **Develop campaigns.**

   Craft campaigns that speak directly to the needs and motivations of your target audience.

4. **Launch your campaigns.**

   Test across different media channels to gauge return on investment (ROI) initially, and then increase investment after you've determined which channels yield the best results.

5. **Measure ROI.**

   Be sure you're tracking and measuring impact across all your channels. Whether your investment is time or money (or both), understanding which channels pay the greatest dividends for each target audience helps you invest wisely.

6. **Fine-tune your campaign.**

   Make adjustments and then head back to Step 1 and run through the process again. Monitoring results and fine-tuning your approach enables you to optimize results.

# Chapter 9

# Creating a Winning Career Site

Your career website is your career channel hub and shop window, the focal point for your employer brand. From this hub, you can branch out to other online properties, including social channels (LinkedIn, Glassdoor, Twitter, and so on) and job boards (CareerBuilder, Monster, Indeed, and so on). Your career website also gives you a convenient destination to send prospects for more info; you can link back to your career website from social channels, email and text messages, announcements for job openings, career-oriented press releases, comments and replies you post anywhere on the web (where appropriate), and all other relevant communications with prospects.

In its most advanced form your career website can provide a rich, multimedia brand experience. If suitably impressive, it draws the targeted prospects as they search for relevant job vacancies, and it streamlines the application process, so highly desired candidates are more likely to complete and submit their applications.

Given its vast potential to attract the right people and the key role it plays in your employer branding efforts, your career website deserves considerable time, effort, and expertise. In this chapter, we offer guidance on how to create a career website that showcases what you have to offer as an employer, draws the right talent to your organization, and ushers them through the application process.

# Making a Great First Impression

Your career website may be the first encounter a prospect has with your company. In this role, the website handles the initial meet and greet, so it needs to be attractive, impressive, and engaging.

**TIP**

Think of your career website as a funnel. At the top of the funnel is the landing page, where everyone even remotely interested and qualified to join your organization arrives. At the bottom is the Apply button for a specific job. The space between the two is the path that the prospect must follow. This is the space you need to populate with valuable content and active engagement to convince the right prospects to click that Apply button.

In this section, we focus on the top of the funnel — designing a career website that attracts prospects and delivers an experience that encourages them to explore what your company has to offer.

## Checking off landing page essentials

When you're selling a home, your real estate agent will tell you to focus first on curbside appeal. After all, if prospective buyers are turned off by their first encounter with the house, they're likely to drive off instead of stepping inside for a closer look. This curbside appeal concept applies to your website's landing page, as well. If your landing page is shabby or difficult to navigate, potential prospects, especially the most qualified candidates, are more likely to leave than linger. To impress visitors and draw them into your site, make sure your landing page contains the following items:

>> **Attractive, engaging design:** You can base your career website design on your corporate/customer website design to maintain a consistent brand, but modify the design to make it more appealing to the talent you're trying to attract.

>> **Compelling vision statement and/or recruiting tagline:** Compose a brief, catchy phrase or a single sentence that clearly and concisely conveys why candidates should consider joining your organization. Your vision statement or recruiting tagline should spark curiosity, evoke passion and pride, and inspire visitors to continue engaging with the site.

**TIP**

When composing a vision statement or recruiting tagline, do some competitive research. Your company may offer a "World of Opportunity," but so do half a dozen others in your space. Be distinctive.

>> **Banner or photos reflective of your company's culture and employees:** A banner may be a photo of a typical workspace, showing people working in a creative, fun environment or a button-down professional office. For example, the banner on the Airbnb career page (www.airbnb.com/careers) shows a guy with his shirt not tucked in sitting on an overstuffed chair and a gal off to the side walking with her dog; the image exudes a sense of fun, creativity, and comfort.

**TIP**

Use photos of real employees. Stock photos are an immediate turn-off to candidates trying to gauge your culture.

>> **A list of or link to current job openings:** Your employer branding efforts will drive both active and passive job seekers to your career site, so make it easy for them to find your jobs. Position your list of openings or some sort of navigation to your list of openings prominently above the fold on your landing page.

>> **Intuitive navigation:** Find out what prospects need to know most about careers or openings at your company, and make it easy for them to get there. For example, you may include a navigation bar along the top that contains links to pages where prospects can view current job openings, departments, locations, and information about your company's culture.

**REMEMBER**

Layout is key. Position all the core components you want job seekers to see, such as a Search Jobs button and social links, above the fold. Approach your career site as would a marketing maven and think user experience (UX). The simpler you make it for users to navigate their way through the funnel, the better.

## Integrating with your social properties

Of all your online properties, your career website is probably the easiest to maintain. All you need to do is keep the list of job openings up to date. The rest of the site remains mostly static. Once a year, you may tweak the copy or do a major overhaul just to keep the site looking fresh and to add features that weren't available a year ago.

Unfortunately, a static site, regardless of how amazing it is, doesn't earn the loyalty of returning visitors. The solution: Integrate your more dynamic online properties — your social media channels, such as LinkedIn, Glassdoor, and Twitter — with your static website. Social website integration enables you to provide a real-time employee-driven narrative about the organization, while your base copy remains static.

# RECRUITING WITH A VISION AT PALANTIR

Palantir is a Palo Alto–based data analytics company that recruits technical talent in one of the most competitive hiring climates on the planet. The day we visited, Palantir's careers page had a banner photo of a young worker wearing earphones looking intently at a what appeared to be a panel of three large computer screens. The subtle message: This company employs tech-savvy individuals, who can work independently. Less subtle are its tagline and vision statement, which appear front and center over the banner:

## THERE IS SO MUCH LEFT TO BUILD

At Palantir, we work for the common good — within our organization and with other organizations around the world. We're building a future where data can be leveraged to serve people, create value, and improve quality of life.

Palantir interns apply their knowledge to real-world problems from day one. Learn more.

## OPEN POSITIONS

No matter where you're based, or which team you work on, you'll be part of a group of people working together to build solutions to mission-critical problems and a company that values the very best ideas. There's a role for you here — where you're a new grad or have years of experience.

Examine this landing page more closely:

- **Tagline:** The tagline, "There is so much left to build," conveys a sense of vision, purpose, and opportunity. It suggests that the company has a place for people who yearn to build something that really matters. The word *build* can be applied to job, career, company, or even oneself. The tagline clearly speaks to movers and shakers — people who create and lead.

- **Vision statement:** The vision statement sets the stage for the work done at Palantir — work for the common good, work within the organization (locally), and work around the world (globally). "Building a future" resonates with the tagline of there being so much left to build. The work is "data" driven to "create value" and to "improve quality of life," suggesting that the company cares not only about the work but also about how that work can improve people's lives and ensure a better future.

- **Appeal to interns:** Just below the banner is a special appeal to interns, indicating that Palantir has an active internship program and that it values interns enough to single them out. Clicking the link directs users to a microsite that focuses on recruiting interns (for more about microsites, see the later section "Creating Job Microsites").

- **Open positions:** Palantir doesn't make visitors click a link or page through menus to find a list of openings. On the landing page, just above the fold is the text "OPEN POSITIONS," which lets visitors know they can scroll down for a list of openings.

Visit the career pages of top employers, especially those that compete for the same talent you're trying to attract. Check out their taglines and vision statements and closely examine how easy or difficult it is to navigate to the list of job openings or the page where visitors can search for openings. Use what you discover to perfect your own career website.

All social platforms have numerous prescripted *plugins* that you can easily add to any web page by copying and pasting the script into the source code for the web page. For example, LinkedIn has several tools that automatically generate custom JavaScript code to add LinkedIn functionality to a web page. LinkedIn plugins include Follow Company, Company Profile, Company Insider, and Jobs You Might Be Interested In. You can add a plugin that users can click to follow you on Twitter. YouTube and Vimeo also feature video embed codes that you can paste into the web page's source code to include a video on the page.

Just as you use your social channels to drive traffic *in* to your career website (see Chapter 11), use your website to drive traffic *out* to your social channels.

## Optimizing for mobile

More users are spending more time accessing the web via smartphones than ever before, so design your website accordingly. Among web designers and builders, creating websites for mobile devices including smartphones calls for *responsive design* — a fluid approach that enables a website to adapt to the size of the screen on which it's viewed, so it looks great on any device and doesn't require the user to engage in cumbersome left–right scrolling to view content that appears off-screen. Responsive websites deliver a similar candidate experience, regardless of whether the visitor is on a desktop, tablet, or smartphone.

Embrace *mobile-first design;* that is, design your site to look great on a mobile device and then work toward making it look great on larger displays. In the past, web developers designed for larger screens first and then tried to scale the site down for mobile devices. Now that more people are navigating the web using mobile devices, developers are taking the opposite approach — mobile first.

## Staying a step ahead of the Joneses

Although a career website is relatively static compared to the more dynamic social media channels, consider updating your site annually to take advantage of the latest web technologies and design practices. For example, in the not-so-distant past, web developers insisted on keeping important elements above the fold and dividing content into multiple pages. Keeping key elements above the fold is still important, but long pages with fewer links out to other pages are more common. With the increasing popularity of the mobile web, users have become more accustomed to scrolling, so long pages have become more acceptable, and they provide all related content on a single page, so users don't have to click through a trail of links.

Another trend in web design is the tile layout or card layout, made popular by Pinterest. A page may have several cards or tiles that break information into more digestible chunks. Phenom People is a tool that allows you to build tile-based career sites that target and serve content based on your user profile. The Careers at Phenom People site (`http://careers.phenompeople.com`) employs this approach on at least a portion of its landing page. Each card represents a different business function: Customer Success, Implementation, Product Development, Sales, and Other.

Rather than a static site structure for all visitors, sites that use a tile format are often widget based and enable you to provide a tailored experience to visitors via browser-based cookies; for example, a product manager in Singapore may see product development job listings in the Asia-Pacific (APAC) region, while a sales associate in New York receives a list of job openings in the company's sales department in the Northeast U.S. region. This targeted approach allows you to hyper-tailor content to the talent you're recruiting.

# Delivering the Goods: Content

When you have a clear idea of the look, feel, and function of your career website, you're ready to turn your attention to the most important component of any website — content. As you gather and create content for your website, follow these guidelines:

>> Align your content with your employer value proposition (EVP; see Chapter 4).

>> Tailor your content to the different talent groups you're recruiting.

>> Write job descriptions that attract the right people and make everyone else think twice about applying.

>> Streamline the application process, so exceptional candidates aren't turned off by an onerous chore.

In this section, we address each of these guidelines in greater detail.

# Aligning your website with your employer value proposition

The two most basic objectives of any communication strategy are to engage your target audience and convey your message. An additional objective, from the employer branding perspective, is to ensure that the collective result of your communication is a more positive and distinctive brand image. To achieve this objective, consult your EVP (see Chapter 4) for guidance when producing content and messaging. Your core positioning statement and brand pillars point the way to the type of content and messaging you need to be posting on your career website and social channels. For example, if your core positioning statement is "Shape the future of sport" (Adidas), your career site may pitch certain job descriptions in a way that shows how that particular position contributes to shaping the future of sport, or you may include employee achievements that contribute to shaping the future of sport.

**REMEMBER**

You can reinforce a positive and distinctive brand image to some degree by consistently framing and branding your content, but ideally, your content must also help to reinforce consistent brand associations. A series of employee-focused stories may engage the target audience; personalize the corporation, making it more attractive to graduates; and prompt candidates to apply. All of these are worthy communication objectives. However, content falls short of effective brand communication if it doesn't also demonstrate and dramatize the key characteristics of the organization you want potential candidates to associate with your company.

**WARNING**

Don't obsess over brand control. Not all content and every message needs to align with a brand pillar. The objective is to ensure that you have enough consistency in the overall content mix to communicate the desired employer brand associations.

## Tailoring content to target groups

Writing branded content about your company and what a wonderful place it is to work is relatively easy, but it may not resonate with specific talent groups. What makes a company a great place to work for marketing people isn't what makes it a great place to work for programmers, product development specialists, or operations analysts. Target content to different talent groups. Here's how:

>> **When developing content, consult personnel in the talent areas you're targeting.** For example, if your company is in dire need of software developers, ask the software developers in your company to be involved in content development. Ask them to produce content, make suggestions, or at least review content before posting it to your career website. Nobody knows more about what appeals to a certain talent group than the people in your company who belong to that group.

>> **Provide a balanced mix of content throughout your website to showcase various departments and personnel that have openings you need to fill, such as administration, business development, engineering, design, operations, and legal.** You may want to include more content for talent that's a higher priority or give such content more prominence on your career website, but provide at least some content that speaks to each talent group you recruit.

>> **If your value proposition differs substantially for different employee populations, consider creating a separate page for each talent group and populate that page with content that speaks more directly to each group.** You may even want to create a microsite that focuses on recruiting high-demand talent (see the later section "Creating Job Microsites" for details).

**REMEMBER**

Trying to appeal to everyone often appeals to no one. Overly general messaging fails to resonate with any given target group. Identify key talent groups, and ensure your career website clearly conveys your EVP to your most coveted prospects.

## Writing effective job descriptions

Job descriptions are one of the least evolved tools in the corporate recruiting tool belt. They tend to be written for the benefit of the employer, not the employee. When writing job descriptions, don't simply list job features and qualifications (employer needs); focus more on how the position is likely to benefit the candidate (employee needs). Focus as much on the feel as the facts.

**TIP**

Here are a few suggestions on how to infuse your job description with both facts and feel:

>> Add links to additional content and messaging, such as press releases, awards, employee blogs, multimedia, company social channels, and so on. Linking to addition content makes the job description more dynamic and interactive.

>> Include a 30-second video of the hiring manger talking enthusiastically about the specific position in the company and the unique work environment and camaraderie the department fosters.

>> Share stories of employees in similar roles and their career growth.

>> Include LinkedIn profiles or other social profiles of team members, so the prospect can envision how cool it would be to work with these extraordinary individuals.

- >> Embed photos or videos of the office that reveal the company culture.

- >> Include infographics and other visual media to convey the opportunity being presented.

**REMEMBER**

Prospects may not view job descriptions until after they investigate a potential new employer, but they're just as likely to encounter a job description when they take the first step on their job search journey. A high percentage of active job seekers start their search on the Internet using job-related terms instead of the names of specific employers.

## STEER CLEAR OF BOILERPLATE JOB DESCRIPTIONS

Many job descriptions are based on outdated notions that can't be quantified, such as "excellent teamwork," just pulled off the shelf from the last time the role was filled five years ago. When recycling in this way, companies often fail to give prospects a true sense of what the company is like — its culture, its teams, its perks, and its physical office space. They try to convey the soul of their organization in text alone and tend to rely too much on the landing page as the place to share images, videos, and employee profiles.

Today's prospects are busier (and more distracted) than ever. You have a limited window to capture their attention, particularly when targeting high-demand talent. A boilerplate job description won't do it; it doesn't give prospects a reason to explore your jobs. They want to know about deliverables, success measures, growth plans, and perks, along with what their desk might look like, what tools they might use, and what their colleagues are like.

As Matt Lampheer, TMP Worldwide's EVP for Digital Marketing and Strategy, comments:

The differentiation of a job from company X and a job from company Y is often negligible in displaying job information despite what may be on the home page of a company's career site. Since jobs are often the first step on a potential candidate's journey, there is a significant opportunity to differentiate at the job level. We shouldn't be talking to software engineers in the same way we speak with administrative people. Not marketing-speak or overarching company news, but messaging and content relevant to the role.

Good writing always places the needs of the reader over those of the writer. As you compose job descriptions, imagine yourself selling the job to the ideal prospect.

**TIP**

Here are three suggestions to increase the availability and impact of a job description:

>> **Make it mobile.** Assume your primary audience will be reading the job description on a mobile device.

>> **Make it meaningful.** Avoid boilerplate templates and laundry lists of expectations.

>> **Make it dynamic.** Add photos, videos, and links to bring the job to life.

**TIP**

Consider using tools such as Clinch (`www.clinch.io`) to frame job descriptions with other relevant contextual content. Such content may include day-in-the-life video profiles, photographs of the working environment, and tailored brand messages that highlight aspects of the overall employer brand promise that are known to be most relevant and important to the type of people targeted for the role.

## Making it easy to apply

Face it, applying for a job can be annoying and frustrating. You come across that amazing job, spend hours getting your résumé and application together, submit your application, jump through a series of hoops, and then wait . . . and wait . . . and wait. This is the unfortunate reality for most job seekers today. Here are a few suggestions to make your application process less painful:

>> **Apply for a job listed on your career site.** How long did it take? How pleasant was the experience? Did you ever hear back about the status of your application? If you received a reply, did it have a personal touch or was it obviously a stock template? Applying to your own jobs is a great way to understand the application experience. It can be eye opening, revealing why your drop-off rate is so high and applications are so few.

>> **Optimize for mobile.** Make it easier for mobile users to navigate the application. Use white space. Keep sentences short. Don't overdo the word count. Be sure to keep this in mind when writing the copy for your career site.

>> **Audit the application process.** Using tools such as Google Analytics (`http://analytics.google.com`), find out where applicants are dropping out of the process and focus your efforts on those points. While you're at it, eliminate any nonessential steps and nonessential fields on the application form.

>> **Manage expectations.** Let the applicant know upfront how much time the application generally requires to complete and how the process will unfold. Consider adding FAQs to your auto-response application receipt confirmations to help set expectations when candidates apply (more on that in the next section).

>> **Provide feedback.** Inform applicants of where they are in the application process and how much further they need to go. After an applicant submits an application, send a timely confirmation message with some indication of when the applicant can expect to hear back.

Approach the online application process as an opportunity to find out more about potential candidates instead of as a way to weed out unqualified applicants.

## Personalizing your response letters

Most companies confirm receipt of the application by sending an impersonal, computer-generated email. Such letters typically say nothing more than "We received your résumé. Thank you for applying." That's what applicants have come to expect; yes, the bar is *that* low. The good news is that this standard, impersonal approach presents you with a golden opportunity to exceed applicants' expectations.

Here are a few suggestions for adding a personal touch to your response letters and proactively addressing candidates' questions and concerns:

>> **Include graphics.** Most recruiting emails are text-only, which is dull. Add a colorful, branded header image and one or two interesting or entertaining graphics in the body of the message.

>> **Provide a hiring process overview.** Remove the mystery of applicant volume, how applications are evaluated, the interview process, and the time frame.

>> **Let candidates know when they can expect to hear back.** You can relieve a lot of anxiety simply by managing expectations. If applicants know they won't be contacted for six weeks, they're much more patient and understanding.

>> **Lighten up.** Use appropriate humor or some other approach to connect with the applicant on a more personal level and alleviate any tension. Aim toward shifting the balance in tone from professional to personal.

>> **Give applicants something to do.** Include a link to check the application status and links to social channels where you post additional jobs content. Candidates always wonder "What else can I do?" This answers that question.

Keep your EVP in mind when composing response letters. The overall appearance and tone of your letters must align with your core positioning and brand pillars. To brand your company as the fun, creative place to work, for example, make sure your letter is both fun and creative.

When composing a rejection letter, show some compassion. Acknowledge the fact that rejection letters can disappoint and discourage job seekers. Let the applicant know how stiff the competition was and how difficult the choice was. Do your best to make the candidate feel good about herself and her qualifications and hopeful in her job search.

# Creating Job Microsites

A *job microsite* is a small independent website, separate from the primary career website, that's focused on recruiting a specific set of candidates. For example, a company may launch a job microsite devoted exclusively to recruiting college interns or recent college graduates. You can also create microsites based on business unit or function.

Each microsite delivers content that's tailored to the specific needs and interests of the targeted talent group. When candidates enter certain search criteria, the search results direct them to the relevant microsite. For example, if a potential candidate searches for a job in systems engineering, the person is directed to a microsite that presents relevant job openings and a richer assortment of context-specific content, such as:

>> Details about the company's internship program

>> A broader introduction to the specific business function or unit

>> Information about the site and location

>> Job-specific images and video content, which may include relevant employee profiles or a personal message from the hiring manager

>> Messages that your research or experience suggests are the most appropriate for this talent group

>> Links to other relevant jobs

This kind of context-rich framing has already become commonplace in consumer content — music, for example. The application Shazam enables you to connect a song you're listening to (or simply searching for) with a wide range of relevant content. Options include downloading the song, watching it on YouTube, accessing information about the artist or concert tour dates, and, of course, sharing this content with your social contacts. Job microsites enable you to do the same thing with job content.

**»** **Turning rejected applicants into brand advocates**

**»** **Tapping the power of talent communities**

# Chapter **10**

# Developing Your Talent Network

Traditionally, people seeking employment have engaged in networking to find the best jobs. In this chapter, we turn that model on its head to explain how you can network to find the best employees. After all, the underlying principles and benefits are the same:

**»** Networking extends the reach of both the company and the candidates, exposing both to opportunities they may never have considered on their own.

**»** Networking filters out bad employees and employers, saving both parties time and resources.

**»** Those who know both the company and the candidate are uniquely qualified to serve as matchmakers.

With the explosion of professional and social networking venues, including LinkedIn, Glassdoor, and Twitter, networking is an increasingly powerful recruiting and selection tool. In this chapter, we show you how to harness your community connections to find, recruit, and select top talent for your company.

# Leveraging the Networking Power of Current and Former Employees

Collectively, your current and former employees can be an employer branding goldmine. They know what it's like to work for your company, at least a few of them are probably well connected to talented prospects, and they have a vested interest in bringing the best people into the company — people they'd like to work with and who will contribute to the company's success and earn kudos (and possibly a bounty) for the employee who referred them. And even if an employee isn't well connected, that person can sing your praises as a top-notch employer, thus contributing to your efforts of building a positive employer brand reputation.

In this section, we reveal the benefits of employee referrals and explain how to encourage and facilitate referrals from current and former employees.

## Understanding why referrals make great hires

Referrals are broadly considered one of the best sources for hires — and for good reason. Because of their relationships with their inside contacts, referred candidates typically have a much better view of your organization, culture, team, and how work gets done. They apply with eyes wide open about subtle job-related nuances that don't show up in job descriptions. This insight enables them to make well-informed decisions about how your opportunity aligns with their own interests, work style, and aspirations.

On the hiring side, you can reverse-engineer the preceding paragraph to make a case for why referred candidates tend to make better hires. They've been more deeply prepped for the opportunity, including some of the less desirable aspects of the job, and are being recommended by someone who knows them firsthand and vouches that this new hire is a good fit. Essentially, referral candidates are pre-screened by someone in your company who has a vested interest in that candidate's success.

According to a recent study by Jobvite (www.theundercoverrecruiter.com/ infographic-employee-referrals-hire), several key statistics illustrate the value of referrals:

>> **Employee referrals have the highest applicant-to-hire conversion rate.** Only 7 percent of those applying for a position are referred by employees, but they account for 40 percent of all those eventually hired.

>> **Applicants hired from a referral begin their position quicker than applicants found via job boards and career sites.** Referrals begin after 29 days compared with 39 days via job boards and 55 days via career sites.

>> **Sixty-seven percent of employers and recruiters reported that the recruiting process was shorter for referrals.**

>> **Fifty-one percent of employers and recruiters reported that recruiting referrals was less expensive.**

According to a report by iCIMS (`http://bit.ly/2bPLwma`), employee referrals at large companies account for nearly 40 percent of all new employees hired. When rates at smaller companies are added in, the percentage drops to 24 percent. If your rate is any lower than 25 percent, you need to figure out how to get there, which is the subject of the next section.

The nearby sidebar reveals how Dell significantly improved its *employee referral program* (a recruiting program that encourages and often rewards employees for discovering talented people who are eventually hired by the company). However, not all organizations have the size or resources to apply these approaches. The guidance we provide in the following sections are designed to help any size company build an employee referral program from the ground up.

## Setting up an employee referral program

Every company should have an employee referral program, and an effective program doesn't need to be a budget buster. Most established referral programs include bonuses, but studies have shown that bonus amounts and referrals don't necessarily have a direct correlation. Incentives for referring talented individuals to an employee's workplace are inherent in human nature. People want to work with their friends, people they admire, or those they can learn from. It's in their own best interest to bring those types of people into the organization, assuming they're a good fit.

However, employee referrals don't happen without some impetus. You have to develop programs that provide awareness of current hiring needs, publicly recognize referral successes, and creatively encourage employee involvement. As you build or strengthen your employee referral program, strive to create a program that achieves the following goals:

>> **Promote hiring awareness.** One of the biggest mistakes companies make is creating referral programs, even investing in large bounties, but not having any mechanisms to ensure employees are aware of the talent being sought or the positions that need to be filled. Some referrals happen organically, but success depends largely on awareness. Given this fact, the first step in building a successful referral program is ensuring that your employees know what jobs are open.

# FIXING DELL'S EMPLOYEE REFERRAL PROGRAM

The following case study from Dell illustrates how organizations can evaluate, adjust, and reframe their employee referral programs to significantly improve outcomes. (This case study was shared by Dell on HR Open Source at www.hros.co/case-studies.)

Dell knew it had serious challenges with its employee referral program given the volume of complaints in many locations. These comments were not isolated, and they came from multiple sources, including employees, recruiters, and hiring leaders. Dell was expending a significant amount of time to constantly monitor and manage queries and complaints. It realized that there was an inconsistency in understanding of the program so referral rates were all over the map — in some locations very low (single-digit percentages). Dell decided to take a step back to objectively review all the operational components, assess its challenges, map solutions, and implement enhancements that could take its referral program to the next level.

Some of the challenges Dell uncovered during its discovery process included:

- **Lack of consistent policy interpretation:** No global program owner was in place, and the policy was managed and interpreted differently country by country. This included eligibility differences, payout time frame differences, and so on. Also no regional owners or points of contact for employees or recruiters were available to respond to questions or issues.

- **Manual process:** Recruiters were spending their own time to manually track referrals on spreadsheets that sat on their desktops. Not only was this a poor use of the recruiter's time, but if one of them left, referral payouts were dropped, creating exceptions, requests, and frustrations on the part of the employee and payroll.

- **Inability to pay out for those making referrals in other countries**

- **Inability to accurately track global spend**

- **Manual data entry errors:** Managers had to manually key in referral numbers. Even with the payout matrix (which helped), sometimes the amounts keyed in were wrong, causing major issues with team members on the back end.

- **Inconsistent promotion and understanding of the program**

- **Inconsistent referral payments:** Some countries didn't have an agreed-upon amount and would have to wing it.

- **Incorrect logging:** Fewer than half of all referrals were properly recorded, creating manual work country by country to determine referral payout percentage.

- **No social sharing of jobs**

Dell set about to completely redesign its referral program with a heavy focus on prioritizing referrals and alumni activation. These efforts led to the following results:

- **A 50 percent to 125 percent increase in global referral hires:** Dell's global employee referral rate doubled from 19 percent in 2010 to 38 percent, and over 50 percent in some locations.

- **A 20 percent decrease over three years in cost-per-hire:** The new global referral program was one of several initiatives that resulted in this cost savings.

- **More accurate global forecasting:** Consistent values in USD payouts resulted in clearer insight into spend by location, level, and business unity, enabling the recruiting team to more accurately and effectively update and inform the business.

- **Consistent time frames for payouts**

- **Much more accessible and flexible referral data:** More flexible data gives recruiters the ability to filter by job grade, function, region, and business unit to share with the organizations they support.

- **Enhanced global participation in enterprise resource planning:** Employees have clear guidelines on things such as cross-country referrals, payouts and timing, referral levels, amounts, and so on.

- **Realized administration time savings roughly equal to one full-time employee**

- **Consistent monitoring of exceptions:** Better monitoring enables Dell to easily identify and address policy or tool issues.

- **Improved documentation (in multiple languages):** Well-documented employee referral policies help to support any payout or denial of payout with a clear reason.

- **Centralized tracking of referral sources:** Improved tracking results in better reporting, dashboards, forecasting, and visibility.

**TIP**

Consider creating a weekly/monthly newsletter that highlights open jobs across your company. If you hire a high volume, highlight the key openings and be sure to hyperlink to jobs to make them easy to share. Newsletters are also a great way to share recent referral hires and publicly thank the source of the referral.

» **Prioritize employee referrals.** Put a system in place that streamlines the evaluation and hiring process for referred candidates and quickly acknowledges and thanks employees for making referrals. The quickest way to demotivate employees from making referrals is to sit on the applications of referred candidates.

- >> **Keep employees in the loop.** To maintain engagement with your referring employees, keep them posted regarding the status of the candidates they referred. Consider developing a "white glove" approach for referrals to ensure employees and referred candidates are kept in the loop and receive timely updates.

- >> **Publicly recognize referrers.** Public recognition is a great way to get employees involved in your referral program. Seeing their peers participate and be recognized helps employees understand how your organization values involvement in your employee referral program.

- >> **Motivate and reward in creative ways.** Many companies limit their referrals to cash bonuses, but money alone may not be the best incentive. Think of other fun, creative perks, such as time off, donations to the employee's charity of choice, smartphones, laptops, trips, travel vouchers, tickets to concerts or plays, and so on. You can even gamify the system, awarding bigger prizes for more and better referrals or for discovering talented people to fill key positions in the company. Have fun with it, and be sure to promote it broadly.

TIP

Maintain impeccable records on employee referrals, and encourage employees and the talented people hired through the referral program to share their stories of success in your employee referral program. Such stories can provide your company with valuable content to further the goals of your employer branding efforts in addition to expanding employee participation in the program.

## EXPERIENTIAL INCENTIVES AT InMobi

If you've ever been to India, you know that motorcycles are a common method of communication. Instead of embracing the traditional cash bonus programs, InMobi incentivized its employees by offering a motorcycle as a reward for successfully referring an engineering manager (https://business.linkedin.com/talent-solutions/blog/employee-referrals/2015/when-it-comes-to-referral-bonuses-this-company-proves-that-experiences-beat-cash).

To create additional buzz around its program, InMobi parked the motorcycle in the middle of its office. Every day employees walked by the shiny new hot rod, and had a constant reminder to refer talent.

This was the beginning of InMobi's shift from cash incentives to "experiential incentives," and it took the referral program from 20 percent to 50 percent in the span of a year.

# Building an alumni talent network

Employees are wise to follow the age-old adage "don't burn your bridges on the way out," but the same holds true for employers. Former employees can be a great source of referrals. They may even return to a company as valuable *boomerang hires* —former employees who return to the company. Here are a few suggestions for creating your own alumni talent network:

**TIP**

>> **Put someone in charge of building and maintaining your alumni talent network.** Don't assume that "if you build it, they will come." Someone in your company needs to be in charge of encouraging and rewarding participation in the network and monitoring activity.

>> **Create a place to meet online.** You can create an alumni talent network online via social platforms, such as LinkedIn and Facebook. This meeting place serves as a social glue that maintains the bond between former employees and your company, as well as their bond between each other and with former colleagues still working at your company.

If any unofficial alumni group already exists, reach out to its founders or facilitators to gauge their interest in launching an official alumni talent network.

>> **Retool your exit interview.** Instead of handing departing employees their final paychecks and saying goodbye, encourage them to stay in touch and remain active in your alumni talent network. Follow up with an email invitation to join the alumni talent network along with a list of benefits and instructions on how to join and participate.

>> **Encourage current employees to join.** Former employees typically have strong bonds with current employees, so provide all employees the opportunity to stay in touch.

>> **Host alumni talent events.** Cocktail parties, alumni outings, professional retreats, and so forth provide alumni with opportunities to stay in touch, hone their skills, and further their careers.

>> **Extend employee referral incentives to former employees.** Don't lose a potential source of employee referrals when employees are leaving your company. Let them know that they can continue to reap the benefits of your employee referral program.

# NURTURING BOOMERANG HIRES AT CA TECHNOLOGY

CA Technology is a global technology firm with an active practice of "boomerang" hiring. The Talent Acquisition Marketing and Operations teams wanted to establish a way to actively engage with previous employees and to create a talent community of these potential candidates who may consider returning to the organization. They saw the key advantages of staying connected to their alumni because of their understanding of CA's corporate culture, processes, and goals. They also saw this alumni candidate pool as natural brand ambassadors who can be utilized to help amplify the CA Talent Brand in the marketplace. Finally, they saw a reduced burden on the business when it comes to onboarding, because these candidates already know how to perform the role in the way required at the company.

CA Technology launched a formal boomerang talent community to more effectively engage and cultivate these hires. The objective and scope were to create a talent community of CA Alumni that the company can actively engage with for branding activations and rehire. The operations team developed a process where, on a quarterly basis, an invitation was sent to any former employees who left the company at any time during the previous two quarters (on the first of the year, the company would invite ex-employees from July 1 to Sept 30) to join the exclusive Alumni Talent Community. This group of people will be fully searchable by the company's talent acquisition team. To maintain engagement and provide a level of exclusivity, the talent acquisition marketing team created an engagement plan that generates alumni-specific content distributed on a monthly basis to cultivate a high level of engagement from the community. Twenty percent of those invited joined the new alumni talent community. The program launched in 2016 so hire metrics are limited, but company leadership expects a measurable increase in boomerang hires as a result. According to Craig Fisher, head of marketing, talent acquisition in the Americas:

> Workers see jobs more as projects which can be done with many different employers over a career. They change jobs every two or three years, so the goal of talent acquisition must shift from being not just a great place to work, but a great place to come back to. We must court our boomerangs. If we play our cards right, the best workers will work with us again and again in some capacity. At CA Technologies we went to great lengths to track *and* attract our potential boomerang hires back to the organization. The results have been outstanding. When they come back, we must make work so compelling, vital, and urgent that our workforce feels constantly challenged, appreciated, and that they are continually growing. We must give them the tools to be more efficient. And we must make it easy for them to work when and where they want.

# Boosting Your Rejected Candidate Referral Rate

For every candidate you hire, dozens, hundreds, or even thousands more are rejected. Every single one of these candidates is a potential source of candidate referrals and is a potential brand advocate or detractor. For these two reasons, and others not mentioned here, you need to invest some time, effort, and resources in creating a positive candidate experience (CX). For details on how to create a positive CX, turn to Chapter 15. Part of your focus in creating a positive CX is to generate rejected candidate referrals (RCRs). Here are a few suggestions on how to increase your RCR rate:

>> **Treat all candidates with respect and compassion.** The application and selection process is very emotional. Express your appreciation for the time and effort they invested in applying for the job, answer any questions they have, and respond from a position of empathy.

>> **Manage expectations on your career website and in your job descriptions.** If your company typically receives hundreds or thousands of applications for the jobs posted or for a particular position, include this information on your career site and in the job description, so applicants have a realistic expectation of their odds and will be more understanding if they receive an auto-generated rejection letter.

**TIP**

Consider setting up a system that automatically responds to applicants after they submit their applications and presents them with FAQs about the application, review, and interview process. This is an easy and automated way to manage expectations and help applicants understand the process the moment they apply.

>> **Keep candidates posted regardless of the decision.** Candidates who don't hear back from you are likely to write off your company. They won't apply for future openings, and they certainly won't do you the favor of referring talented candidates your way. Send rejection letters or emails informing them of your hiring decision.

>> **Let them down easy.** Rejection is emotionally deflating. Let candidates know that they're valued even though they're not your candidate of choice for a particular position. Remind them of the stiff competition for the job. Let them know whether you plan to keep their applications on file and consider them for future openings.

>> **Ask them for candidate referrals.** You'll get rejected candidate referrals only if you ask for them. Encourage rejected candidates to monitor your career website for future openings, apply for any they're qualified for, and refer other qualified candidates to your career site.

**REMEMBER**

The online transparency available through social media, including LinkedIn and Glassdoor, makes it easy for rejected candidates to publicize and amplify both positive and negative candidate experiences across various channels. That's reason enough to create a positive CX for all applicants.

# Creating Your Own Talent Communities

A powerful way to network for talent is to create your own talent communities. A *talent community* is a forum where individuals with shared skill sets and interests can gather and interact both personally and professionally with each other and with the company's leadership, management, and HR personnel. From a recruiting perspective, a talent community is a talent pool that can meet the current and future hiring needs of the company.

**WARNING**

Don't create a talent community to serve solely as a passive audience for job openings and company updates. A true talent community is focused on engagement. Members extract value primarily from peer-to-peer exchanges.

To create and build a vibrant talent community that attracts the talent your organization needs, take the following steps:

1. **Analyze your target audience.**

   Who are the ideal members of your talent community? What are their drivers? Consult your persona maps (see Chapter 8), and consider other segments you want to target, such as alumni, function/skill groups, specific locations, students, and so on.

2. **Select a platform for hosting your talent community.**

   Your platform options include the following:

   - *Social platforms:* Social platforms, including LinkedIn and Facebook, are very effective for hosting talent communities. You can find ways to add specific host value, such as special content or access to your employees, discounts, and so on.

   - *Candidate relationship management platforms:* The advantages of these platforms is that they're designed to support recruiting, they likely integrate with your applicant tracking system, and they enable advanced segmentation and targeting of talent. The disadvantage is they often don't allow peer-to-peer sharing, so they're really more for creating and managing dynamic talent pools than true communities.

### 3. Establish the ground rules.

Write a description of the community, its purpose, its potential member benefits, and its ground rules (rules of engagement). Include this information in the group description when creating your group and in email invitations to join the group. Let members know what the group is about, why it was created, what's expected of them, and what's prohibited.

### 4. Create a community management plan.

Most online communities require a community management plan, especially in the community's early days, to help drive conversation, answer questions, and moderate posts. When an online community is well established, you're more likely to see members self-moderating undesirable or abusive behavior.

**WARNING**

Protect against spammers. Social platforms can be a haven for spammers. Have a process in place to quickly review and approve posts to ensure your members aren't being spammed. A quick review and approval process is key, because members are likely to perceive lengthy review processes as over-regulation, which will discourage engagement. Streamline any review process so the community can share and engage freely.

### 5. Measure recruitment success.

You can't adjust what you can't measure. Have a system in place to track the following metrics:

- Number of referral applicants
- Number of referral hires
- Time to fill for referral hires
- Retention of referred hires
- Cost per referral hire
- Referral hires by team/manager/location
- Referrals by employee

These metrics provide insight into the effectiveness of your talent community in generating referrals, so you can make well-informed adjustments.

### 6. Launch your talent community.

When everything is in place, send out invitations and publicize the talent community on your career website, in company newsletters, and through other means, so you can quickly populate the community with engaging talent.

Key to the success of any talent community is two-way communication:

>> You can communicate with members.

>> Members can communicate with you.

>> Members can communicate with each other.

Two-way communication is the real differentiator for a true talent community. Many candidate relationship management platforms and applicant tracking systems have a talent community feature, which is popular with many Fortune 500 companies. These platforms are a great way to capture passive talent, or active job seekers who aren't a good match for any of your current openings, but they're often used more for *push messaging* — strictly to send messages, such as job openings and company updates. That's not a community.

# Chapter **11**

# Engaging Talent through Social Media

When it comes to finding jobs through social contacts, not much has changed; people have always networked socially and professionally to find great jobs and connect with first-rate employers. What has changed is *how* people socialize and network. Increasingly, people are spending more time connecting with personal and business contacts online and less time in person. And a large portion of the population networking online is made up of the tech-savvy talent in highest demand.

As always, to recruit top candidates, you need to be where they are and rise above the rabble. You need to establish a presence on the social media channels your targeted talent tune into, whether it's Facebook, LinkedIn, Twitter, Snapchat, Glassdoor, some other channel, or all of the above. You need to offer something distinctive and valuable to attract your targeted talent. And, perhaps most important, you need to stimulate and maintain positive engagement. In this chapter, we explain how.

# Getting Your Head in the Game

Gone are the days when recruiting teams debated the value and return on investment (ROI) of social engagement. In today's world, the question isn't *whether* you should be on social, it's *where* to show up and *how* to engage. In this section, we tackle those two key questions.

**WARNING**

Don't venture into any social platform without a clear strategy. Establishing a presence merely for the sake of being there is likely to do more harm than good.

## Where to show up: Choosing social channels

The first issue you need to address is where the candidates you're trying to reach are hanging out — which social platforms they're using. If you've performed the persona mapping exercises in Chapter 8, you should have a sense of the social networks your target talent is likely to use to network and to research employers and a general mapping of their motivations and interests. (If you haven't read Chapter 8 yet, now would be a good time to do that.) Sizing up your target audience enables you to develop a content strategy that cuts through the noise and allows you to begin pulling prospects into your engagement funnel.

**TIP**

Choose one platform (probably LinkedIn or Glassdoor) to focus on first, and use it as your pilot platform. As you gain success on one platform, you can expand your efforts to other social platforms more easily and confidently.

## How to engage potential candidates

After you figure out *where* your targeted talent hang out and what they're interested in, you can begin to focus on *how* to engage them. Of course, you need to tailor your approach to your audience and to the each social platform you use, but you also need to follow some general guidelines that apply to all audiences and to social media as a whole, as we explain in this section.

### Play by the (unwritten) rules

Every social media platform has its own terms of service and other rules of engagement, but when you're using any of these platforms to build an employer brand, we recommend that you also follow these four rules that will enhance your success:

» **Establish a clear purpose.** Whether you're using social media to reach active or passive job seekers, promote your employer brand, or build a community of employees and targeted talent, think about exactly what you want to achieve. Your purpose will guide your choice of social media platforms to use, how you target talent, and even the content you choose to share.

» **Add value.** Be generous. Inform, inspire, and entertain. How you define value varies based on your goals and objectives, but assuming you're using your social channels to attract talent, value is almost always more than just jobs. Jobs are only valuable to active job seekers who are looking for a position in your field, industry, or location. That's a tiny slice of the overall population pie you can reach on social. When you have a diversified content stream, you're able to appeal to a much broader audience. Many may not be in a position to consider jobs with you today, but providing value to them opens up the door for future consideration, likes, shares, +1's, and referrals.

» **Diversify your content stream.** Share a diversified stream of content, including industry news and information, behind-the-scenes looks at the employee experience and culture, job search resources, recognition/awards for being a quality employer, community and sustainability initiatives, and so on. If you're using social solely to post job openings, you won't see much engagement.

» **Embrace the real-time dynamic.** Instant gratification drives engagement on social media; users demand content the instant it's available and expect a reasonably timely response to comments they post or questions they ask. Social gives you the power to share content in real-time and gives candidates the freedom to message you in real-time. Social media success depends on two-way communication. If you're going to launch a social channel, be prepared to monitor it and to answer and engage your audience. Fail here, and you'll soon have a reputation as an employer who doesn't care.

**REMEMBER**

Contribute to relevant discussions. Whether someone asked a question in response to a post you shared or you've been notified about a conversation about the changing landscape of your industry, respond and join the discussion. Position your company as the leading expert in the industry.

## Finding your social media marketing voice

Success on social media often goes hand in hand with a distinctive but consistent tone of voice. Just as in consumer branding, consistency across social channels provides a familiar framework for candidates and prospects to get to know you and engage with you.

**REMEMBER**

Make your tone of voice an extension of your employer value proposition (EVP; see Chapter 4). It should reflect the core components of what you offer and strive toward offering as an employer. It typically should align with, but not necessarily mirror, your consumer brand voice. Consistency leverages the partnership with marketing as you execute your employer brand strategy.

Because the ultimate aims of consumer branding (get customers to buy your products or services) and employer branding (attract the *right* talent and get them to apply) differ, so may your tone of voice. Consider making your employer brand voice a little less corporate and more personal and engaging. Your goal is to display the humanity in your organization through intentional storytelling and other means. A less formal tone is more likely to connect with prospects on social platforms.

**WARNING**

Don't treat social media as an extension of your job board. A job board is merely a broadcast, a one-way channel. Social media is a two-way channel in which you interact with prospects to form the type of relationship that eventually enables employers and employees to find the right match.

# Laying the Groundwork

Before you venture out into the world of social media, be prepared. Having software in place to facilitate the management of your social properties and a budget available to cover the costs of any advertising and sponsored content prevents you from having to scramble for these necessities at the last minute. Speaking of minutes, you also need to set aside some time to manage your social properties.

## Choosing a social dashboard

One of the tools that can help you manage social platforms is a social dashboard. Your social dashboard enables you to manage all your social channels, posts, engagement, and metrics from one central location, which is vital for efficiency, follow-through, and reporting. Plenty of options are available ranging from free to enterprise, including Hootsuite (www.hootsuite.com), Buffer (www.buffer.com), Sprout Social (www.sproutsocial.com), and others.

**TIP**

New dashboards launch (and are shuttered) monthly, so consider choosing a well-established dashboard.

# Budgeting for ads and sponsored content

The majority of content you share on social media is organic (unpaid), including any general post you share in any format across any social network. Organic content can be liked, shared, or +1'd, increasing its reach. Most platforms, including Facebook and Instagram, use algorithms to determine which content appears in users' news feeds. The more engagement around a particular piece of content, the more likely others will see it. This feature is great for amazing content, but it can bury the content you most want users to see, such as openings for key positions, hiring initiatives, a new career site, employer brand campaigns, and so on. Sponsored content/ads are one solution.

Sponsored content allows you to pay (usually on a pay-per-click basis) to have designated content advertised to a certain audience. You can be very specific about the profile you're targeting (for example, web developers within a 50 miles radius of 90405 who are passionate about Drupal and PHP), and your ad is served up to them. This is a very effective way of getting targeted visibility on key jobs and campaigns.

TIP

Budget for social ads and activate them on an as-needed basis. The majority of your content is likely to be organic, but sponsored ads and content are a great way to add "juice" to specific campaigns.

WARNING

Use ads to promote designated content and increase engagement, not merely to gain followers. Raising one of the biggest social media vanity metrics — number of followers — doesn't necessarily translate to engagement. (For more about paid ads and related topics, see Chapter 12.)

# Making time for social media

At this point, you may be wondering whether this social media thing is going to eat up all your time. If you let it, it will. If you're smart and disciplined, it won't. Many tools are available to streamline social media management, such as Buffer (mentioned earlier), which can schedule your tweets and automate some of your postings. You can also use tools for improving the impact of your efforts, such as Crowdbooster (www.crowdbooster.com), which tells you what times of day your tweets will reach the most followers.

REMEMBER

Although these tools help, be prepared to dedicate a certain portion of your week, including some time every day, to monitor and manage your accounts. Many large organizations split social duties between several members of the recruiting or HR team. Some assign these duties to a single individual. Managing the social properties for corporate recruiting requires time, effort, and focus, so plan accordingly.

# Recruiting on LinkedIn

LinkedIn is typically the first tool in most organizations' branding portfolios. It's certainly no stranger to recruiting, with more than 90 percent of recruiters using the platform to find talent. In this section, we touch on the key areas of focus for achieving recruiting success on LinkedIn.

We don't provide step-by-step instruction on how to use LinkedIn; for that, consult LinkedIn's online help system or check out *LinkedIn For Dummies*, 4th Edition, by Joel Elad (Wiley).

## Building your Company and Career pages

On LinkedIn, you can create a Company Page to showcase your organization, its products or services, its culture, and other attractions (see Figure 11-1). You're allowed a base level of customization at no cost. Enter the standard info — about the company, location, website address, industry, company size, and so on. You also have the option of adding a banner and a logo. You can further customize your content, look, and feel by upgrading to a premium account.

**FIGURE 11-1:**
A sample
Company Page
on LinkedIn.

After you've created your Company Page, click the Careers tab and customize your Career Page. Again, LinkedIn allows you a base level of customization at no cost. For additional customization options, you can upgrade to a Silver or Gold Career Page, each of which provides additional features, such as a clickable banner, customizable modules, analytics on who is viewing the page, direct links to recruiters, video content, and more.

LinkedIn recently updated its Company Page format to make it even more employer brand friendly. Now you can upload photos, feature executives and key employees, and even highlight employee-contributed blogs from the LinkedIn Publisher platform.

## Posting regular status updates

Posting regular status updates is key to promoting your company's corporate, customer, and employer brand on LinkedIn. Posting compelling, relevant content builds engagement and community and raises the visibility of your Company and Career pages. You give your followers a reason to engage, share, and return for more, regardless of whether they're currently looking for a job. This engagement fuels discovery and helps draw new followers to your page and ideally to your jobs.

TIP

LinkedIn has dedicated significant resources toward building more robust employer branding capabilities into its platform. It has released several branding resources to help organizations in this effort, so be sure to search for its most recent resources.

TIP

Video in particular is a great way to highlight your culture and shine a spotlight on your employees. You can also include links to employer branding campaigns you have on other networks.

## Measuring and optimizing engagement

Analytics and fine-tuning are crucial to any social media strategy. Without analytics, you have no real sense of whether your efforts are making an impact. This is where LinkedIn adds value by providing real-time engagement analytics directly beneath each post. This indicator enables you to see what kind of content interests your audience most and adjust accordingly.

TIP

Click the Analytics tab of your Career Page to access valuable data and insight into your audience — including clicks, likes, comments, shares, followers acquired, and engagement percentage (see Figure 11-2). These metrics are useful tools to help you continually recalibrate and refine your content.

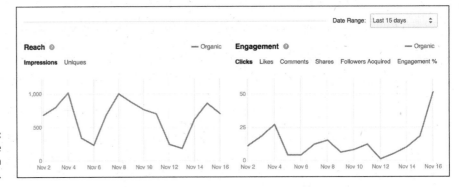

**FIGURE 11-2:**
Company Page
analytics on
LinkedIn.

Another interesting widget in the analytics dashboard is the "How You Compare" dashboard, which reveals how your follower count compares with that of other organizations. This metric gives you some perspective on how you're doing on LinkedIn and may point the way to some best practices you'd be wise to emulate.

## Having employees update their profiles

Today's candidates are savvy shoppers. They're researching companies and colleagues before, during, and after the interview process. What will they discover when they view your employees' LinkedIn profiles? That answer may determine whether they pursue your company or head to greener pastures.

**REMEMBER**

Your employees are brand ambassadors; help them shine by providing training and guidance on creating a compelling professional LinkedIn profile that reflects positively on your organization. If you have a culture video or other employer brand collateral, ask employees to embed it in their Experience section. In their Current Experience section, have them describe what they do and why they enjoy it. These subtle additions can pay huge dividends when candidates research your organization.

# Giving Job Seekers a Backstage Pass with Glassdoor

Glassdoor is a popular social media jobs site that helps employers across all industries and sizes build their brands, monitor their reputations, advertise their jobs, and promote their companies to a highly researched, highly selective candidate pool. Its social media component provides job seekers with a backstage pass to find out more about companies from the people who work there. By advertising job openings and engaging with prospects on Glassdoor, you have a unique opportunity to influence candidates at the moment they're making career decisions, resulting in higher-quality applicants at a significantly lower cost-per-hire compared to traditional job boards.

To get started with Glassdoor, sign up at www.glassdoor.com/employers and follow the prompts to create your company profile. You can then start promoting your employer brand, by doing the following:

>> **Monitor your reputation and employer brand.** A convenient dashboard delivers a real-time snapshot of how the organization is perceived by employees, former employees, and job seekers. You can quickly see profile visits over time (awareness), company rating (brand reputation), CEO approval rating, company followers, sponsored job performance, top job clicks, and more. Dig deeper for detailed demographics of candidates visiting your profile, ratings trends (including the percentage who would recommend your company), interview trends, and competitor comparisons.

>> **Encourage your employees to write honest, candid, and detailed reviews about working at the company.** Job seekers value transparency, and nobody knows better than your employees what working there is really like. One of the byproducts of such encouragement is the organic cultivation of *internal brand ambassadors* — employees who can help amplify a company's recruitment message to job seekers in the form of endorsements and referrals.

>> **Advertise job openings.** By promoting open jobs on a channel where job seekers are already researching and choosing employers, you can make a welcome first impression and start influencing, attracting, and nurturing top candidates. As a bonus, well-informed job seekers who aren't a good fit self-select, so you're likely to see a smaller, stronger pool of applicants and need only half the résumés to make a hire.

>> **Read and reply to comments and reviews.** By staying abreast of comments and reviews — both positive and negative — you can spot trends that validate current policies or call for positive organizational change. By having people inside your company post replies, you demonstrate that your organization cares about its people, and you provide prospects with the information and insight they need to make a well-informed decision about working for your company or applying for a certain position.

**TIP**

Always reply in a nondefensive voice that acknowledges both the reviewer and the issue or challenge being raised.

# MAKING THE CASE FOR GLASSDOOR: FACTS AND FIGURES

If you're uncertain whether Glassdoor is worth your time and effort, check out the following statistics, which make a strong case for adding Glassdoor to your employer branding toolkit:

- Glassdoor has public profiles on more than 540,000 companies worldwide; approximately 30 million monthly visitors; and millions of company reviews, salary reports, interview reviews, and benefit information.

- Ninety percent of job seekers say it's important to work for a company that embraces transparency (Glassdoor U.S. Site Survey, January 2016).

- Three out of four job seekers on Glassdoor value reviews and ratings from employees within the company when making job decisions (Harris Interactive Survey for Glassdoor, 2015).

- Sixty-two percent of job seekers on Glassdoor say their perception of a company improves after seeing an employer respond to a review about their company (Glassdoor U.S. Site Survey, January 2016).

- Eighty-nine percent of Glassdoor users are either actively looking for jobs or open to better opportunities, while 64 percent of users are just starting their job search (Glassdoor U.S. Site Survey, January 2016).

- Employers advertising positions on Glassdoor report two times better applicant quality at an average 30 percent lower cost-per-hire compared to traditional job boards (Brandon Hall Group, 2014).

- Sixty-nine percent of job seekers wouldn't take a job with a company that had a bad reputation, even if they were unemployed, but for as little as 1 percent to 10 percent more compensation, 84 percent of job seekers would consider leaving their current jobs if offered another role with a company that had an excellent reputation (*Corporate Responsibility Magazine*/Allegis Group Services Study, October 2013).

With so much at stake, it's imperative that your company establish a presence on Glassdoor and engage with prospects. Regardless of whether you play an active role on Glassdoor, what people say about your organization will affect its reputation in the workforce. By taking the lead, you have the opportunity to influence public opinion in your favor.

>> **Monitor interview feedback.** Use the Glassdoor Employer Center to monitor your company's interview trends, noting the percentage of candidates who report a positive or negative experience. Provide this feedback to the people in your organization who conduct interviews, so they can make any necessary adjustments. Educating interviewers on the company mission, values, and employer brand is essential.

>> **Use analytics to optimize your brand and recruiting.** Brand and talent analytics — gleaned from intelligence found on Glassdoor — enables you to improve your recruiting strategies and candidate appeal. Analytics insight can lead to more accurate hiring projections, investment in more profitable recruitment channels, and improved candidate selection. Proactively targeting the candidates mostly likely to do well in your company reduces the incidence of bad-fit hires and costly attrition.

# Making a Splash on Facebook

Facebook is the 800-pound gorilla of the social media world, and because the platform is so powerful and influential, your company needs to be on Facebook. After all, about 20 percent of the world's population is on Facebook, providing you with an incredible opportunity and tool to build your employer brand.

We assume you're on Facebook and you know the basics. If you need guidance, check out *Facebook For Dummies*, 6th Edition, by Carolyn Abram (Wiley). In this section, we highlight three Facebook features that are excellent for building your employer brand and extending your reach.

## Creating a Facebook Page

Most businesses create a Facebook Page primarily to promote products and services to customers (see Figure 11-3). To use Facebook to build an employer brand, you have the option of using the company's existing page or creating a separate page to build the employer brand:

>> **Use the company's existing Facebook Page.** Depending on your company's size and resources and the focus of the content on the company's existing Facebook Page, you may be able to leverage the reach and impact of that page to share some of your employer brand content, including jobs and workplace culture. The advantage to this approach is that the channel is likely

already established, with set governance, content strategy, and, most important, audience. The downside is you often lack control and have to work through established content calendars to insert your employer brand content.

>> **Build a new Facebook Page.** If you have the bandwidth and resources, you may want to build a separate Facebook Page dedicated to your employer brand, so you have full autonomy and authority over the content, content shares, tone of voice, and engagement strategy. It's a great way to tap into the largest social network, and the 1.7 billion or so active monthly users.

Consult your content marketing strategy, as explained in Part 2 of this book, to determine the type of content you share on your Facebook Page.

*Reproduced with the permission of Universum*

If you're building a dedicated Facebook Page for your employer brand, notify employees and ask them to follow and share the page. You may also want to leverage the established reach (and likes) of your corporate channels with strategic requests to share and promote your content, so their audience becomes aware of the employer brand channel and has the opportunity to get an inside look at the employee experience. For companies with strong consumer brands and existing customer affinity, this is a great way to quickly grow your audience.

## Hosting Facebook Groups

Facebook Groups is another great tool for employer branding, particularly as engagement levels in LinkedIn groups continue to decline. Facebook Groups allows you to create open, closed, or secret groups that allow members to interact, share, and engage with one other.

TIP

Consider creating a private group that includes employees, prospects, and fans. This approach provides a direct way to engage prospects with your existing talent, enabling prospects to ask questions and get a firsthand look at the culture. It also enables your team to identify engaged prospects you may want to recruit.

## Broadcasting via Facebook Live

Facebook Live, recently added to Facebook's portfolio, taps into the resurgence of livestreaming, enabling users to broadcast live video from their mobile devices (see Figure 11-4). You can find a variety of applications for broadcasting live on Facebook; see Chapter 8 for details.

**FIGURE 11-4:**
A sample Facebook Live broadcast.

# Attracting Top Talent on Twitter

Building an engaged network on Twitter can have a huge positive impact on your recruiting efforts, particularly if you're recruiting in fields such as knowledge workers, who tend to flock to Twitter. It's an open platform, meaning anyone can see any content without necessarily following the account, so tweets have the potential of reaching a wider audience. We get into more of that when we discuss hashtags in the later section, "Using hashtags to source candidates."

Again, we assume you know Twitter basics. If you don't know the difference between a hashtag and a price tag, you may want to check out *Twitter For Dummies*, 3rd Edition, by Laura Fitton, Anum Hussain, and Brittany Leaning (Wiley). In this section, we focus on using Twitter to recruit talent.

## Picking up strategies by observing others

Before you venture into any unfamiliar social gathering, whether online or not, hang out for a while and observe how others in the community interact. When you're setting out to establish an employer brand presence on Twitter, observe other Twitter accounts that have strong positive employer brands and take note of the content they tweet, the tone or voice, and how they interact with potential candidates. You can find plenty of role models on Twitter; here are examples of a few good corporate accounts you may want to follow: @NPRjobs, @JoinTheFlock, @PepsiCoJobs, @MicrosoftJobs, @ViacomCareers, @InsideZappo, and @HootsuiteLife.

**TIP**

Try following your peers and competitors on Twitter to find out what they're doing to compete for talent. For a collection of more than 250 brand recruiting handles on Twitter, visit `https://twitter.com/ThisIsLars/lists/brand-recruiting-handles`.

## Using hashtags to source candidates

Most employer branding efforts are designed around *pull marketing* (attracting prospects), but sourcing is a *push marketing* technique that involves proactively recruiting individuals with high-value skills and expertise. We focus on building a strong employer brand, but Twitter is also a good platform for recruiters and organizations to identify and engage with prospects who may not even be in the market for a new job.

When posting job notices on Twitter, include function- or job-specific hashtags in your tweets (for example, #digitalmarketing, #PR, #webdesign, or #accounting). You can find function- or skill-specific hashtags by searching the web for "job seeker hashtags."

Tread carefully when using hashtags. If you're oversharing jobs with event hashtags, you'll likely face blowback for spamming.

You can also use Twitter to source candidates by keeping an eye on hashtags relevant to positions you're trying to fill. For example, if you're recruiting Drupal developers, keep an eye on the hashtags: #Drupal, #DrupalCon, #Drupal8, and so on to see what these communities are talking about and to identify influential developers. If you're recruiting marketing managers, keep an eye on #marketing, #digitalmarketing, #marketingresearch, #mktg, and so on.

Plenty of tools are available to help you identify influencers within various hashtag communities. Here are a few to check out:

>> **Google Trends:** www.google.com/trends

>> **Audiense:** www.audiense.com

>> **Hashtags:** www.hashtags.org

>> **What The Trend:** www.wthashtag.com

Sourcing local talent? These tools and others enable you to search for people talking about relevant topics within a certain mile radius of your company.

## Engaging prospects

When you're posting tweets, which are essentially very brief, overlooking the necessity of offering followers something of real value is far too easy. Keep the focus on delivering valuable content. Share behind-the-scenes photos or videos to help prospects get a sense of what it's like to work for your company. Share articles and resources about your industry. Join Twitter chats and share your insights and expertise. Interact with your followers. Try to respond to every @mention and question. Engagement and interaction are vital for building community.

## Getting your employees involved

To fully harness the power of Twitter, get employees involved. Candidates don't want to hear only from employer brand managers; they want to hear from peers doing the work they (prospects) may be doing for your company in the near future. They want to talk shop with the people who may someday be their colleagues.

Great talent can recognize similar talent. Consider developing internal programs that encourage employees to share their knowledge and expertise in online communities where you recruit. By increasing their visibility in certain professional circles and establishing themselves as experts in those communities, your employees can expand their own professional networks while helping you identify and attract talented prospects.

REMEMBER

Prospects want to hear from your employees. That product manager you've been wooing wants to see tweets from your product team that will help them get a feel for the work, team atmosphere, culture, and so on. You may share supremely clever and compelling content on Twitter, but you're still an HR guy or gal. You have an agenda to bring talent into your organization, so of course your posts are biased.

## Gauging your Twitter impact

You can use any of several available tools to measure the reach, retweets, impressions, and so on related to your tweeting activity. You should also be measuring applications and hires coming from Twitter through your applicant tracking software (ATS). Use these tools to adjust your campaigns regularly.

You may be tempted to obsess over your number of followers. Don't let that be your primary indicator as to whether your account is successful. If you focus on providing valuable content and engaging your community, followers will come. Focus on this and you'll have something better than followers; you'll have brand advocates who bring you the best talent available.

# Adapting to a New Model: Snapchat

Snapchat is unlike any other social platform. It's all about capturing a moment through a photo or video and sharing it in real time. You can customize these moments with filters, emojis, text, and drawing, but you can't share links, self-promotional "thought leadership" blog posts, or auto-scheduled posts, only moments.

Brands are increasingly migrating to Snapchat and some are finding measurable success. If you've researched your target audience and determined that Snapchat makes sense for your employer brand, then consider following their lead. However, be prepared to develop an entirely new approach.

TIP

Here are some tips on how to use Snapchat to promote your employer brand:

>> **Hand over the keys and the camera.** Let employees take the lead and tell their stories (or whatever) with photos and videos. You're likely to be pleasantly surprised by the results.

>> **Keep it real.** Avoid the temptation to over-edit footage. Staged content comes across as inauthentic.

>> **Embrace low fidelity.** Expectations of Snapchat video quality aren't as high as they are on other social platforms, such as YouTube. Have fun with it!

>> **Showcase your work environment.** Snapchat is a great platform for behind-the-scenes social sharing. Let your hiring managers show the desk/office where their new employee will sit or take a tour of your office. You're only limited by your time and creativity.

>> **Use geofilters.** Custom geofilters are a great way to extend your brand into events. They can be purchased to run during events, and they give you the opportunity to make attendees mini brand ambassadors.

>> **Don't be afraid of lenses.** Snapchat includes augmented reality (AR) lenses you can use to contort faces. Have fun with them, and don't be afraid to incorporate them into your videos and photos to add personality.

>> **Keep an eye on your view count and completion rates.** Snapchat metrics and analytics aren't easy to come by, so just keep an eye on view count, the number of snaps and chants returned to you, and completion rates (the number of viewers who watch a story to the end). Try to get a general idea of what works and what doesn't and make adjustments as needed.

# Leveraging Video

Online videos now exceed 50 percent of mobile traffic and 64 percent of all Internet traffic. These figures continue to rise each year, as does the importance of having a video component as a component of your recruitment marketing efforts. In this section, we offer guidance on how and where to leverage video content and encourage you to focus your efforts on YouTube first.

# Exploring ways to use video in recruitment marketing

Today most companies rely on employer brand videos as the focal point of their employer branding efforts. These videos are usually highly produced montages of employees, testimonials, and campus shots designed to give viewers a look inside the culture of the organization. Here are a few more creative ways to implement video in your recruitment marketing.

## Job descriptions

Job descriptions are often the least interesting component of a recruitment marketing portfolio, yet they're the most common. Consider ditching the static text and include video from the hiring manager or a future colleague. It's a great way to humanize the opportunity and give prospects a more intimate view of what to expect. See Chapter 9 for additional tips on creating compelling job descriptions.

## Social media

The marriage of social media and mobile devices means we all have video production studios in our pockets. Use that studio to share video clips of the office, team, manager, or culture on Instagram and Snapchat.

## Livestreaming: Facebook Live, Periscope, and more

With the rise of livestreaming apps such as Periscope, Meerkat, and Facebook Live, anyone can be a broadcaster. Use these tools to host live chats with the hiring manager and team, tours of the office, and "ask a recruiter" segments. Live streaming allows you to engage directly with your audience, and vice versa, so prospects can ask questions and have direct access to people they may work with in the future.

TIP

Live streaming is particularly useful in providing you with insight into your audience. The information you gather from interactive sessions can help you fine-tune your talent personas.

# Recognizing the importance of YouTube

YouTube is the second most popular search engine after Google, with over a billion unique monthly visitors and six billion hours of video viewed every month. Put that into perspective. In the time it took you to read that last sentence, 24 hours of content was uploaded to YouTube. People generally prefer to hear and see information than read it.

Studies of website usage suggest that people gravitate toward video content, and the trend is growing. This means that if your career site is text heavy and video light, it's likely to be less effective in engaging potential candidates. An obvious illustration is the video employee profile (currently the most common use of video on career sites). It's undeniable that video can convey the personality and feel of a potential employer and its employees far more effectively than a text-based profile, however well written it may be, and personality is precisely what many candidates are looking for.

The other important reason for including more video is that it increases your page ranking on Google. According to the leading technology research house, Forrester, videos are 50 times more likely than text to rank on the first page of Google results. Reflecting the growing use of YouTube as a search engine, Potentialpark's 2014 research revealed that 45 percent of employers now have a YouTube channel, and one-third provide a YouTube connection from their career sites.

# Exploring Chat Platforms and Regional Channels

The big platforms — LinkedIn, Glassdoor, Facebook, Twitter, and Snapchat — aren't the only platforms suitable for promoting an employer brand. Depending on the locations and types of talent you're targeting, you may want to consider dozens of niche platforms to add to your repertoire.

Chat platforms, such as WhatsApp and QQ, with their 900 million active users, have surged in popularity over the recent years. This shift toward chat has caused industry titans such as Facebook and Apple to rethink their messenger strategies and introduce new products with stickers and other customizations that enable users to personalize their content.

**REMEMBER**

Most important, identify your target audience's preferred platforms, and let those platforms drive your strategy. Recruiting in China? QZone should likely be part of your channel portfolio. Staffing a project in India? Be sure to realize that it's Google+'s second largest market. Expanding in Russia? You should be familiar with V Kontakte and Odnoklassniki.

The world of social media evolves rapidly, and dozens of new platforms are being launched and shuttered every year. To benefit from the "first mover" advantage, consider becoming an early adopter. However, before investing too heavily in new platforms, understand how they align with your persona maps and employer brand strategy, and do your best to gauge the platform's potential staying power.

# Building a Social Media Calendar

A *social media calendar* is a schedule detailing what, when, and where (on which social platforms) you post content. It ensures that you remain active and relevant across all your employer brand channels, and it helps you plan and coordinate your social sharing. Planning and coordination become very important as your employer brand efforts mature and become more sophisticated; for example, when the content you share on Twitter to attract software engineers needs to differ from the content you share on LinkedIn to attract marketing professionals.

Table 11-1 shows a sample social media calendar. Yours can certainly be different, but it should include some indication of what you plan to post, the person in charge of creating the content, the nature of the content (for example, the title of a blog post), and where the content is to be posted (Facebook, Twitter, LinkedIn, Glassdoor, Instagram, and so on).

**TABLE 11-1**     **Sample Social Media Calendar**

|  | Author | Facebook | Twitter | LinkedIn | Google+ | Instagram |
|---|---|---|---|---|---|---|
| **Monday** | | | | | | |
| Third-party post | | | | | | |
| Blog post | | | | | | |
| Photo | | | | | | |
| Promotion | | | | | | |
| **Tuesday** | | | | | | |
| Third-party post | | | | | | |
| Blog post | | | | | | |
| Photo | | | | | | |
| Promotion | | | | | | |

|  | Author | Facebook | Twitter | LinkedIn | Google+ | Instagram |
|---|---|---|---|---|---|---|
| **Wednesday** | | | | | | |
| Third-party post | | | | | | |
| Blog post | | | | | | |
| Photo | | | | | | |
| Promotion | | | | | | |
| **Thursday** | | | | | | |
| Third-party post | | | | | | |
| Blog post | | | | | | |
| Photo | | | | | | |
| Promotion | | | | | | |
| **Friday** | | | | | | |
| Third-party post | | | | | | |
| Blog post | | | | | | |
| Photo | | | | | | |
| Promotion | | | | | | |

Chapter **12**

# Making the Most of Recruitment Advertising

n Chapter 5, we cover the basics of developing recruitment advertising campaigns — establishing campaign objectives, writing a creative brief, choosing the right creatives in your organization to work with, and writing attention-grabbing taglines. What we don't cover in that chapter is how to execute your recruitment advertising campaigns. That's where this chapter comes in.

In this chapter, you discover the various methods and channels through which you can execute an effective recruitment advertising campaign, including search engine marketing, paid media, job boards, and direct contact with candidates. We bring you up to speed on what your options are and provide the information and insight you need to choose the best methods and channels for your recruitment advertising campaigns. We also provide tips and other suggestions to help you get the most out of whichever methods and channels you choose.

**REMEMBER**

The success of any recruitment advertising campaign depends on the relevance and value of the content, event, or activity that advertising campaign promotes. See Chapter 6 for more about developing relevant and engaging content. The purpose of recruitment advertising is to draw attention to your content, and when advertising and content are well coordinated, your content has a much better chance of gaining traction and perhaps even going viral.

# Raising Your Employer Brand Profile in Search Engine Results

Many of the most talented prospects use online resources and information in their job search. In fact, a recent study by Pew Research Center revealed that among those in the United States who've looked for work in the past two years (2014–2015), 79 reported using online resources and information in their job search, with 34 percent claiming that Internet resources were the most important in helping them find a job. Furthermore, job seekers were just as likely to use the Internet as to turn to their personal or professional networks when searching for jobs. To track down the information and resources they need, many job seekers rely on Google and other search engines.

The moral of this story is that if you want to improve your chances of being discovered by job seekers online, you need to make sure that links to your career website and other online recruiting centers appear near the top of the search results when job seekers search for the positions you need to fill. To achieve a higher search engine ranking, harness the power of search engine optimization and search engine marketing:

>> **Search engine optimization (SEO):** SEO involves numerous techniques to raise the ranking of online content in search engine results organically (without having to pay for it). Techniques center on giving search engines the information they need to properly index the content, so the search engine can determine which content is most relevant to what users are searching for and display links to that content near the top of the user's search results. Techniques include publishing relevant content, using keywords that users are likely to search for, tagging images and videos, linking to related content within your own site, and having popular external sites with similar content link to content on your site. SEO is a component of search engine marketing.

>> **Search engine marketing (SEM):** SEM involves paying search engine companies for the privilege of having your content appear more prominently when a user searches for specific content you want them to be aware of on your site. On Google, for example, you often see sponsored links at the top of search results that may be labeled "Ad" to indicate that someone paid to have that link promoted to the top of the list. Search engine companies typically offer two SEM options: pay per view (PPV) and pay per click (PPC).

The importance of SEO and SEM in recruiting candidates is becoming more important as Google increasingly becomes the hub of preference for job seekers. Although people still visit company websites, social career websites such as Glassdoor, and job boards such as Monster and Indeed, more and more job seekers are using job title and location keywords via general search engines such as Google to initiate their job search.

In the following sections, we offer guidance on how to improve your search engine ranking through the use of SEO and SEM.

## Using search engine optimization to improve your site's search engine ranking

**TIP**

Go to Google, search for your company name followed by "jobs," and then scroll through the search results to see where the link to your career website shows up. If it's not on the first page, you have some work to do. Here are a few suggestions to place you on the path to improving the search engine ranking for your online career content via SEO:

>> **Make your site mobile friendly.** Search engines can determine whether a user is conducting a search from a mobile device, and it may exclude from its search results links to any content that's not mobile-friendly.

>> **Post great content regularly.** The best way to achieve a high search engine ranking is to earn it with content that's relevant and valuable to the job seekers you're trying to attract. (See Chapter 6 for more about developing great content.)

>> **Harness the power of keywords and phrases.** Search engines may use *keyword density* (the ratio of keywords to total words on a page) to determine how relevant that content is to something a user is searching for. Be aware of keywords and phrases, and use them as a way to "describe" content, but don't overuse them. Use them strategically on your career site, in job descriptions, and in all your online recruitment marketing.

>> **Engage visitors.** When you engage visitors, and they post comments, they're constantly updating your site with fresh content, which search engines love. Be sure your career site has a way for visitors to post comments.

Consider adding a blog to your career site, if you haven't already. By posting relevant content regularly (at least twice a week) and having visitors post content, you build a large target for search engines. Invite employees to share content, as well.

**TIP**

>> **Leverage the power of backlinks.** Links that point to your site from other sites may raise your search engine rank. Link everything you post on the web back to your career site or page, including any social properties you manage, such as a LinkedIn or Facebook Page. Likewise, when you post an opening on a job board, include a link that points back to your career site.

**TIP**

Have your recruiters and employees include a link to your career site on their LinkedIn and other social profiles. The more pages referring web users to your site, the better your chances of getting a higher ranking.

>> **Use internal links to help search engines crawl your career site.** Search engines index only the pages they can find. Structure the content on your site in a hierarchy so that all pages ultimately link to the site's home page.

>> **Submit your career site to search engine indexes.** Most search engines will find your career site on their own, but it doesn't hurt, especially if your career site is new, to submit it to the top search engines, including Google, Bing, Yahoo!, and Ask.com.

>> **Avoid cheap tricks.** Packing content with keywords is likely to result in having your site penalized by search engines for cheating.

**REMEMBER**

You're not entirely in control of your search engine ranking. Search engines customize the search results for users based on the user's location, browsing history, social settings, and so forth. Two users searching for the same job are likely to receive a different arrangement of search results.

For more about SEO, SEM, and other forms of online promotion, check out *Digital Marketing For Dummies,* by Ryan Deiss and Russ Henneberry (Wiley). For more specific coverage of SEO, pick up a copy of *SEO For Dummies,* by Peter Kent (Wiley).

## Gaining traction with search engine marketing

When you need to raise your search engine ranking in a hurry or you're looking for a way to more effectively target certain talent, consider paying for a higher search engine ranking. With SEM, such as Google AdWords, you can target or exclude geographical areas, set your daily budget and how much you're willing to pay per click, create your own ad(s), and specify the keywords and phrases you want to trigger your ad(s) appearing in the search results. To optimize SEM results and your return on investment (ROI), follow these suggestions:

>> **Don't pay for what you're already getting for free.** If you're already showing up near the top of the search results for the keywords and phrases you're targeting, don't pay for advertising. Use your budget to shore up weaknesses in your recruitment advertising or to promote specific job openings.

>> **Be specific with keywords and phrases.** Use exact matching and keyword exclusion (negative keywords) to produce more targeted search results. With keyword exclusion, you can prevent your ad from appearing in the search

results if it includes a specific word; for example, if you're advertising for an electrical engineer, and you're getting a lot of traffic from people searching "software engineer," you can enter "software" as a negative keyword, so your ad doesn't appear when a user includes "software" in his search phrase.

>> **Fine-tune the destination.** If a user clicks one of your pay-per-click ads, make sure she lands on a page that's likely to provide the information she expected. For example, if you create a PPC ad to promote a job opening for a CEO, make sure that ad links to the page devoted to that job opening and not to the home page of your career website.

>> **Start low when choosing how much to pay per click.** Your ad doesn't need to be at the very top of the list. If it's in the top three, that's usually sufficient.

>> **Track and tweak.** Keep track of PPC activity and tweak your messaging to see how users respond. Minor changes in your messaging can significantly improve results. Track both your click-through and conversion rates:

- **Click-through rate (CTR):** This metric tells you how many people are clicking your ad to learn more. The higher your CTR, the more your ad is connecting with the desired audience. If your CTR is lower than 1 percent, you need to adjust your ad copy.

- **Conversion rate (CR):** If your ad leads to a call to action, such as "apply for this job," the CR represents the percentage of times a person who visits your site after clicking your ad performs the call to action — in this example, the percentage of people who click the button to apply for the job. An average CR is about 2 percent, an outstanding CR is about 5 percent, and a mind-blowing CR is 10 percent or higher.

>> **Boost SEO with SEM.** Coordinate your SEO and SEM efforts. As you increase your PPC efforts, you're likely to get a boost in traffic from organic search results (those you're not paying for). Use the same keywords and phrases in your SEM as you do in your SEO to help search engines associate those keywords and phrases with your company.

TIP

Not to give Google free advertising, but if you want to get the most for your SEM buck, consider spending it on Google AdWords. Google is the world's largest search engine, accounting for 72 percent of all global searches.

# Sizing Up Paid Media Channels

The world of advertising has seen substantial shifts over the past ten years. Traditional channels such as TV, radio, and print advertising have lost ground to web, social, and mobile advertising. These changes reflect a shift in behavior in how media is consumed. The recruitment marketing world has experienced a similar shift in the media used to reach talent. Like the general population, candidates are relying more on online content to find out about employers and the jobs they advertise and less on job listings in newspapers and other print media.

The effects of this technological transformation on candidate behavior are already being reflected in organizations' future media planning and recruitment advertising. In our global employer brand practice survey, we asked participants to rate the relative impact of different media channels on perceptions of their employer brand, and anticipated future changes in investment. The results confirmed a significant shift toward social media and away from print, third-party recruiters, and job boards. This reflects similar findings from Potentialpark's global survey of job seeker behaviors, although some significant variations clearly exist between regions.

In this section, we provide guidance to help you decide which media channels are likely to give you the most bang for your buck in terms of recruitment advertising and introduce the growing trend toward programmatic media buying.

## Evaluating your potential media mix

Traditional media channels still exist, but recruitment marketers now have a broader range of options to consider. Traditional media include the following:

>> Print (newspapers and magazines)

>> Radio

>> Television

>> Billboard

>> Events

>> PR/publicity

>> Recruitment marketing materials

>> Direct mail

As interest in traditional channels diminishes, these more modern media channels are growing in popularity:

>> Websites

>> Blogs

>> Social media

>> SEO and SEM

>> Podcasts

>> Mobile apps/games

>> Web advertising

Which media you choose for your recruitment advertising depends almost entirely on your audience and budget, especially on the media preference of the specific talent you're targeting. If you're advertising for game developers, for example, you may want to do something creative with mobile apps or online games to attract the talent you're looking for. Or, you may want to advertise in magazines that are popular with game developers.

**REMEMBER**

The "best mix" for recruitment depends on variables most suitable for each individual hiring situation. The most important three questions to ask yourself when applying that to your hiring initiatives are the following:

>> **What platforms are my prospects using?** You won't bring a golf club to a baseball game. Similarly, you won't advertise jobs on platforms your audience doesn't use.

>> **What budget do I have?** Assuming you have a budget to allocate, you need to assess the cost/value/return on investment (ROI) of different platforms. This consideration ties into the next question as well. A billboard isn't an effective recruitment advertising channel if you're hiring only one call center specialist. If you're hiring a thousand call center specialists, the investment may be worth it.

>> **Are these hiring needs evergreen or one-off?** Evergreen jobs are positions that come up regularly during hiring cycles. They tend to be aligned with a company's core business and may include roles with higher turnover. Investment in recruitment advertising for evergreen hiring should be viewed differently, and with more budget allocated, because you'll have similar hiring needs on an ongoing basis and the advertising campaign will continue to bear fruit.

**REMEMBER**

With more and more people searching for jobs on the web, you're always wise to invest resources in a career website and blog and in social media channels. Building an online presence is a very cost-effective way to build your employer brand while taking advantage of the growing preference among job seekers for online media.

# Programmatic media buying

*Programmatic media buying* (programmatic for short) is an approach to advertising that automates ad placement to more accurately target the desired demographic. You, the advertiser, enter your budget, choose media and platforms, specify keywords, set your goal, create one or more ads, and enter other parameters. Based on the parameters you set and the vast amount of analytical data that the programmatic platform has access to, the platform chooses which ad to display and where and when to display it to achieve the maximum return on your advertising dollar — or at least reach the ROI goal you set.

Programmatic offers several benefits over traditional online advertising, including the following:

>> You, the advertiser, don't need to negotiate separately with various media producers to place ads.

>> Programmatic determines ad placement based on analytics (real data) instead of guesswork. The assumption (rightly so) is that compared to humans, artificial intelligence (AI) will make better ad placement decisions.

>> Ad placement and audience response is continually monitored, and advanced algorithms adjust the campaign to maximize reach and impact.

Although programmatic is used primarily to purchase online advertising, many companies are exploring ways to use it to sell advertising through traditional media, including print advertising and TV ads.

Some estimates project that over $100 million of job ad spend will have been programmatic in 2016. If you're still not convinced programmatic recruiting advertising is right for you, consider these advantages:

>> **You can save time.** By using a centralized platform such as Appcast, recruiters can create ad campaigns that span almost every online/digital platform they want to reach.

>> **You can increase candidate quality.** The nature of programmatic advertising means you're reaching candidates outside of typical channels, thus expanding your outreach efforts to a much broader candidate pool (for example, advertising to a software engineer in a maker hobbyist website). (Maker hobbyists are part of a high-tech subculture that uses a copy/paste approach to invent new gadgets using existing devices.) Recent studies have shown an 8 percent increase in finalist candidates identified through programmatic versus job boards and aggregators.

>> **You can reduce cost-per-applicant.** Programmatic advertising has features such as the ability to end campaigns after a certain threshold of applicants has been reached.

# Getting the Best out of Job Boards

The demise of the job board is greatly exaggerated. According to a recent study from ERE Media (www.eremedia.com/tlnt/they-may-be-slipping-but-job-boards-are-still-the-top-way-to-find-a-job), 25 percent of job seekers cite commercial job boards as the source of their applications. Job boards may not be en vogue like they used to be, but they can still be very effective when used for the right roles in the right markets. According to a 2016 study by SilkRoad (http://hr1.silkroad.com/l/61532/2016-04-22/256qhk), job boards are still the second-rated source of hire, with Indeed accounting for 43 percent of that traffic.

**TIP**

To get the most value from job boards, consider your audience. For example, if you're in the market for technology and IT talent, Dice (www.dice.com) may be the best place to post openings. HCareers (www.hcareers.com) is the place to go if you're looking to hire talent in the hotel and hospitality industry. Post openings on SalesGravy (www.salesgravy.com) to recruit candidates with sales and customer service experience. Understanding what platforms are being used for what job types is your first step to success with job boards.

## A JOB BOARD ON THE RISE: INDEED

The rise of Indeed is a great illustration of the changing nature of the job board. With traditional job boards, such as CareerBuilder and Monster, companies pay to post specific jobs or have their websites *scraped* (harvested for job listings). Indeed and similar job boards are aggregators that pull jobs from a variety of sources, including career sites. They're one-stop shops for job seekers looking for a broader pool of opportunities.

Indeed's scraping technology enables it to serve a much broader talent pool. According to SilkRoad, Indeed yields two and a half times as many hires as all the other top external sources combined. After Indeed, the next largest external source for interviews is CareerBuilder (8 percent), followed by recruiting agencies (5 percent), craigslist (5 percent), LinkedIn (5 percent), campus recruiting (3 percent), and Monster (2 percent).

# Adding a Personal Touch with Direct Engagement

No recruiting tactic is more effective than contacting and engaging with a prospect on a personal level. Imagine recruiting the top college baseball or football players for a professional team. You certainly wouldn't post an ad in the newspaper or even on Monster in the hopes that your top pick would notice it and respond. You'd need to initiate contact, engage the recruit, and then convince the player to join your squad. The same is true when you're trying to fill a high-demand position at your company: To succeed, you need to personalize your approach and cut through the spam, as explained in this section.

**REMEMBER**

Advertising at scale still can't be personalized for the direct one-to-one or one-to-few messaging that's likely to convert top candidates to fill high-demand positions. You need to make it personal.

## Personalizing your message

Writing a generic letter or job description is easy, because you don't have to do much research, include research, or understand your audience. You simply describe the job and what *you* or *your company* needs. Personalizing your message requires getting to know the prospect(s) you're reaching out to, demonstrating your interest in them, and addressing *their* needs. Take the following steps to develop more personal messaging and engagement:

---

### INCREASING YOUR RESPONSE RATE

Personalizing your recruitment efforts will significantly increase your response rate. Here's what a Yahoo! recruiter had to say about personalizing contact with prospects via email:

> In my personal experience, the more personalized the email, the better the response rate. For example, when I send a mildly tailored email, I usually get a 25 percent response rate. However, when I really customize the email and show the candidate I've done my homework, the response rate jumps to 60 [percent] to 70 percent. More important, when they do respond to me, I usually get something like, "It's so refreshing to be contacted by someone who has done their homework." That's important to me because it sets the tone for our conversation and gets the candidate more willing to hear about the opportunity I have in mind for them.

Personalizing your initial contact with a prospective candidate warms that person up for subsequent engagement. It turns cold calls into warm calls.

---

>> **Prioritize positions.** You probably don't have the time or resources to personally recruit every candidate. Focus your personalized recruiting efforts on filling key positions.

>> **Do your homework.** Conduct a thorough search of the web to find out more about the candidate, including the person's alma mater, past employers and positions, major accomplishments, interests, and so on. You may even be able to find out what sort of position and employer the person considers to be ideal.

>> **Be specific.** Whether you're writing a letter or a job description, details are key to personalization.

>> **Tailor your message to your audience.** Mention something specific about the person you're contacting — perhaps his alma mater, what he majored in, a previous position he held, a place he worked, a paper he published, or something else that shows you did your homework and put some effort into getting to know him. Tell him *why* you're contacting him. "You have a great background" is the same line a dozen other recruiters have used that week. Explain what it is about his background that makes him so well suited for the position and why you think he'd love to work for your company.

**TIP**

Don't get creepy. Mentioning someone's marital status, his children, or other personal details may make the person uncomfortable, as if you've been spying on him. Try to stick to relevant job-related details, such as education, certifications, experience, and professional accomplishments.

>> **Reach out on social channels.** Social channels are great for getting to know candidates personally prior to contacting them to come and work for you.

>> **Go old school: face-to-face.** If and when appropriate, try to meet the candidate in person, perhaps over coffee or lunch. Nothing is more personal than an in-person, face-to-face meeting.

## Cutting through the spam

It's never been easier to contact talent, and it's never been harder to cut through the spam and seize their attention. The recruiting world is awash with bad templates from lazy recruiters who treat email and LinkedIn InMails as a spam machine. Those generic templates lie dormant in junk mail folders, as busy candidates ignore the drone of mass communications.

**TIP**

Here are a few suggestions to help you cut through the spam and get your message across:

>> **Avoid templates.** Many recruiters lean too heavily on generic templates for mass outreach. This approach may work for some positions where prospects are more likely to switch jobs, but it has little chance for niche or in-demand talent. This doesn't mean every email must be handwritten, but it does mean a degree or personalization is required to convert.

>> **Minimize jargon.** "I have an outstanding value proposition full of synergies with your portfolio." Bingo! Unless you were playing buzzword bingo, that jargon-filled message will likely result in a swift click of the Delete button. Use real language. Talk like a human being. That natural vernacular is more likely to be relatable, capturing a prospect's attention and increasing the chances of a response.

>> **Make it visual.** Scroll through your inbox. What captures your attention? Probably not the plain text emails. Perhaps it's the newsletter with the branded header? Take a page out of email marketing's playbook and use tools like MixMax to create dynamic emails with images, videos, links, and other assets to help your email stand out.

>> **Personalize everything.** Any initial outreach to a candidate should include at least one personalized element that demonstrates you've taken the time to explore her background. With the amount of information on the social web, there are very few true "cold calls."

>> **Include a specific call to action (CTA).** Why are you contacting this person and what are you looking for? A referral? An application? General networking? Be clear about your intent so candidates know you appreciate their time and understand why you're contacting them.

By cutting through the spam and delivering a personal message, you significantly improve your chances of connecting with a candidate and engaging her in a discussion that's likely to convince her to join your organization.

# Chapter **13**

# Making a Splash on Campus

olleges and universities are fertile grounds for recruiters. Every year, these educational institutions produce a fresh crop of eager, intelligent, and often highly gifted individuals who are well prepared to enter the workforce. You also have the option of teaming up with schools to create internships in which you can groom students, over the course of their college years, for an entry-level position within your company. Internships are a great way to test the talent, reap the benefits of low-cost labor, and contribute to creating a well-trained workforce — all at the same time.

To tap into this workforce of the future, you must appeal to and engage with students, which requires an understanding of who they are, what they want, what they offer, how they search for jobs, and what sorts of messages are likely to catch their interest and compel them to engage. It also involves teaming up with colleges and universities to establish a presence on campuses and to connect with students on their home turf. In this chapter, we explain how to do all of this and more.

# Marketing to College Students

Marketing to college students presents both a challenge and an opportunity. The challenge is how to reach, appeal to, and engage an audience that may be unfamiliar to you; if you've never gone to college or it's been a while, you may have trouble connecting with students and delivering messages that resonate with them. The opportunity is that you have a niche to target; if you're able to tune in to your audience, you can more narrowly focus your content and messaging to maximize impact. In this section, we provide guidance on how to meet the challenge and seize the opportunity.

## Understanding the student/graduate mind-set

Whether you're a recent graduate still close to the student mind-set or a baby boomer in the twilight of her career, it's important to find the right approach when marketing to students. Here are a few suggestions:

» **Build relationships with students and younger employees.** The best way to tune in to your audience is to mingle with members of that group, ideally face-to-face but also online via social media. The more you engage, the more comfortable, capable, and confident you'll be writing content that connects with that group.

» **Put yourself in their shoes.** Empathy and compassion go a long way. Recognize what they're going through as they put themselves out there in a competitive job market.

» **Find out what else they want.** People want rewarding work and a fat paycheck, but find out what else they want — opportunities to advance or learn new skills, take on new challenges, work in a creative and fun environment, and so on.

» **Put their needs first.** Although you certainly want to recruit talent that helps the company meet its goals, putting students' needs first improves your ability to attract and engage with that talent.

**WARNING**

As you work to develop your university outreach and engagement, don't try *too* hard to connect with students. In 2016, an alleged email from a Microsoft recruiter trying too hard to connect went viral. In an effort to seem youthful and hip, the author weaved in words like *bae, hella noms,* and *dranks.* Unfortunately for this recruiter, the recipient's roommate got hold of the email and tweeted it for the world to see. Needless to say, the Internet had a field day with that gaffe.

# Attending to key touch points

A crucial tactic in an effective student/graduate recruiting program is to establish a presence where students go to find information about careers and job openings. Take a holistic approach by considering possible touch points, making sure they align to convey the story and messages you want to get across, and building a presence around those touch points. Key touch points include the following:

» **A university career microsite:** A *career microsite* is a special area of your website, or a separate website altogether, devoted exclusively to a certain talent group, such as college interns. (For more about microsites, see Chapter 9, and check out the nearby sidebar for an example.) Depending on how many interns or new grads you hire, you may want to launch a microsite exclusively for interns or college grads or a university website for both.

» **Social media:** As your employer brand journey progresses, you're likely to have several social media channels dedicated to employer brand and recruiting. Twitter, in particular, is a very effective channel for recruiting interns and graduates, because it allows you to use hashtags to get your content in front of the right audience. After you've identified your target schools and programs (see the later section "Choosing Schools Wisely"), search online for hashtags for schools or events on your list. You can then include these hashtags with targeted tweets about intern or new-grad opportunities.

**TIP**

Event hashtags are a great way to engage attendees *before* an event by sending tweets letting students know you'll be there. You can also tweet or post photos on Instagram or Snapchat before, during, and after events. Consider posting photos of your booth, former interns from the school, or graduates who now work at your company.

**WARNING**

Don't overuse hashtags for recruitment marketing, or you may cross over into spammer territory and draw the ire of students.

» **Recruitment marketing:** Your recruitment marketing materials should clearly convey your employer value proposition (EVP) in a way that resonates with students. (See Chapter 4 for more about developing your EVP.) Whether you're creating banners, microsites, videos, or social campaigns, you should be answering the question, "Why should I work for Company X?"

» **Career fairs:** Career fairs remain a big component in many companies' university recruiting strategies. Consider how you come across to students, because they're likely to form perceptions about your company based on their career fair experiences. Here are some tips to help you succeed in this area:

- **Show up with fresh, engaging, and branded signage and recruitment marketing materials.** These items create the all-important first impression.

- **If possible, bring current or former interns, especially those who've been converted to full-time and/or have graduated from that school.** At the very least, bring employees who work in the key fields/positions you're recruiting to fill (again, best if they're alumni). Students want to talk with people who can give them the inside scoop of what it's like to work at your company in the field they're pursuing. Candid answers from people who are doing the work the students will be doing helps drive conversation and conversion. First-person accounts of the experience of interning/working at your company have the greatest impact.

- **Bring tablet computers with your career site bookmarked.** Allow students to share their LinkedIn profiles with the click of a button. Include a monitor with a video loop of your employer brand video or testimonials from interns. Demonstrating that you're a modern company with the technology to match has more impact than fancy swag with your logo on it.

**WARNING**

Whatever you do, don't bring a paper sign-up sheet. It may seem superficial, but today's students grew up with smartphones and tablets. They'll draw assumptions about your company based on your technology or lack thereof.

## A CAREER MICROSITE TO BE PROUD OF

Adobe's career microsite dedicated to university recruiting (www.adobe.com/careers/university.html) is a great model to follow. The site includes content tailored specifically to interns and recent grads. Content on the site not only appeals to target groups, but also provides a distinct path and journey for each. The microsite greets prospects with the requisite tagline and vision statement we discuss in Chapter 9:

**Shift your future into high gear.**

When you come to Adobe as a university student or graduate, you'll work side by side with the tech industry's biggest thinkers and creators to help change the world through digital experiences. You'll be welcomed into a community that loves to dream up groundbreaking ideas and make them real. You'll join forces with master statisticians and serial entrepreneurs, experience designers and engineering fellows, community activists and women who swim with sharks — and you'll stand out for who you are and what you bring to the team.

Experience Adobe. Watch the video >

Your tagline and vision statement and the structure and content of your university career microsite must be tailored to the needs of your audience and your company, but Adobe's is an excellent model to spark your own creative ideas.

# Evaluating regional differences

If you're recruiting in different regions around the world, tailor your university recruiting playbook to the different regions. A one-size-fits-all approach is less effective and may even do more harm than good if cultural differences are ignored. As you develop your student outreach and engagement strategy, account for language and cultural nuances in the local markets where you recruit.

REMEMBER

If you're driving university recruiting in unfamiliar regions, engage local employees and do your homework on customary approaches before implementing your strategy. Increase sensitivity to differences in language and culture is particularly important for large multinational organizations that have university recruiting led from a central location, such as the United States.

# Converting interns

Many organizations use their intern programs as a feeder system for talent and for good reason: Interns make great hires, because they're already accustomed to the organization's culture and way of doing things. Internships also give companies the opportunity to test-drive the talent — to gauge their fit and assess their abilities before making a full-time commitment.

TIP

To reap the benefits, you first need to attract, engage, and convert prospective interns. How do you make that happen? Here are some suggestions for developing an internship program that builds a following and drives conversions:

>> **Make the work meaningful.** The best way to convert interns is to ensure their work is meaningful. If you treat your interns as filing clerks, your conversion rates will struggle. Make sure their experience is immersive and exposes them to some of the tasks they would see as an employee. This gives them a sense of what to expect and allows you to gauge their enthusiasm, commitment, and ability before making a full-time commitment.

>> **Assign well-trained managers to interns.** Either have the intern report to a bona fide manager or provide basic management training to any employee who oversees an intern. Having employees who aren't actual managers managing interns is a common practice, but those nonmanagers still need to know how to manage. Lack of management training can lead to a negative intern experience, or worse.

>> **Check in often.** Ensure that managers have regular check-ins with their interns throughout their internship so that interns feel supported. An internship may be someone's first experience in a professional setting, which can be frightening, intimidating, exhilarating, or all of the above.

>> **Try to create real deliverables.** Design your internship program to give interns real-world experience. Ideally an internship should include a project or deliverable she can list on her résumé or LinkedIn profile. This tangible achievement may open doors for her in the future (even if it's not with your company). The experience is also something the intern will share with her peers, which may create buzz and strengthen your employer brand for future university internships and hiring opportunities.

>> **Socialize interns internally.** Introduce high-potential interns to hiring managers in your company, so these interns see the breadth of opportunities in your organization. You don't want to invest in a quality intern only to lose that person to your competitors.

>> **Make sure that entry-level opportunities are visible.** Inform interns of all the entry-level opportunities. Consider sharing a newsletter or email of jobs on a regular basis, particularly toward the end of the internship period. You may have tremendous opportunities for students, but if they don't know about them, your conversion will be low.

TIP

Survey and measure. The old adage that you can't fix what you can't measure certainly applies to internships. Survey all outgoing interns to gather information and insight about their experiences — what went well and what didn't. Also, track conversion and retention. This data helps you understand where your best intern teams are so you can identify and scale their best practices and spot trouble areas where you may have weak roles or managers.

## Designing an attractive graduate program

*Graduates* are a mix of undergrads who went directly into graduate programs and experienced hires with a mix of real-world employment and advanced education. When developing a graduate intern recruiting program, follow the suggestions in the previous section, keeping in mind that grad students are more experienced, and their value drivers (what draws them to your company) will be different. Align your employer branding efforts and value drivers more closely with those for full-time hires. Here are some grad student value drivers to consider:

>> **Opportunities for tangible accomplishments:** Graduate interns typically are looking for hands-on experience with deliverables they can list on a résumé.

>> **Commensurate compensation:** Most graduate interns expect a compensation program commensurate with their level of education and experience.

>> **Graduate career opportunities:** Because graduate students are more experienced, they're often more "skilled up" and ready to make an immediate

impact. Be sure your recruitment marketing and engagement efforts convey the career opportunities for graduate-level hires. Peer testimonials and peer interviews can get strengthen that message.

TIP

When marketing to graduate students, showcase real-world contributions of your graduate interns and success stories of interns who've become full-time employees in your company.

## Balancing targeting with diversity

Diversity is an important component to university recruiting, and for good reason: Organizations thrive when their workforce reflects the breadth of diversity in the marketplace. According to the Society for Human Resource Management (SHRM), racially diverse teams outperform nondiverse teams by 35 percent, yet 41 percent of companies say they're "too busy" to implement diversity initiatives. If you have a similar disconnect in your organization, it needs to be addressed.

REMEMBER

Balance your efforts at targeting certain talent groups with a commitment to increasing diversity in your organization. A conscious and proactive diversity focus in your student/graduate recruiting strategy enables you to infuse your organization with diverse talent and begin building your reputation as an inclusive employer that values diversity. Of course, effective diversity efforts go well beyond university recruitment, but this is one direct way to ensure your company is regularly infused with diverse talent.

TIP

Here are a few ways to enhance your diversity outreach initiatives:

>> **Reach out to diverse student organizations.** Most universities have a broad range of diverse student organizations. Identify them and build relationships over time (through sponsorship, social engagement, hosted events, and so on) so that the students are familiar with your organization and see the inclusive opportunities.

>> **Be mindful of your signage and recruitment materials.** Review and audit your marketing materials for gender and cultural bias. You may think that campaign logo is hip and edgy, but if it's overly masculine, you may unintentionally turn away talent. If your recruitment marketing materials include all white males, you may be giving the impression you're not an inclusive environment.

>> **Don't forget the stories.** Highlight the diversity of your workforce in your recruitment marketing materials.

>> **Don't narrow your definition.** Too many companies approach diversity strictly through a racial lens. Be sure to consider all aspects of diversity (race, gender, disability, veteran status, socioeconomics, and so on) when developing your outreach strategies.

# Choosing Schools Wisely

Most leading employers now recognize that they need to do far more than turn up for the conventional round of seasonal, final-year student recruitment activities. They're building deeper, ongoing relationships with university career advisors, student organizations, and target faculties. They're also reaching out to potential candidates much earlier in their academic studies. Paul McIntyre, BP's Global Head of Resourcing, shared the following story which underlines the importance of developing closer relationships with colleges and universities:

> I recently visited the second biggest engineering college in the United States in terms of enrollment and sat next to the dean of engineering at dinner. I asked him who in our industry is doing really well in attracting your highest-quality diverse talent, and what are they doing differently? The dean said, "It really isn't rocket science, Paul. They're simply here more, not just during the recruitment season, but a lot more often and they build personal relationships."

**TIP**

Building relationships requires a great deal of time and effort, and your resources are limited, so choose schools wisely. Look for schools that offer the following:

>> **Key talent your organization needs:** For example, MIT is known for engineering and technology, Yale is a top law school, Harvard has a solid reputation in law and medicine, Johns Hopkins is a leading medical school, the University of Chicago has a stellar business school, and so on.

>> **Motivated career centers or job placement services:** Management of these valuable student services are your inside connection to the college or university. Look for schools that are eager to build relationships with businesses (most are) and, more important, are eager to team up with your company.

>> **Accommodations and perks for student interns:** Schools that accommodate or even reward interns are better than those that don't. Find out how flexible the college or university is with internship programs.

>> **Reasonably convenient geographical location:** If your company is located in Zurich, focusing your university outreach efforts in the United States would be foolish. Work with the career centers to understand the location preferences of the students, and factor that into your selection process.

>> **Diversity:** Recruit at schools with diverse student populations or at a number of schools that collectively have a diverse student population. Google had a reputation for hiring only Ivy League graduates. After multiyear analysis, it learned that the pedigree of school was not an indicator of job performance, so Google took steps to diversify its university partners.

# Supporting College Career and Job Placement Services

Just as your recruiting efforts benefit from putting student needs first, students will also benefit from your putting the needs of the college career and job placement services first. These services need you as much as you need them. Being able to boast about their job placement rates and the quality of the companies that hire their graduates significantly improves demand for what the college or university has to offer. It increases enrollment rates for schools that struggle in that area and makes competitive schools that much more competitive. Give them what they need to succeed, and they'll be much more attentive to meeting your needs.

TIP

Here are a few suggestions on how to attend to the needs of the colleges and universities you choose to team up with:

>> **Provide superior recruitment marketing materials and content.** If the school has a career website or blog, offer to supply content or to write a series of guest blog posts. Generating relevant content for websites and blogs is a constant burden; help ease that burden for them. Print media also tend to be more important for students and graduates, including university publications, student organization publications and career magazines, and alumni magazines.

>> **Attend campus career events and job fairs.** The success of such events hinges on employer participation. Help the school make these events a big hit among the student body.

>> **Build strong relationships.** Building strong relationships with university outplacement offices opens the door to unforeseen opportunities and synergies. Stay in touch with your university contacts even when you're not actively recruiting and even at times during the school year when placement offices aren't so busy.

>> **Lend your expertise.** Bring your recruiters (and managers) on campus to provide jobs search and résumé writing workshops. This is a great way to build affinity with the students and career services, and it also gives you a closed audience that provides more engagement opportunities than a crowded career fair does.

# Reaching Out to Less Prominent Institutions

Investing your recruitment efforts in the colleges and universities with the best reputations for developing the talent your company needs is a no-brainer, but also consider recruiting at less prominent educational institutions. As Malcolm Gladwell points out in *Outliers,* being among the best students in a lower-ranking college has benefits, particularly for science, technology, engineering, and math (STEM) students. Similarly, you can reap many benefits from recruiting at under-represented colleges and universities. These students tend to be just as successful as those at the "elite" schools and generally have more manageable egos and employment expectations. A recent Equilar research study of C-level executives working at Fortune 100 firms revealed that instead of coming from a concentrated number of elite colleges, they came from more than 300 different colleges and universities.

TIP

To connect with students and graduates at lesser-known schools without investing huge amounts of resources, consider the following methods:

» **Engage students in mini projects and competitions.** Partner with local universities to create student competitions where you present real challenges your business faces and allow them to work on solutions. Create coding contests with prizes to gauge proficiency in different technologies.

» **Explore a range of content marketing approaches.** Consider blogs or slide-show presentations tailored to the interests of target student populations.

» **Ramp up referrals.** If you have employees who attended the schools you're targeting for your recruitment efforts, ask them to be more active in referring promising candidates they know who attend or graduated from that school. Employees may be reluctant to refer people they know, but by asking for referrals, you give them permission to do so.

» **Implement remote recruiting.** You can establish a presence in colleges and universities and connect with students without ever setting foot on campus. Video conferencing, online slide shows, and webinars extend your recruitment reach. You can use them to identify, contact, interview, and hire student candidates at remote and under-represented colleges and universities at a fraction of the cost of establishing a physical presence on campus.

# INCREASING EMPLOYEE DIVERSITY AT GOLDMAN SACHS

Goldman Sachs is one of the traditional stalwarts of campus recruiting, currently active on 225 college campuses in the United States alone. Every year, it admits 2,500 undergraduates into its internship program and chooses its new analysts from that group. The company has announced several initiatives to curb bias in its recruitment and selection of college graduates:

- **Expand the number of targeted schools.** Traditionally, Goldman Sachs drew applicants from approximately 400 target schools, including 225 in the United States. In an attempt to draw students from more diverse backgrounds, the company is reaching out to more schools.

- **Increase efforts to reach out to students through social media.** By increasing its use of social media, Goldman Sachs hopes to connect with students beyond even the larger group of schools where it plans to actively recruit.

- **Employ a computerized résumé screening tool.** The tool is programmed to identify traits that the company considers more predictive of career success and longevity, such as grit or life circumstances.

- **Automate more of the interview and selection process.** More of the interview process will be automated and standardized and will occur online, without human interviewers. Automation serves two purposes: It makes the interview and selection process more efficient, so fewer recruiters/interviewers can consider more prospects, and, along with standardization, it reduces the potential for human bias.

- **Discontinue face-to-face on-campus interviews of undergraduates.** The purpose here is to prevent interviewers from being swayed by discussions of shared interests and mutual acquaintances. However, while the new approach reduces the likelihood of bias, it doesn't eliminate it. Recruiting executives will watch the recorded interviews to determine which students move on to the second round, and any subsequent interviews will be conducted by hiring managers at one of the bank's offices. Also, the company will continue its practice of interviewing MBA students on campus.

- **Introduce a personality test.** The personality test will help to automate and standardize the interview process to a greater degree, using more objective criteria than is typically used by human interviewers to determine whether any given prospect is a good fit for the company.

If your organization is looking to increase diversity in its recruitment and hiring practices, you can learn quite a bit from these clever initiatives at Goldman Sachs.

# 4

## Delivering on Your Employer Brand Promises

Deliver a superior employment experience to engage and retain current employees.

Convert employees into powerful, vocal, employer brand advocates helping you to identify great candidates and recruit the best talent.

Make a great first and lasting impression on job candidates, so they feel good about the application and screening process, your organization, and themselves, regardless of the outcome.

Ensure your onboarding process gets new joiners up to speed and performing at their best as soon as possible.

Engage and retain your talent by identifying and responding to local engagement drivers and retention risks, particularly during challenging periods of organizational change such as downsizing, restructuring, mergers, or acquisitions.

# Chapter **14**

# Shaping a Positive Brand Experience

M any sales and customer service reps will tell you that the key to keeping a customer happy is to underpromise and overdeliver. Our advice for shaping a positive *employer brand experience* (what it's like to work at the company) is more nuanced: Keep your promises and continually strive to improve the employment experience. If an employee's experience fulfills or surpasses your employer brand promises, the employee is likely to sing the company's praises, strengthening the brand. If the employment experience falls short of your promises, the employee is more likely to feel cheated and share negative comments with his friends and professional contacts — and your brand will suffer.

In this chapter, we tackle the challenge of delivering an employer brand experience that lives up to your recruitment marketing promises through the design and implementation of consistent people management processes and leadership behaviors.

**REMEMBER**

Delivering an employer experience that consistently lives up to your brand promises is challenging. The larger and more complex the organization, the harder it gets. Because people are involved you'll always find variations in the employment experience largely due to local differences in culture, personality, and priorities.

This diversity is healthy, and brand consistency should never mean uniformity. Nevertheless, your employer branding efforts, including the delivery of a high value employment experience, must accommodate this diversity.

# Applying Customer Experience Thinking to HR Processes

People often take for granted the planning and discipline required to deliver an excellent customer experience. When companies get this right, it often feels easy and natural, much like a great athletic performance, but it generally takes considerable effort to deliver a quality experience on a consistent basis.

Consider the brand experience of an airline customer, and the complex coordination of services required to deliver a distinctively positive experience. More often than not, the process starts online with a digital experience. How informative and easy to use is the website? On the way to the airport can the customer check-in using her smartphone and keep up to date with any changes that may be affecting the flight schedule? How easy is it for the customer to check in her bags? How friendly and informative are the customer service assistants at the check-in desk? Once onboard, how comfortable is the seat? What kind of entertainment is available? How good is the food being served? How attentive is the cabin crew? Getting all these experiential elements right (at a competitive price) lies at the heart of successful customer marketing.

Delivering an excellent employment experience requires a similar coordinated effort throughout the company, often under the direction HR. In this section, we provide guidance on how to put all the pieces in place and rally company leadership to coordinate their efforts.

## Thinking differently about HR

The reason leading airlines pay so much attention to the design and consistent delivery of the customer experience is that airline passengers (especially frequent flyers) can generally choose between providers. Because employees (especially the most talented) are also free to choose between employers, it surely makes sense for companies to apply the same rigor and discipline to managing the employment experience. This has not been the kind of thinking HR has conventionally applied, but the HR function looks set to go through another period of transformation with significant signs of convergence between talent management and customer experience management thinking.

## EMBRACING THE CUSTOMER SERVICE MODEL

In Deloitte's Global Human Capital Trends 2016 report, "The New Organization, Different by Design" (www.deloitte.com/us/en/pages/human-capital/articles/introduction-human-capital-trends.html), the authors arrive at the following conclusion:

> In competition for skilled people, organizations are vying for top talent in a highly transparent job market and becoming laser-focused on their employment brand. . . . The mission of the HR leader is evolving from that of "chief talent executive" to "chief employee experience officer." HR is being asked to simplify its processes, help employees manage the flood of information at work, and build a culture of collaboration, empowerment, and innovation. This means that HR is redesigning almost everything it does — from recruiting to performance management to onboarding to rewards systems.

If your company's HR department isn't already transitioning from the talent management model to the customer service model, it needs to start soon to remain competitive.

**REMEMBER**

Stop thinking of HR as an administrative function and start thinking of it as a customer service department for employees.

## Reviewing your current employment experience

Shaun Smith, the author of *Managing the Customer Experience* (Pearson FT Press), identifies three levels of customer experience (see Figure 14-1), with the ultimate goal of delivering a differentiated branded experience that's not merely reliably good in delivering against service expectations but distinctively great in delivering unique customer value.

The employee experience is generally more complex than most customer service experiences, but your company would benefit from adopting a similar approach. The goal is to climb the ladder from brand busters to brand signatures, as shown in Figure 14-2 and explained in the following sections.

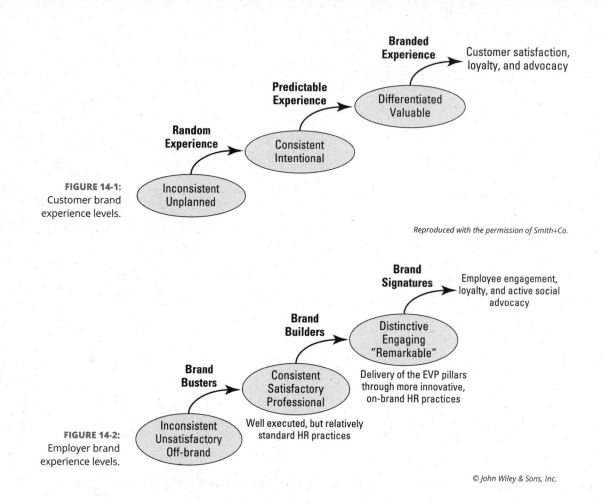

**FIGURE 14-1:**
Customer brand experience levels.

Random Experience

Predictable Experience

Branded Experience

Inconsistent Unplanned

Consistent Intentional

Differentiated Valuable

Customer satisfaction, loyalty, and advocacy

*Reproduced with the permission of Smith+Co.*

**FIGURE 14-2:**
Employer brand experience levels.

Brand Busters

Brand Builders

Brand Signatures

Inconsistent Unsatisfactory Off-brand

Consistent Satisfactory Professional

Distinctive Engaging "Remarkable"

Well executed, but relatively standard HR practices

Delivery of the EVP pillars through more innovative, on-brand HR practices

Employee engagement, loyalty, and active social advocacy

*© John Wiley & Sons, Inc.*

## Spotting brand busters

*Brand busters* are employment experiences that undermine the employer brand for any number of reasons, such as the following:

>> **Inconsistent experience:** Inconsistencies in the employment experience are typically the result of having no people management process in place or executing the process that is in place inconsistently. Induction and orientation processes are prone to these kind of inconsistencies in many organizations.

>> **Unsatisfactory experience:** Employees are typically dissatisfied with the employment experience as a result of poor process design, insufficient investment, or both. In many organizations, employees are most often disappointed with career development and mobility.

>> **Off-brand experience:** The preceding two brand busters may relate to any aspect of the employment experience, but an off-brand experience is more

specific to your employer brand promises. If you promise "a world of opportunities" but have no process or investment in place to advance employees' careers abroad, then you have a classic brand buster on your hands.

In small to medium-size companies, a strong leadership presence and tightly knit culture can sometimes deliver a consistently positive employment experience with very few formal people management processes. In larger companies, an absence of well-designed and well-executed processes almost inevitably leads to significant inconsistencies. Even with well-designed processes, insufficient time and investment applied to training and communication lead to similarly poor or inconsistent employee experiences.

## Identifying brand builders

*Brand builders* are consistently positive employment experiences resulting from professional, well-executed, but relatively standard HR procedures. To step up from brand busters to brand builders, all you need to do is figure out what your competitors are doing well and follow their lead. You don't need to do anything special.

## TRANSITIONING HR TO A MARKETING MIND-SET

Traditionally, HR has been far more focused on and driven by best-practice benchmarking than marketing. Establishing "effective" best-practice processes has been regarded as the general goal of HR process design and a sufficient foundation for supporting business performance. This is very different from marketing-think, where establishing points of parity with key competitors is only one part of brand development. The other goal of brand development is to identify points of difference. From a marketing point of view, this is by far the more important task. The greater the parity, the more you need to rely on reducing price or investing in your distribution to win customers. The greater the difference (as long as you've chosen the right points of differentiation), the more you can hold your price and expect customers to beat a path to your door.

When you apply this thinking to HR, you soon realize that many organizations place too much focus on applying the same people management practices as their competitors and far too little focus and investment on innovating distinctive ways of working that will help them stand apart from their talent competitors. As for customer marketing, if your organization offers essentially the same employment experience as your competitors, then you need to rely far more on money to attract and retain. If you build a more distinctive employer brand experience, attracting people to join and stay with you for other reasons should be easier.

### Raising the bar: Brand signatures

If your organization has successfully turned brand busters into brand builders, and has a consistently positive and professional approach to people management process, the next level to aspire to from an employer brand perspective is the development of *signature experiences* — elements of your company's employment experience that make the experience unique and superior to that offered by competitors. Signature experiences are of value to employees and to the organization, but they also serve as constant reminders of the company's culture and values.

Signature experiences may be different by degree, in terms of the amount of emphasis or investment dedicated to the underlying process or practice. For example, you may have a career path model that is similar to other companies, but better because you invested more than your leading talent competitors in the kind of software that enables employees to map out different career options and training requirements. Alternatively, the employment experience could be different in kind, which means it includes elements unique to your organization. These generally require greater investment in imagination than money.

Signature experiences may define processes that are so central to the organization, they could be seen by many as defining its core ethos, such as Kaizen, Toyota's continuous improvement process, or GE's lean-thinking Work-Out. In other cases, it simply represents a distinctive aspect of the business such as IBM's online collaborative Jam sessions. Some companies, including Google and Virgin, seem to be naturally drawn to creating signature experiences.

For additional guidance on how to create signature experiences, see the later section "Designing signature experiences."

# Engaging in Touch-Point Planning

People management involves a wide range of ritualized processes and HR "products" that can be described as *employee touch points* — stages in a process where HR interacts with, or has the opportunity to interact with, employees (see Figure 14-3). Planning these touch points is a key step in developing extraordinary employment experiences — those that rise to the level of signature experiences.

## Conducting a touch-point review

Touch-point planning involves reviewing the current alignment of people management practices with the EVP, setting priorities to turn employer brand busters into brand signatures, and identifying opportunities to reinforce or develop new brand signatures.

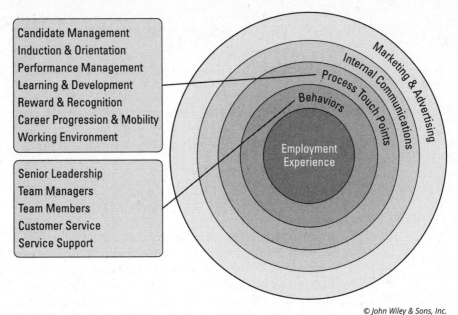

Candidate Management
Induction & Orientation
Performance Management
Learning & Development
Reward & Recognition
Career Progression & Mobility
Working Environment

Senior Leadership
Team Managers
Team Members
Customer Service
Service Support

Marketing & Advertising
Internal Communications
Process Touch Points
Behaviors
Employment Experience

**FIGURE 14-3:**
Employer brand experience touch points.

© John Wiley & Sons, Inc.

**WARNING**

Don't restrict touch-point planning to processes that fall within the governance of HR; instead, include everything that may have a significant effect on the internal employer brand experience, including employee communication, facilities management, and the working environment. Starting with a relatively broad framework provides more opportunities to identify potential signature experiences.

The ideal approach to conducting a touch-point review is to do customized research into employees' perceptions of the different aspects of the employment experience (the touch points shown in Figure 14-3). This research may take the form of focus groups with key employee segments or a more extensive quantitative survey.

**WARNING**

New joiner surveys and employee engagement research may provide some useful insights, but these methodologies often fail to provide the kind of granular information required to diagnose satisfaction with specific people management processes, and very seldom provide the kind of information required to diagnose alignment with an EVP.

If you don't have access to detailed research data, you can still conduct a touch-point review. We've found that the HR leadership team, HR centers of excellence, and other relevant functional heads generally have a good enough understanding to conduct a top-line review of people management performance and alignment.

For each of the areas under review, rate the brand consistency and alignment of both the process design (how things are supposed to work) and practices (how they actually work).

**TIP**

Consider color-coding each touch-point category according to its buster/builder/signature status to create a useful visual summary of the overall results of this exercise. Many companies use a traffic-light system, with green designating on-brand, orange designating room for improvement, and red designating an urgent need to redress.

## Touch-point action planning

The "big picture" touch-point review discussed in the preceding section makes it far easier to see what needs to be done to bring the employment experience into alignment with the EVP. The most obvious place to start is an assessment of current HR priorities in light of your touch-point analysis. If the EVP has been developed with this forward plan in mind, then you should see a reasonable match between areas of recognizable stretch and HR improvements already underway or in the HR pipeline. The next step is to identify the gaps, and you do that by answering the following questions:

>> **What *must* you do to address remaining and significant brand busters?** If key areas of the employment experience conflict with your brand promises, how well you're delivering in other areas doesn't matter; the brand will always be compromised.

>> **What *should* you do to exploit the most immediate opportunities to strengthen the brand through more effective people management or create more signature brand experiences?** This relates to touch-point improvements that should be relatively easy and inexpensive to implement given sufficient commitment from the leadership team.

>> **What *could* you do given the right resources and budget to deliver further improvements over time?**

Having established your priorities, the next step is to address the changes that may need to be made to redesign people processes and practices. This may involve redesigning the process itself or, if the shortfall in employee experience relates to the consistency or style of implementation, you may need to redesign or reinvest in training and communication.

Your facilities management may fall within this process framework, but shaping the overall design of the working environment is generally a much bigger question. If you're considering the right kind of architectural design for a new build, or reconfiguring the workplace design of an existing building, consult your EVP. Most leading companies now have a very conscious desire to reflect the brand values within the design of the workplace, and you can find many excellent examples of this in the book *I Wish I Worked There!* by Kursty Groves with Will Knight (Wiley).

# Designing signature experiences

You have two major ways to create a signature experience: Do it more or do it differently. Doing something more than your competitors generally requires a strong HR business case and strategic investment from the leadership team. Doing something differently may not require as much investment in time and money, but it requires imagination both from the team that designs the experience and the leaders who sign off on it. In the following sections, we explain each of these approaches in greater detail.

## Doing it more

Making something a signature of the organization by investing significantly more time or money than others tends to be more powerful (than doing it differently) from an employer branding perspective, because it generally implies more deeply held cultural values. A good example of this is McDonald's, a company that for many years invested significantly more in training and development than the rest of the quick-service restaurant sector, with McDonald's University one of the first of its kind in the corporate world. Another example is Toyota, whose dedication to quality has long been enshrined in its Kaizen approach to continuous improvement. In both of these cases, the company has developed a reputation for offering something different by degree (doing it more) from its talent competitors without necessarily doing anything particularly innovative in terms of process design.

To develop this kind of signature experience, you need to create a strong business case for investment in an area of people management where you believe that special focus will deliver significant returns in terms of engagement, performance, and brand reputation. McDonald's believes that its superior training and development leads to better product quality, customer service, and talent retention. Toyota, whose business was severely tested a few years ago through problems with its braking system, believed that it was able to survive the crisis because of its widely recognized, long-term dedication to quality (it was an isolated problem that could be fixed rather than a more widespread organizational failure).

## Doing it differently

Doing something differently often comes from investing more time and money in something, but this isn't always the case. This kind of signature generally results from a belief within the organization that there's always a better way, and that way is often different from the road taken by everyone else. In this case, companies simply take a different approach to the way they design their processes. A good recent example of this is Accenture, which completely redesigned its performance management process to save both time and money, and make it more effective. Here are some more examples:

>> **Google:** Google's success as an employer can be partly explained by its phenomenal success as a business, but its distinctive approach to people management has undoubtedly made a significant contribution to its long reign at the top of every list of best places to work. Who hasn't heard of "20 percent time"? If you haven't, it refers to Google's policy of encouraging software engineers to spend one day a week on a personal passion project, unconnected with their regular work. Other creative Google initiatives include the "pets at work" policy, 24/7 gourmet food, and the famously fun working environments (slides, ski-lift meeting rooms, and so on). This may sound like the recipe for every tech startup, but important cultural differences between the leading Silicon Valley players are reflected in their choice of brand signatures.

>> **Apple:** Apple is far less laid back than Google. It doesn't encourage 20 percent time or have evident work-life balance policies. Clearly, Apple demands extreme dedication and hard work. As its career site states:

> A job at Apple is one that requires a lot of you, but it's also one that rewards bright, original thinking and hard work. None of us here at Apple would have it any other way.

Apple's people management policies are designed to reinforce self-reliance. The company underplays the notion of career paths to encourage people to actively seek out their own information and contacts about opportunities around the company. Apple also spends a great deal less on benefits than its immediate competitors do. After researching the company's approach to talent management Dr. John Sullivan concluded: "Apple's offerings are Spartan when compared to Google, Facebook, and Microsoft."

Another signature difference is Apple's 10:3:1 approach to innovation, which involves up to ten teams working in isolation from each other on the same product area. Then, following a formal peer review, the resulting product mock-ups are pared down to three, and then down to one. Unlike most other companies, Apple makes a virtue of silos and secrecy to eliminate any threat of groupthink. You can't argue with Apple's success.

>> **Facebook:** Facebook's approach is almost the exact opposite of Apple's. "Being open" is a core feature of Facebook's belief system, and this means doing everything possible to encourage openness and collaboration between its employees, which includes standing desks that help to create a much more open working environment (in addition to a healthier posture). It means providing new joiners with complete access to Facebook's computer code. It also informs two of Facebook's signature innovation processes:

- Hackathons involve eight-hour, all-night sessions involving large groups of employees brainstorming new product concepts.

- Project Mayhem events are 27-hour sessions, focusing on mobile product ideas, which generally require more planning time.

In addition to reinforcing a distinctive employer brand, signature employer brand experiences help to engender a distinctive brand attitude, generate distinctive brand behaviors, and ultimately reinforce the kind of distinctive customer service style that adds value to the customer experience and differentiates an organization from its competitors.

## QUICKEN LOANS'S CHEESE FACTORY

Quicken Loans provides a great example of a company that has developed a signature way of describing and delivering a key component of its employment experience — its employee ideas generator. Quicken Loans is on a constant mission to do things better, or "build a better mousetrap," as they like to say. And what better way to do that than to arm the mousetrap with delicious cheese? To bring this to life, Quick Loans created the "Cheese Factory," a section of the company's intranet site that allows team members to propose ideas (or nuggets of cheddar) for the mousetrap. To make it as easy as possible to post new ideas, the company also provides a mobile app so team members don't need to be at their desks, or even in the office, to suggest ideas or process improvements. Every idea that is posted is displayed on the Cheese Factory site for a week, and team members are encouraged to vote and comment on the proposals. The ideas are then rated yea or nay.

Ideas appearing on the Cheese Factory have varied widely, ranging from the types of free snacks provided in the company's "kitchens" to improvements to its mortgage process and the types of companies and real estate that Quicken Loans should consider acquiring. All ideas, regardless of size and scope, are posted, voted upon, and considered. Each month, the five best ideas that were submitted are recognized in a company-wide email from the Cheese Factory, with the team members behind those ideas being rewarded with cash ranging from $100 to $250.

One shining example of an idea that originated from the Cheese Factory is Rocket Fiber, the newest gigabit high-speed Internet currently being installed in the entire downtown urban core of Detroit. Rocket Fiber, which will soon be available to all businesses and residents living in the central business district and beyond, began as an idea submitted by Quicken Loans engineer Marc Hudson through the Cheese Factory.

Chapter **15**

# Making a Positive Impression on Candidates

elivering an exceptional employer brand experience begins long before people join your organization and extends beyond your employees. It begins with your content marketing and recruitment advertising, when many candidates get their first glimpse of your organization and start to form their initial expectations. It then ramps up slowly as candidates submit applications and undergo screening — their first actual experiences with your organization.

If you receive plenty of applications from well-qualified candidates, your screening process may be brutal, but it can't feel that way to prospective new hires. When candidates apply for a position, they're often at their most vulnerable, and the application and screening process can be very emotional, particularly for those who don't make the cut. To make a positive first and lasting impression, develop an application and screening process that makes them feel good about themselves and your organization, regardless of the outcome. And for those who do make the cut, develop and implement induction and orientation processes that make the onboarding experience as smooth and pleasant as possible. In this chapter, we explain how to do just that.

# Building Candidate-Friendly Application and Selection Processes

Many organizations approach the application and selection processes as an exercise in thinning the herd — rejecting the weakest candidates until only the best of the best remains. Like the process of natural selection, this approach is cold and cruel and can make unsuccessful candidates feel bad about themselves and bitter toward your organization. Even worse, those rejected candidates are likely to become an ongoing source of negative word-of-mouth advertising that damages your employer brand.

REMEMBER

Although you're looking to fill a position with the most qualified candidate whose personality and values mesh with those of your organization, keep in mind that every applicant is a human being with emotions and struggles. While you certainly can't hire everyone, you can make your application and selection processes feel more personal, thus preventing applicants from feeling like cattle being led to slaughter.

In this section, we explain how to build more personal and compassionate application and selection processes that enable applicants to interact with your organization in a positive way, retain their dignity regardless of the outcome, and become a lasting source of positive word-of-mouth advertising that reinforces your employer brand.

REMEMBER

Organizations with durable brands stay *on brand* — they approach key strategic decisions in the context of their brand identities. Apple is hip and fun. Disney is magic. Google is connecting people to information. Coke makes you happy. Toyota stands for affordable reliability.

## Designing a professional and courteous application and selection funnel

Assuming an applicant has already established a certain number of employer brand expectations through exposure to your recruitment advertising and content marketing (see Part 3), you should consciously wire these same brand attributes into the application and screening process. Perhaps even more important, and more fundamental, is to be sure that your application and interview processes are professional and courteous, as explained in this section.

### Focusing on the application process

One way to reinforce a positive brand impression throughout the application process is to focus your efforts on treating candidates with courtesy and managing their expectations. Here's how:

>> **Treat every applicant with respect.** Applying for a job can be an emotional experience. Be sure you're building a candidate experience that's empathy driven. However tough the screening process may be, applicants should emerge with their dignity intact.

>> **Set clear expectations.** Be upfront about the number of applications you expect to receive, when applicants will be notified that their applications have been received and whether they've been selected to be interviewed, how long the process will take, and when you expect to have the position filled. By managing expectations, you reduce the disappointment that may convert a rejected applicant into a brand detractor.

>> **Acknowledge applications promptly and with gratitude.** Have a system in place to acknowledge the receipt of an application within a day or two of receiving it. Thank applicants for taking the time to complete and submit their applications. Avoid making applicants feel as though their applications have been sucked into the "black hole," where they're never acknowledged.

>> **Let people know where they are in the process.** Keep candidates updated throughout the process. If your applicant tracking system (ATS) has the capability to show candidates where they are in the process, use it.

>> **Keep the candidates you've chosen to interview in the loop about the screening process.** Let candidates know whether they'll be interviewed in person or online, whether the interview will be automated or conducted by a person, and so on. Also keep candidates posted regarding the number of interviews required and where they are in the process.

>> **Communicate decisions promptly and clearly.** As decisions are made, keep the applicants informed. Most candidates will appreciate even bad news if it's delivered in a timely manner, because it shows you respect their time.

These steps reflect basic acts of decency that reflect well on the brand. Candidates selected for interviews will feel they've made the right choice to pursue the opportunity. Those who fail to make the grade will feel they've been dealt with professionally; even though they may feel bad about the result, they're more likely to feel good about your organization.

REMEMBER

Candidates are just as likely to share their negative experiences as they are to share their positive experiences. CareerBuilder's research suggests that the majority of people who've had a bad experience during the application and selection process will tell at least three of their friends, and a significant number will tell considerably more.

## Interviewing applicants

This same respect and consideration shown during the application stage should carry over to those you choose to interview. Make sure candidates know what to expect. This doesn't mean providing candidates with a list of 50 questions they may be asked during the interview. Instead, provide candidates with some general information about the interview format, the interviewers, and the type and level of preparation required:

>> **Describe the interview format.** For example, explain whether interviews will be conducted via video or in person and whether all candidates for the position will be asked the same questions. Details about the interview format may include the interview type — standard (question-and-answer format), behavioral (for example, "Describe a time when you disagreed with a supervisor"), or situational (for example, "How would you respond in the following situation?").

>> **Provide information about the people conducting the interview.** You may want to let candidates know whether to expect to be interviewed by one or two people or a panel. You may want to relieve any anxiety by explaining that the interviewer(s) are not there to judge but to help determine whether candidates are the right fit for the position. Or you may provide additional details, including the names of the people who will conduct the interview and their positions in the organization.

>> **Describe the level of preparation required and suggest ways to prepare (or not).** You may, for example, inform candidates that they can't possibly prepare for the interview. Or you may want to offer additional guidance, such as, "Bring a portfolio of your work and be prepared to discuss it" or "Be prepared to discuss specifically how your education and experience have prepared you for this position" or "Bring any questions you have about our organization and the position you're interested in."

McKinsey, a leading global management consulting firm, provides an excellent example of this kind of selection process prebriefing.

> For those of you feeling anxious about interviews with McKinsey, relax. Our interviewers aren't there to grill you, or laser in on your weaknesses, or destabilize you with trick questions. In fact, they're smart and caring people who are eager to find your strengths, especially in unexpected places.

McKinsey goes on to describe the two types of interviews involved in the selection process:

>> **Experience interview:** The experience interview is designed to explore people's strengths and accomplishments.

>> **Case interview:** The case interview is designed to test people's problem-solving abilities.

McKinsey provides a number of practice tests and coaching tips to help people perform at their best but advises candidates not to overprepare:

> Familiarizing yourself with the content and structure of the interviews — and broadly framing the areas you want to cover based on the attributes we've described above — is enough. We are not looking for "the most prepped."

## Handling selection and rejection with sensitivity

You can't speak with job seekers without hearing them refer to the "black hole," where applications go immediately upon submission never to be acknowledged by the employer. It's an all-too-common result of recruiting apparatuses that are built for speed and scale and lack the empathy and humanity the industry *should* be known for.

Considering taking the following steps to convert rejected candidates into brand advocates or at least reduce the changes of converting them into brand detractors:

» Always be respectful of a candidate's time.

» When a hiring decision has been made, notify all applicants in a timely manner.

» If possible and appropriate, provide feedback that may help the candidate with future applications and interviews.

» If possible, offer guidance that may help the candidate find a job that's a better match for his knowledge and skills or recommend positions that the candidate may not have considered.

» Considering sharing job search resources that may help the candidates in their search.

» Thank any applicants you meet for their interest and time and wish them all the best in their continuing job search.

» If the door is open for future consideration, be sure to let them know.

» Avoid any sort of phrase like "We'll keep your résumé on file." Most candidates see this as a token gesture.

**REMEMBER**

Applying for jobs is an emotional experience. It's part of a major life-changing decision that ranks right up there with getting married, starting a family, and buying a house. Yet too many organizations treat talent like a commodity and build recruiting engines driven solely by efficiency. In doing so, they lose sight of the personal impact these decisions have on the people they're trying to hire.

Creating a recruiting process that's based on empathy gives you a golden opportunity to create advocates out of the people being rejected, and not just those you're hiring. Building a process infused with empathy requires significant time and attention to detail, but it can have a huge positive impact on your employer brand. Your organization will build a strong reputation as the employer who cares and who treats all applicants as people, not as commodities.

## Tailoring your application, screening, and selection process to your EVP

After ensuring that your organization's application and screening processes are both professional and courteous, the next step is to tailor your application, screening, and selection processes to reinforce the key pillars of your employer value proposition (EVP):

1. **Create a two-column table.**

2. **In the left column, list the key pillars of your EVP.**

3. **In the right column, create a list of ways to demonstrate each EVP pillar in the various stages of the application, screening, and selection process.**

Table 15-1 provides an example of what a portion of such a table should look like. The example is from a leading global company that required every manager involved in conducting interviews to take a day's training to fully understand not only the professional standards required, but also the importance of reinforcing the company's EVP through the way they conducted each interview.

**TABLE 15-1** **Example of EVP Pillars Aligned with the Interview Process**

| EVP Pillars | Demonstrated through the Interview By |
|---|---|
| Enabling and empowering people | Ensuring the candidate is given every opportunity to perform to the very best of his ability |
| | Helping the candidate understand what you're looking for |
| | Making the candidate feel comfortable |
| | Using open-ended questions |
| | Remaining impartial (avoiding judgment cues during the interview) |
| Responding to individual needs | Clarifying what the candidate is looking for |
| | Remaining attentive and approachable |
| | Actively avoiding stereotyping |
| | Providing time at the end of the interview for candidate questions |

**REMEMBER**

You're assessing candidates, and they're assessing you. These are important moments of truth for your employer brand promises. If your proposition promises flexibility, then you need to make sure to build flexibility into your process design. If you've claimed to be a progressive and innovative employer, for example, you should find a way to demonstrate this commitment through the innovative approach you take to interviewing and selection.

# Ensuring a Positive Brand Experience through Induction and Orientation

Once you've made an offer and it's been accepted, you may think that you can take your foot off the employer brand marketing pedal. Nothing could be further from the truth. Onboarding talent in the right way is just as important as recruiting the right talent. If you succeed, high expectations will fast-forward into high engagement and high performance. Get it wrong, and disappointment will lead to disengagement and early attrition.

In this section, we present best practices for onboarding new hires. We start by bringing you up to speed on the fundamentals and then provide more detailed guidance for preboarding and welcoming new hires and ramping up engagement and performance right out of the gate.

## PROOF THAT FORMAL ONBOARDING PROCESSES WORK MAGIC

In Aberdeen Group's recent research among nearly 200 organizations, it discovered that those with the most advanced onboarding practices retained 86 percent of their employees over the first 12 months compared with 56 percent among the "laggards." These leading orientation methods also helped to ensure that 77 percent of newly hired employees met first-year performance expectations compared with only 49 percent among those less advanced in their orientation practices. Despite this proven performance impact over one-third of organizations were found to have no formal onboarding processes.

The moral of this story: Invest the time, effort, and expertise in developing effective onboarding processes, and you will reap the benefits of increased retention and improved productivity.

## Focusing on the fundamentals

As you launch your efforts to deliver a positive brand experience through induction and orientation, focus on mastering the fundamentals first. Here are the five onboarding practices that are essential to effective employer brand engagement and identification as well as to hastening the new hire's *time to performance* (the time required for a new employee to begin paying dividends):

>> **Set global standards while allowing for local tailoring.** Set up a consistent global onboarding process across your organization to ensure close alignment with the EVP, effective application of technology, and consistent feedback and metrics. As with other employer brand management processes, give other divisions in your organization the freedom, within certain constraints, to localize the standards and practices to meet the needs and preferences of regional cultures, local business units, and specific talent segments.

>> **Start orientation early and stretch it out.** Successfully onboarding new employees requires a great deal more than a day-long induction session. As soon as the selected candidate accepts the offer, start some form of preboarding process (see the later section "Preboarding new hires" for details). Extend your orientation to a period lasting 3 to 12 months. (See the later section "Designing an extensive orientation process" for details about structuring an effective orientation program.)

>> **Establish clear ownership and ensure seamless teamwork.** HR generally owns the onboarding function, but it's definitely a team sport. The reason a

formalized process is required is because effective onboarding requires the close coordination of many different functions within the business. Prior to onboarding new employees, make sure the following departments are onboard:

- *Recruitment team:* Responsible for ensuring a smooth handoff of the new employee to the department that person is assigned to and to other members of the onboarding team.

- *HR management:* In charge of the overall delivery of onboarding, providing support to hiring managers and updating the process to meet the changing needs of the business.

- *IT and facilities:* Tasked with ensuring new employees are appropriately equipped and enabled from day one.

- *Learning and development:* Responsible for evaluating the learning and development needs of new employees and providing the educational and training resources required. Responsibilities include the provision of e-learning support through induction and orientation.

- *Line management:* Takes the leading role in welcoming new employees and orienting them to their new roles and to colleagues and bringing them up to speed on performance objectives.

» **Leverage technology.** Technology can play a highly effective role in guiding both new joiners and hiring managers through the onboarding process, as well as providing a more consistent on-brand experience. Technology support may include task flow management (prompting and tracking the checklist of information and tasks required throughout the process), socialization (building a communications and support network), and cultural orientation (through videos, learning modules, and games). A number of these services can be built onto an existing human resource management system (HRMS) or ATS, but the best in breed according to benchmarking research conducted by the Aberdeen Group are custom-built portals that are fully integrated into the wider talent management system, such as Workday Recruiting.

» **Leverage the power of data to optimize performance.** Onboarding provides an important data set that that enables you to measure key performance indicators (KPIs) such as quality of hire. IT links the data collected during the hiring process, data collected during subsequent performance management, and data gathered during development processes to provide full-stream visibility into the employee life cycle. Linking these three data sets enables organizations to better understand the kind of interventions required during onboarding to ensure people feel fully engaged and accelerate to full performance in the shortest possible time.

## ONBOARDING PROCESSES IN THE REAL WORLD

Your organization should also think about how it can best communicate the distinctive culture and brand identity of the organization. In her *Harvard Business Review* article "What It Means to Work Here," Linda Graton describes three orientation processes designed to provide a clear understanding of the distinctive organizational culture that candidates were joining:

- Whole Foods Market treats each department in a store as a highly empowered, entrepreneurial team whose members have complete control over who joins the group. In this organization, the onboarding process involves a four-week trial period, during which team members vote on whether a new hire stays or goes; the trainee needs two-thirds of the team's support to be accepted as a permanent member of staff.

- At the software services provider Trilogy Software, new recruits undertake an intense three-month onboarding process which provides a compelling and immediate illustration of the way the company operates. In the first month, new recruits participate in creative projects teams of around 20 people, overseen by more senior and experienced mentors. In the second month, the project teams are reconfigured into smaller breakthrough teams charged with the fast-track development of new product or service ideas, business models, prototypes, and marketing plans. In the third month, some recruits continue working in their breakthrough teams; others find alternative sponsors elsewhere in the company. Upon completion, candidates undergo rigorous evaluation before being redeployed to different parts of the organization.

- At the storage solution retailer, The Container Store, the onboarding process is heavily weighted toward product knowledge. This starts with Foundation Week, five full days of intensive briefing on the company's values, processes, and products, and continues throughout the first year with an average of 235 hours of formal training (more than 20 times greater than the retail industry average).

As you can see from these examples, the onboarding process is unique to the organization. No one way is right or best. You need to think about moving a new hire from point A to point B in a certain period of time and then carefully think about the best way to accomplish that goal. Think not only about bringing a new employee up to speed on her job responsibilities but also about integrating her into the organization's community.

## Preboarding new hires

Recruiting a candidate shouldn't stop the moment he accepts an offer, and neither should your employer branding efforts. Because most recruiting structures are transactional, they stop as soon as the selected candidate accepts the offer. This is a real risk for recruiting, particularly considering the competition for top talent in today's markets. You can be assured your competitors aren't slowing down in their efforts to woo your new hire.

Make your offer more "sticky" by developing a plan to have the hiring managers, team, peers, and others involved in recruiting your new hire maintain communication during those vulnerable weeks between offer acceptance and start date. Here are a few things to consider in order to create a "white glove" onboarding experience:

>> **Create an onboarding checklist for everyone who has a stake in the new hire, including your hiring manager/team, recruiting, HR, facilities, and IT.** Establish clear expectation of who will do what and when, in order to ensure a smooth onboarding experience.

>> **If the recruiter is making the offer, have the hiring manager follow up within 24 hours.** Your hiring manager should congratulate the new hire, answer any questions, and make herself available for anything that comes up.

>> **Assign a contact person to each new hire.** Make sure the person has a point of contact at all times for any questions.

>> **Have someone check in with the new hire every week.** Don't let the new hire fall off the radar.

>> **Help new hires make a graceful exit from their current employers.** Prep them for the exit/notice meeting, potential counteroffers, work transition, and so on. Understand that this is an emotional experience for some employees, and let them know you're there to support them.

>> **Send the new hire any resources, documents, links, and so on that help with understanding the company, team, role, and so on.** *Be sure to let them know that this "research" is entirely optional.* They may be buried with transition work for their current employers, so don't add to that stress or pull focus by adding mandatory preboarding reading.

## Providing a warm welcome

Starting a new job is as stressful as it is exhilarating. By making your new hire feel welcome and attending to her creature comforts, you can mitigate the stress and ease the transition while initiating your retention efforts.

Consider adding one or more of the following steps to your onboarding process to create a pleasant and memorable onboarding experience:

>> Send a welcome letter signed by the hiring manager and members of the department or team that will be working closely with the new hire.

>> Prepare and send the person a detailed itinerary of her first week, including any and all orientation sessions.

>> Prepare the person's workspace to provide everything he'll need — desk, chair, computer hardware and software, sticky notes, and so on. Be sure that IT sets him up with a network username and password. Nothing sucks the wind out of day one more than waiting hours to get a computer set up.

>> Schedule a team lunch or happy hour near the end of the person's first week.

>> Assign an onboarding ambassador to answer questions and shepherd the new hire through the first couple of weeks.

>> Provide a tour of the building.

>> Schedule meetings with senior leaders.

>> Introduce your new hire to others new/recent hires.

>> Check in at the end of week one.

>> Schedule regular (weekly at least) check-ins during the first 90 days.

>> Establish clear goals, deliverables, and priorities for the onboarding period.

## Designing an extensive orientation process

Many organizations allocate only a day or a few days to orienting new employees, but for best results, extend your orientation period to three months at the minimum and up to a year. Create a three-column table, like the one in Table 15-2 with the scheduled time periods in the left column, the onboarding phases in the center column, and objectives for each onboarding phase in the right column.

**TIP**

Consider adding a fourth column for assigning each onboarding phase/objective to the department(s) or individual(s) responsible for that phase/objective.

**TABLE 15-2**     **Phases of Onboarding at the LEGO Group**

| Time Period | Onboarding Phase | Objective |
| --- | --- | --- |
| Acceptance to arrival | Preboarding | Setting expectations |
| Day 1 to Week 1 | Induction | Welcoming and equipping |
| Week 1 to Month 1 | Orientation | Connecting the dots |
| Month 1 to Month 3 | Integration | Building a network |
| Month 3 to Year 1 | Acceleration | Getting up to full speed |

Chapter **16**

# Engaging and Retaining Your Talent

Most of this book is about *getting there* — getting started with employer branding and kicking it into high gear to attract, engage, and retain the talent your company needs to meet its business objectives. This chapter is about *staying there* — maintaining your company's competitive advantage in the heat of the battle for top talent and even extending your lead (or at least closing the gap between you and the talent leader in your industry).

In this chapter, we focus on three ways to increase or at least maintain engagement and retention: by marrying your employer value proposition (EVP) and touch-point planning to ongoing employee engagement surveys, identifying and responding to retention risks, and managing engagement and retention through difficult times, such as during mergers and acquisitions.

## Conducting Engagement Survey Action Planning

*Engagement survey action planning* involves developing a plan for improving your employee engagement based on feedback from employee engagement surveys.

(For guidance on how to conduct an employee engagement survey, see Chapter 3.) In this section, we present the conventional approach to conducting engagement survey action planning followed by two methods for developing plans that are better aligned with your EVP and employer brand strategy.

## Considering the conventional approach to engagement action planning

Most employee engagement surveys are followed by a period of action planning, which is very often a localized process. The management team of a branch, division, or department receives a report that presents the survey results from its employees and is instructed to respond to the following information:

>> **Employment attributes:** The aspects of the employment deal that the employer is responsible for delivering, such as professional development, opportunities for advancement, or a workplace that encourages and facilitates a healthy work-life balance

>> **Engagement driver ranking:** A ranking of the importance of these employment attributes in terms of their linkage (correlation) with employee motivation, advocacy, and loyalty

>> **Employee favorability scores:** An indication of how well the organization is perceived to be performing by current employees in relation to the most important of these employment attributes

>> **Benchmark comparison:** An indication of how well the local group is doing in relation to each attribute as compared to industry benchmarks

Table 16-1 provides an example of conventional employee engagement analysis.

Having highlighted these priority areas, local management teams are expected to generate action plans to address the shortfalls in favorability relating to the most important engagement drivers. For example, in response to the data in Table 16-1, the action planning would focus on finding more effective ways to deliver the three engagement drivers that employees scored low to moderate: career opportunities, empowerment, and work-life balance.

**REMEMBER**

The advantage of local action planning is that it promotes greater ownership and accountability for delivering engagement drivers. Given the feedback presented in Table 16-1, for example, the local management team could do more to highlight existing career opportunities that its employees may be unaware of. They could also commit to giving employees additional freedom and responsibility in how they perform their jobs and introduce a flexible work environment that would be conducive to employees' achieving a healthy work-life balance.

**TABLE 16-1** **Conventional Engagement Driver Analysis**

| Employment Attributes | Engagement Driver Ranking | Employee Favorability | Benchmark Comparison |
|---|---|---|---|
| Our company is committed to developing professional expertise among its employees. | 1st | High | Positive |
| We are provided with opportunities to advance in our careers. | 2nd | Low | Negative |
| Our company empowers its people to make a difference. | 3rd | Moderate | Average |
| We are provided with the flexibility required to achieve a healthy work-life balance. | 4th | Low | Average |

However, this localized approach may not be the most effective way to deliver sustainable solutions to issues that are often more deeply rooted in operational structure and culture of the organization. In the following sections, we recommend two approaches that are likely to have a deeper and more positive impact on employee engagement.

## Leading with your EVP

The goal of employee survey action planning is to determine how well your company is delivering on its end of the bargain. The goal isn't necessarily to give employees everything they want (if that were even possible). To ensure that whatever actions you take to improve the employment experience align with your EVP, you need to include survey statements and questions that reflect your company's key EVP pillars. Here are a few examples of survey statements that are more reflective of a typical EVP:

>> We are a purpose-driven, customer-focused company.

>> We work as one team across the organization.

>> We empower our people to make a difference.

>> We are committed to developing our employees' expertise.

Your survey can also include more generic statements and questions to gauge the relative importance of what employees value regarding engagement drivers that aren't highlighted in your EVP (engagement drivers that employees value over what you provide). Feedback from these statements and questions may highlight potential shortcomings in the employment deal that could lead to disengagement or reveal strengths that you may want to add or emphasize as part of the employment deal if and when you revise your EVP.

Within this strategic context, employee engagement analysis becomes a three-step process:

1. **Assess how engaged employees are by the key pillars of the employment deal.**

2. **Evaluate how well employees perceive that their employment experience reflects these EVP pillars.**

3. **Assess other potential areas of engagement and disengagement that may represent important additional opportunities or threats to internal employer brand perceptions.**

**REMEMBER**

Always conduct employee engagement analysis within the wider strategic context of your EVP, never in isolation from the EVP.

As with the conventional method for analyzing employee engagement, engagement drivers from EVP-led surveys are ranked by strength and presented with their employee favorability scores and benchmark comparisons, as shown in Table 16-2. Note, however, that the employment attributes are aligned with core EVP attributes and that the table includes a section for other important engagement drivers that aren't currently highlighted as priorities in the EVP.

**TABLE 16-2**     **EVP-Led Engagement Analysis**

| Employment Attributes | Engagement Driver Ranking | Employee Favorability | Benchmark Comparison |
|---|---|---|---|
| **Core EVP Attributes** | | | |
| Our company is committed to developing professional expertise among its employees. | 1st | High | Positive |
| Our company empowers its people to make a difference. | 3rd | Moderate | Average |
| We are a purpose-driven, customer-focused company. | 8th | High | Positive |

| Employment Attributes | Engagement Driver Ranking | Employee Favorability | Benchmark Comparison |
|---|---|---|---|
| We work collaboratively as one team across the organization. | 15th | Low | Negative |
| **Other Important Engagement Drivers** | | | |
| We are provided with opportunities to advance in our careers. | 2nd | Low | Negative |
| We are provided with the flexibility required to achieve a healthy work-life balance. | 4th | Low | Average |

Examining the EVP-led engagement feedback in Table 16-2, the primary EVP-driven conclusions would look something like Table 16-3.

**TABLE 16-3**    **EVP-Driven Conclusions**

| Engagement Driver | Conclusion | Action Needed |
|---|---|---|
| Developing expertise | Strongest EVP pillar in terms of current experience and engagement | Protect, strengthen, and celebrate. |
| Employee empowerment | A key engagement driver; needs to be strengthened | Explore and address the barriers preventing employees from feeling empowered. |
| Purpose-driven customer focus | High employee favorability score, but not among the top engagement drivers | Although this attribute is perceived to be true, it appears to be relatively unappreciated by employees. Explore ways to improve communication to make it more engaging for employees. |
| One team | Unengaging and poorly delivered | A key focus area for both communication and touch-point planning, because teamwork between business units and departments is of significant importance to organizational performance. For teamwork to improve, employees need to understand and be engaged by the benefits of a "one team" mentality. |

**REMEMBER**

When determining the action needed in response to feedback, give as much attention to building on strengths as you do addressing potential weaknesses. This balance is often missing in more conventional approaches to engagement action planning. Also, don't assume that a low engagement importance score is fixed in stone. For example, when Coca-Cola Hellenic first introduced its "Passion for Excellence" EVP, excellence did not appear among the top ten engagement drivers in its employee research. Two years later, after a significant effort to build employee pride and engagement with "excellence," it was scored among Coca-Cola Hellenic's top five most important engagement drivers.

Secondarily, the data listed after "Other Important Engagement Drivers" (refer to Table 16-2) suggests that the perceived lack of career opportunities and flexibility for achieving a healthy work-life balance are potentially in danger of undermining employee engagement. However, these items must be put in context before deciding on an action plan. This company may have decided to maintain a relatively flat organizational structure that limits the opportunities for career advancement, but not for learning and expertise, which remain the main focus of the employment deal. It may also favor buying talent as opposed to building talent, which accounts for the relatively high employee score for competitive salaries. In this case, the action would be to reemphasize and reinforce the more positive aspects of the deal, including the ability to grow expertise, and accept that many people will stay with the organization for three to five years rather than five to ten years. However, the company may have some room to maneuver on flexibility and work-life balance. EVPs should never be fixed in stone, and these attributes may need to be incorporated going forward to strengthen engagement.

## Leading from the top

Local planning has some advantages regarding ownership and accountability, but the action plans produced from such an approach are often superficial, because more deep-rooted change is required from the top to make a sustainable impact. In the light of the employee engagement survey data and analysis, the leadership team should revisit the EVP and overall HR/talent strategy and decide whether to adhere to some of the existing strategies (for example, whether to lean toward buying talent rather than building it), or introduce new strategies for addressing emerging issues such as workplace flexibility. Provided with a framework from the leadership team, local management can more effectively focus on how to execute the strategy at their local level.

**REMEMBER**

Leading from the top also involves requesting, listening, and responding to feedback from local action-planning sessions. Sometimes on-the-ground feedback provokes a rethinking of company-wide strategy. For example, if the majority of the local teams report back that the "buy" talent strategy is causing serious problems, it may need to be revised. Local input can also provide an opportunity to support similar solutions being generated at the local level that could be made more efficient and effective if they were laddered up to become a company-wide strategy. For example, implementing a centralized plan is likely to be far less expensive than having each local unit develop and communicate its own initiative.

# Ongoing Engagement and Retention Processes

Employee engagement research and action planning tends to take place on an annual or biannual basis, which is generally sufficient for this type of major undertaking. However, supplementing this long-cycle activity with other more regular and frequent engagement activities is beneficial. In this section, we present four ongoing processes that serve to maintain engagement and retention.

## Conducting team briefings

One way to promote engagement on a more regular basis is to set up a *team briefing process* — a communication cascade and feedback process managed by internal communications but delivered locally through line managers and team leaders. A typical team briefing process goes like this:

1. The central internal communication team prepares a core brief containing important information, news, and directives from senior leadership and distributes the core brief to regional or business units.

2. Each regional or business unit supplements the core brief with information that's more specifically relevant to the local employee population and distributes the completed brief to frontline team leaders.

3. Frontline team leaders deliver the briefing to team members, preferably in a group setting.

The team briefing provides opportunities for

» Employees to receive a briefing from their immediate managers on the most important company-wide issues of the moment (reinforcing each team manager's position of authority)

» Employees to ask questions and discuss how leadership directives can be implemented most effectively locally

>> Local team leaders to provide feedback from their team to ensure leaders have a clear understanding and immediate feel for how communication is being received on the front line

When an EVP has been established, this briefing process provides a useful means to reinforce the key themes underpinning the employment deal. For example, based on the core EVP attributes presented in Table 16-2, the central communication team running the process would ensure that the key themes of "purpose-driven customer focus," "one team," "empowerment," and "developing expertise" would be regularly reinforced and celebrated with relevant examples and stories from around the business.

The frequency of team briefings varies from organization to organization. Many companies deliver this kind of briefing on a monthly, bimonthly, or quarterly basis, while other companies do it weekly. The founders of Google, Larry Page and Sergey Brin, host an "all-hands" briefing every Friday, which they call they their TGIF (Thank God It's Friday) calls. Mark Zuckerberg takes a similar approach at Facebook.

**TIP**

When possible, conduct face-to-face briefings. Many companies deliver briefings via email or teleconference, which may be more efficient, but research suggests that these methods are far less engaging for employees than face-to-face group briefings.

## Engaging in key people-management conversations

In addition to delivering team briefings, line managers should make effective use of important one-to-one conversations with employees during key occasions on the people-management calendar. At Standard Chartered Bank, these opportunities for an "engaging conversation" are tied to the following five key process touch points, each of which involves individual employee discussions:

>> Objective setting

>> Half-yearly performance review

>> Full-year performance review

>> Learning and development review

>> Reward review

What makes the conversation engaging is the ability of the line manager to do the following:

>> Fully listen to and understand the employee's perspective, which is much more difficult than it sounds.

>> Focus on the things the employee has done well. (Recognition is vital to engagement.)

>> Align the individual to what the team/company has achieved or is trying to achieve (to reinforce a strong sense of shared purpose).

>> Provide clear and constructive direction on what needs to be improved to build on success. (Avoiding areas of underperformance is never an effective path to sustained engagement.)

# Identifying and responding to retention risks

Within your employee engagement survey, ask employees about their intentions to stay with the organization. The employee research firm Willis Towers Watson uses two questions to diagnose retention risk. The first addresses the employee's likelihood of leaving, and the second addresses the employee's desire to stay or leave. The responses to these two questions provide four categories of retention risk indicators, as shown in Table 16-4.

**TABLE 16-4** **Categorizing Retention Risk**

| Employee Group | Attributes |
|---|---|
| Stayers | Not likely to leave in the next two years. Would prefer to remain with the organization even if a comparable opportunity arises. |
| Soft stays | Not likely to leave in the next two years. Would not prefer to remain with the organization if a comparable opportunity arises. |
| At risk | Likely to leave within the next two years. Would prefer to remain with the organization even if a comparable opportunity arises. |
| Leavers | Likely to leave within the next two years. Would not prefer to remain with the organization if a comparable opportunity arises. |

According to Willis Towers Watson's research, leavers and at-risk workers account for around one-quarter of all employees. Here are some of the insights from the research that are useful to bear in mind when seeking to address ongoing retention risks:

>> **Retention-risk employees are often high performers.** Over one-third of high-retention-risk employees are exceeding performance expectations. People don't simply leave because they're failing to perform. They often appear to be doing very well, but are either unhappy for other reasons or open to poaching from talent competitors.

>> **High-risk employees are only slightly less likely to be engaged than their low-risk counterparts.** A common misconception is that those most at risk of leaving are predominantly disengaged. Willis Towers Watson's research suggests that only around a third of those identified as high-retention-risk employees tend to be disengaged and over a quarter are otherwise highly engaged.

>> **Retention risk can occur at any time.** High-retention-risk employees are more likely to have been with their employers between one and five years, but the evidence suggests that people can be retention risks at any point in their tenure. On average, one in four high-retention-risk employees have been with their current employers for more than ten years.

>> **High-risk employees are frequently frustrated by slow career progression.** A perceived lack of career advancement opportunities is the second most frequently cited reason for leaving an organization.

>> **High-risk employees are often concerned about their financial status.** They're about 70 percent more likely than low-risk employees to say that financial concerns and worries are keeping them from doing their best work.

>> **High-risk employees are more likely to embrace change.** Most of them say they enjoy new experiences, embrace change, and are happy to take risks to get more out of life. Many of the qualities that give people the entrepreneurial skills and agility that many employers look for are the same qualities that make people more likely to leave an employer for better opportunities elsewhere.

## Establishing an early-warning system

Employee research and leavers' surveys can give you a collective indication of retention risk and identify some of the most important drivers, but you need to take a more proactive approach to identify early signs of retention risk among individual employees. A number of leading companies have introduced early-warning systems for attrition. These systems are designed to provide a more structured and consistent process for identifying employees' probability to quit by assessing leading behavioral indicators. Where there is perceived to be a relatively high level of retention risk within a team, this kind of assessment should ideally be made on a quarterly basis.

Here are some of the leading behavioral indicators any line manager should consider looking out for in relation to each member of her team:

>> **Career progression:** The employee has been designated high performance and/or high potential but has been in the same role for two or more years with no clear future progress communicated in terms of role expansion, promotion, or career path.

>> **Peer advancement:** The employee has colleagues at a similar level who've been recently promoted, with no similar indication of future progression for the employee.

>> **Desire to move:** The employee has asked for a promotion or lateral move in the past 12 months without success. The risk increases for every unsuccessful internal interview.

>> **Desire for increased compensation:** The employee has expressed overt dissatisfaction with her compensation package on at least two occasions.

>> **Role fit:** The employee has expressed lack of clarity, interest, or challenge in his assigned role.

>> **Role qualification:** The employee appears to be significantly over- or underqualified for her assigned role.

>> **Management:** The employee has expressed dissatisfaction with the level or quality of supervisory/management support.

>> **Work environment:** The employee has expressed dissatisfaction with the physical or social working environment (cooperation and support from immediate colleagues).

>> **Personal:** The employee is undergoing a significant change in personal circumstances; for example, marriage, childbirth, or death of parents or other close relatives.

TIP

Provide managers with a checklist of retention-risk indicators and instruct them to use the list to flag potential retention-risk employees, particularly those identified as high performers or having high potential or those in critical roles. Further instruct them to take the necessary steps to try to establish the seriousness of the risk through conversation with the employees involved and take appropriate steps to address and mitigate the risk.

# Maintaining Attraction and Engagement in the Midst of Organizational Change

The uncertainty that accompanies reorganizations can damage attraction, engagement, and retention unless managed proactively by HR and line management. In this section, we offer guidance on how to navigate reorganizations, acquisitions, and mergers while maintaining the strength of your employer brand.

## Navigating a reorganization

Given the constant need to adapt to changes in the market environment, many companies must reengineer, restructure, and right-size their organizations on a regular basis. Ideally, these organizational changes are planned in advance in order to seize future opportunities, but the reality is that companies are just as likely to be reacting to changes they would rather have avoided.

To maintain positive internal and external employer brand perceptions through these challenging times, do the following:

>> **Be sure you have a clear rationale for making the change.** Very often leadership teams spend too much time communicating what needs to change and not enough time explaining why. By helping employees make sense of the changes required, leaders promote a stronger sense of involvement, ownership, and engagement.

>> **Clarify the future destination.** Even though changes may be driven by apparently negative forces such as competitor success or failing demand, establish clear future objectives. Linking change to future goals signals proactive leadership and promotes a greater sense of confidence, forward momentum, and engagement among employees.

>> **Provide support.** Change can be stressful and difficult, but it can also be reinvigorating depending on how well supported employees feel to make the necessary change. When organizational change is required, provide sufficient change management to ensure that employees receive the necessary training and support to make the required transition.

>> **Signal continuity as well as change.** Organizational change can represent a significant moment of truth for the EVP and employer brand. Where possible, do your best to keep faith with the existing pillars of the employment deal, even though sacrifices may be required elsewhere. For example, when a company is downsizing, the company must maintain its promises to remaining employees in key areas such as training and development.

>> **Look for the upside in your external communication.** Prospective candidates recognize that organizational change can represent improved opportunities, as well as potential risks. Incorporate any significant internal change programs into your external recruitment communication and sell the upsides of the change. For example, a company that's shedding certain types of employees may signal a positive response to technological change, particularly if it's increasing its hiring in other areas. Just be sure you're delivering your rationale for the change both internally and externally as clearly and constructively as you can.

## Smoothing the transition during an acquisition

When experiencing a merger and acquisition, employees recognize very quickly that mergers of equals are relatively rare. For organizations that have grown through acquisition, incorporating smaller rivals or simply extending their geographical footprint, there tends to be little argument over which employer brand is going to dominate. In such a case, the process is most akin to employee orientation. Though the acquired organization may keep its name for a period of time, a key objective is for the acquired company to adopt the company values and the employer brand identity of the more dominant company as quickly as possible.

TIP

To smooth the transition, set out a clear migratory path to the new identity, alongside a clear and positive statement of the new EVP/employment deal that acquired employees are entering into.

## Rebranding a merger of equals

Where a merger and acquisition is being more overtly positioned to employees as a merger of equals, most clearly marked by a corporate rebranding, the argument is stronger for developing a new EVP and employer brand. In this case, EVP development should represent an important part of the merger-and-acquisition process, signaling that both leadership teams and employee populations have an equal say in the marriage. When this is managed effectively, the likelihood of maintaining engagement is much greater, because the new EVP serves as a tangible signal of the companies' joint desire to forge not only a new corporation but a new culture and identity, drawing on the best of both parties.

# 5

# Measuring the Success of Your Employer Branding Strategy

Measure the immediate impact of your employer branding initiatives in terms of media reach and audience engagement.

Quantify the efficiency and effectiveness of your employer branding initiatives in terms of cost-per-hire, time-to-hire, and quality of hire.

Measure the longer-term impact of your employer branding efforts by examining brand awareness and reputation; employee engagement, performance, and retention; and overall brand vitality.

Fine-tune your employer branding activities to address changes in the talent market, and refresh, improve, and maintain your competitive edge.

Chapter **17**

# Gauging Your Immediate Impact on Audience Engagement and Hiring

All employer branding efforts have a short-term and a longer-term impact. You can measure the short-term impact according to how effective your recruitment marketing efforts are in attracting suitable candidates to the vacancies you need to fill. The longer-term impact has more to do with employer brand reputation and how existing employees feel about the employment experience.

In this chapter, we focus on the short-term impact of recruitment marketing activities. Gauging the ultimate success of these activities involves calculating your return on investment (ROI); it involves measuring the number and quality of applications you receive in relation to the amount of time and money invested. To determine how to evaluate the longer-term impact of your employer branding efforts, turn to Chapter 18.

# Linking Recruitment Marketing Activities to Objectives

To gauge the effectiveness of your recruitment marketing activities, you first need to match activities to objectives and establish measures of success. Is success measured by the number of applications you receive, the percentage of applications you receive from highly qualified candidates, the number of people who share a job posting on Facebook, or something else entirely? By linking recruitment marketing activities to specific objectives and establishing metrics, you can more accurately gauge the effectiveness of your efforts. Take the following steps:

1. **Identify the different recruitment marketing activities you're undertaking.**

   Marketing activities may involve setting up a career page on Facebook, launching a job microsite, or posting an opening on a job board. To further complicate the process of measuring the success of a marketing activity, realize that each activity has several components:

   - *The channel:* Where the marketing message appears — for example, LinkedIn, your own microsite, a job board, a magazine that's popular with the talented individuals you're targeting, a pay-per-click (PPC) advertising campaign, and so on.

   - *The recruitment marketing message:* What you're trying to convey; this could be a recruitment advertising headline, the implication of a social post, or the key points you're trying to communicate in a specific section of your career site. Clearly, most recruitment marketing content contains a number of different points, but for the purpose of measurement and analysis try to identify the leading message.

   - *The content format:* The format of the message (for example, advert, employee profile, or career story) and the medium in which it appears (for example, text, image, audio, or video).

   The purpose of distinguishing between these three components is that they each contribute to the end result. However, all three components work together. To maximize reach and impact, you need to work toward sending the right message in the right format through the right channels. See Chapter 5 for additional guidance on finding the right mix, but keep in mind that finding the right mix also requires some trial and error with the help of analytics to determine what's working and what's not.

2. **Establish objectives for each activity.**

   Objectives may include the number and percentage of qualified applicants in a specified period of time, the number of people who view the message (reach), the number of people who share a social post (engagement), the cost per qualified applicant, and so on.

3. **Establish as a clear a link as possible to the end results.**

   Trying to link marketing activities to end results can be challenging, especially when you're conducting recruiting activities via social channels; however, the following sections of this chapter provide guidance on how you can best achieve this linkage.

**REMEMBER**

Not all employer branding initiatives are clearly linked to specific objectives and outcomes. A recruitment advertising campaign developed to fill a specific vacancy clearly has a desired objective. However, while social campaigns follow many of the same conventions as traditional advertising, such as consistent formatting and messaging, they're typically focused more on building brand awareness and engagement than on generating applications, so they require different forms of measurement and evaluation.

# Measuring the Effectiveness of Recruitment Advertising

Recruitment advertising is the easiest marketing activity to evaluate, because it involves an investment in creative development and media buying and a return on investment in the form of applications for one or more vacancies. In this section, we cover the metrics to use to measure the effectiveness of your recruitment advertising campaigns.

## Advertising costs

Advertising costs include the expenses involved in creating and placing advertising content:

>> **Creative development cost:** The total investment in creative development and production of core advertising assets. These expenses apply to ideation, copywriting, photography, and the creation of advertising templates. Creative development cost is generally easier to identify if it's outsourced to an agency; otherwise, you need to calculate the cost based on the time and materials used.

- » **Variable advertising cost:** Customization or adaptation of the advertising templates and assets to meet specific local needs. These expenses are for additional copywriting, design, photography, and so on.

- » **Media cost:** Investment in paid media channels, including online job boards, pay-per-click advertising, programmatic media buying, and so on.

## Audience exposure

*Audience exposure* is a measure of the number of people an ad has been presented to or the number of times an ad has been presented, regardless of whether anyone notices it or acts on it. You can measure audience exposure in the following two ways:

- » **Reach:** The total number of people who've had an opportunity to see your message at least once through a specific channel. Where possible, measure reach in terms of key target audiences — the talent you're trying to attract.

- » **Frequency/impressions:** The number of times an advertisement has been presented through a specific channel.

## Engagement

*Engagement* is a measure of how effective an advertisement has been in achieving the desired objective. Two common measures of engagement in recruitment advertising are click-through rate and applications:

- » **Click-through rate (CTR):** The percentage of visitors to a web page who click on the advertisement to access your career site or job microsite or view other recommended content.

- » **Applications:** The number of applications generated by a campaign or a particular advertisement.

## Source of application and source of hire

Source of application and source of hire are two metrics for tracking down and identifying the recruitment advertising campaigns, channels, messages, and formats that are most effective in achieving the desired objectives:

- » **Source of application (SOA):** The advertisement that sparked a prospect's interest in the company, which ultimately led to the prospect submitting an application. Because prospects typically investigate a range of employer sources before making an application, SOA can be a complex metric. However, the increasing sophistication and use of *cookies* (a tiny piece of data sent from a website to a user's browser to record a trail of sites the user visits) have increased the ability of applicant tracking systems (ATSs) to identify the SOA.

>> **Source of hire (SOH):** The advertisement that sparked a prospect's interest in the company, which ultimately led to the prospect being hired. Similar to SOA, SOH provides clearer insight into the quality of the applicants from each advertising channel and campaign, particularly when combined with quality-of-hire data.

## Analyzing the effectiveness of recruitment advertising

After gathering the data related to advertising costs, audience exposure and engagement, and SOA/SOH, analyze it carefully to answer the following questions:

>> Which media channels, recruitment marketing messages, and formats (text, photos, videos, and so on) are most effective in generating the most applications from qualified candidates?

>> Which media channels, recruitment marketing messages, and formats are most efficient in terms of cost per applicant? (See the later section "Analyzing Your Overall Recruitment Marketing Strategy Success" for details.)

>> How does the total ROI of recruitment advertising compare to that of other sources of applications, including referrals, recruitment agencies, internal recruiters, and investment in search engine optimization (SEO)?

# Measuring the Effectiveness of Social Campaigns

The objective of social content marketing tends to be brand engagement and relationship building instead of drawing attention to immediate job opportunities. Some companies post a lot of job adverts or alerts on social channels, but people in these communities often regard such postings as feed clutter, and these adverts are more likely to damage your employer brand than enhance it. For this reason the measures used to evaluate social campaigns and individual posts tend to be different from those generally used to evaluate recruitment advertising.

In this section, we cover the same metrics used to measure the success of recruitment advertising (cost, exposure, engagement, and SOH), while explaining how to apply each metric in a different way to gauge the success of social campaigns.

## Social media costs

The costs of conducting a social media campaign are similar to those for a recruitment marketing campaign. They both cover the cost of creating the content and getting that content in front of prospects:

>> **Content development cost:** These costs cover sourcing, copywriting, photography, and time spent by employees generating and posting content and engaging with prospects who post comments. Content development also includes the time spent developing an editorial calendar to ensure that your company is posting relevant content regularly.

Although social media content development may be outsourced, it's generally more effective when it's produced internally and with the participation of current employees.

>> **Media cost:** Placement of content on social media channels can be free (organic), but companies are increasingly paying for sponsored posts to reach target audiences.

## Audience exposure

On social channels, audience exposure is measured in terms of *reach* — the number of people who've had the opportunity to view a post or the number of people who've had one of your posts show up in their news feeds. On social channels, audience exposure can increase significantly through the number of times a post is shared (earned media reach) on the same social channel or in other channels, as when a post goes viral.

## Engagement

Social campaigns offer numerous opportunities for the audience to engage with the content. Here are some of the engagement metrics you should consider to determine the success of a given post or campaign:

>> **Likes/favorites:** The number of likes is a measure not only of engagement but also your reach and the relevance and value of the content you posted.

>> **Comments:** Comments represent a step up in terms of content interaction, because they require more thought and effort on the part of an audience member. However, you need to consider both the number and nature of comments — how many comments are posted and whether they're positive, negative, or neutral.

>> **Shares:** A form of earned media reach (as opposed to paying for sponsored content), shares extend the potential impact of your content within target peer groups and are an excellent indication that people who viewed the content like it (or hate it) enough to share it with their friends and colleagues.

>> **Click-through rate (CTR):** Although the primary purpose of social content isn't always to direct traffic to your career site, one of your job microsites, or to other suggested content, sometimes that may be your objective. In such cases, CTR becomes an important metric.

>> **Engagement rate:** The total percentage of people who've had the opportunity to view your content and who've chosen to engage with it in at least one of the ways described in this list.

>> **Applications:** The objective of most social campaigns is to build employer brand awareness and create a positive impression of the employer brand on the target audience. However, you may post some content on social channels with the purpose of encouraging people to apply for a particular vacancy or submit an application for future consideration; in such cases, the number of applications is a key metric.

## Source of application, source of hire, and source of influence

Depending on your objectives, you may launch a recruitment campaign on one or more social channels to fill a vacancy or to improve employer brand reach and reputation. Choose the following metrics to measure the success of your campaign relative to your objectives:

>> **SOA and SOH:** Even though social campaigns tend to be delivered in a more storylike format, they can contain one or more links to job-related information. This may result in a social post becoming the first source of awareness for an employment opportunity that ultimately leads to an application or hire. If you're using social to generate applications and fill vacancies in this way, SOA and SOH are relevant metrics.

>> **Source of influence (SOI):** Using cookies to track where people go on the web after reading social content you posted can help you determine whether certain posts are likely to have influenced them as they seek more information prior to making an application. This SOI data can be very useful in identifying the relationship between social engagement, applications, and hires.

## Using the results of your analysis to enhance your recruitment marketing

As you gather and analyze the data to evaluate the success of individual social campaigns, use the insight to improve the overall effectiveness of your recruitment marketing:

>> **Short term:** Identify which social campaigns, topics, and formats generate the highest levels of reach and engagement, and use those findings to adjust and tune your communication strategy on an ongoing basis.

>> **Medium term:** Analyze the data to determine which attributes from your employer value proposition (EVP) resonate most strongly with your target audience, and upweight those attributes in your social campaigns. Depending on your relative return on investment in generating applications, you may also decide to increase or decrease the importance of social media in your overall marketing mix.

>> **Long term:** Over time, you may discover a need to adjust your EVP to align it more closely with the needs, desires, and aspirations of the talent you're trying to attract.

# Measuring the Effectiveness of Career Site Content

Career sites remain an important link in the chain between employer brand awareness, interest, and application, so measuring and monitoring the effectiveness of your career site content and making adjustments to improve results are vital. In terms of metrics, career sites share the qualities of both recruitment advertising and social campaigns. Like recruitment advertising, career sites often promote specific job openings, and the success of the career site content can be measured in the number of applications generated and the quality of applicants.

Like social, some career site content is intended primarily to increase employer brand awareness and improve the company's reputation as an employer.

In this section, we focus on specific metrics to consider when measuring the effectiveness of your career site content.

## Career site costs

Career site costs include costs to build, maintain, and update the site itself along with the cost of developing and posting content to the site:

>> **Development cost:** This cost is the amount spent to get the career site up and running. If the site is a section of an existing company website, the cost will be a portion of the cost of the overall site development. If it's a stand-alone or bolt-on site, its cost may be separate. Because site development cost generally represents a relatively large, medium- to long-term investment, allow for depreciation.

>> **Maintenance cost:** Maintenance involves keeping the site up to date, backing it up regularly, and keeping it secure. Whether you manage the career site internally or hire a service, be sure to account for the cost.

>> **Content creation cost:** Creating and posting fresh, relevant content to your career site is key to its success, and it can be costly in both time and money, especially if your career site includes a blog. You may outsource some of your content creation to a third party, but including current employees in content creation tends to improve the site's impact.

## Audience exposure

You can measure audience exposure to your career site by the number of unique visitors to the site. Any website analytics tool, such as Google Analytics (http://analytics.google.com), tracks this important metric. What's more challenging is identifying the reason why you're attracting a certain number of unique visitors. A bump in unique visitors may be the result of successful SEO, search engine marketing, social campaigns, and so on.

TIP

Launching new campaigns or making adjustments to existing campaigns one at a time can help you identify the reason behind an increase or decrease in the number of unique visitors. If you change several things at one time, determining which change is responsible may be difficult to impossible.

# Engagement

You can measure engagement on a career site using several metrics, including page views, time on page, and click-through rates:

>> **Page views:** Page views indicate the number of pages visitors have viewed and which pages they view, so you can gauge interest in certain jobs or topics. However, a high number of page views combined with a short amount of time spent viewing each page may indicate that visitors are having a difficult time finding the content they're looking for.

>> **Average time on page:** This metric indicates whether people are skimming your content or taking the time to read it, which helps you identify which messages and content are attracting and holding people's attention, and which aren't.

>> **Bounce rate:** This metric reveals the number of visitors or percentage of visitors who leave the site after viewing only one page. A high bounce rate indicates that visitors are disappointed in what they find on the site, but it doesn't reveal the reason why. A bounce rate could be due to poor quality content or to a situation in which a visitor was misdirected; for example, a link to your site may have appeared in the search results when someone was searching for something unrelated to the content on your site.

>> **Click-through rate (CTR):** On a career website, click-through rate provides a good indication of the percentage of visitors who act on your content's call to action; for example, the percentage of visitors who choose to submit an application. Click-through rate may also indicate the percentage of those who actually completed the application, as opposed to those who started to apply and then left the site before submitting the application.

# Source of application and source of hire

Career sites are generally incorporated within SOA/SOH data, because many people find potential employers or job opportunities directly through organic search (searches on sites such as Google and Bing). Bear in mind, however, that the importance of career sites tends to be overrepresented as a source in comparison to other potential sources of employer brand awareness, because a career site, by nature, is the last step in the application journey.

## Improving career site effectiveness through analysis

As you look at the data for audience exposure and engagement, they should point you toward sections of your career site or specific pages that visitors are most interested in exploring (page views) and most engaged by (average time on page). High page visits coupled with low time on page suggests that your content on these pages needs to be improved. This information should also be channeled back into your overall employer brand communication strategy, as it can indicate which subjects potential candidates are most interested in. For example, if your diversity content is getting far lower engagement than your flexibility content, then you should not only upweight your career site focus on flexibility, but also consider the overall emphasis you place on flexibility across your overall communication mix (advertising messages, social posts, and so on).

# Measuring Referral Effectiveness

Referral has always been an important SOH, but the increasing adoption of social media has resulted in a resurgence of interest in network-based recruitment. In Universum's recent global best practice survey, 60 percent of leading global employers claimed they were increasing investment in employee referral and 50 percent were increasing investment in alumni referral. With so many companies ramping up their efforts in referral recruitment, you need to monitor your success in this area in order to remain competitive. In this section, we highlight the referral metrics you need to consider.

## Referral costs

Referral costs boil down to the costs of creating the referral program and funding incentives:

>> **Referral program development cost:** The upfront investment in establishing a referral program

>> **Referral campaign costs:** The costs involved in promoting awareness and uptake of a referral program once established

>> **Referral incentives (bounties):** The costs to fund incentives and rewards for those who refer qualified candidates

## Audience exposure

Measuring the total reach of a referral program is difficult, because much of the activity generally takes place through personal communication channels, but you can gain some indication of the numbers involved by measuring the number of applications made that cite referral as a source. This can be further broken down by region, function, job type, and so on to provide an indication of where the program has generated most and least activity.

## Engagement

Engagement, as it relates to referrals, applies to both the engagement of current employees in the referral program and the number or percentage of qualified applicants that result from the referral program. Here are two key indicators of referral engagement success:

>> **Employee advocacy and net promoter score (NPS):** An important base measure, NPS establishes the proportion of employees who claim they would be happy to recommend their employer to friends and family. It provides an important indicator of your company's referral potential.

>> **Participation rate:** The participation rate reflects the percentage of employees who play an active role in the employee referral program by referring friends, family members, and professional contacts to the company.

>> **Referral applicants:** At the end of the day, referral engagement success boils down to the number of qualified prospects who apply for jobs with your company as a result of being referred by a current or former employee.

## Source of application and source of hire

The SOA and SOH for referrals are key metrics on measuring the success of your referral program, and they're fairly easy to measure reliably. Applicants are eager to share information about current or former employees who referred or recommended them, because they believe — and rightfully so — that such a referral or recommendation will help them in landing the job.

**REMEMBER**

Referrals are generally rated as the most cost-efficient source of quality applicants and hires, but you can't be sure if you don't collect the data and do the math. Referral costs combined with SOA and SOH provide an accurate indication of your referral program's ROI.

## Improving referral effectiveness through analysis

The metrics described in this section provide insight into the success of your employee referral program, but they're less helpful in identifying areas of improvement. Referrals may suffer for several reasons, including the following:

>> The employment experience itself needs improvement. If employees don't feel that your company provides an exceptional workplace environment, they're not likely to encourage people they know to apply.

>> The importance of referrals and of building a strong employer brand has been poorly communicated internally.

>> The referral incentives being offered aren't valuable or exciting enough to encourage employees to participate in the program.

To improve participation in your employee referral program, work on improving internal communication and delivery of your employer brand.

**TIP**

In addition to analyzing your own data, compare your results to external benchmarks to gauge your success to that of other companies competing for the same talent. (See "Comparing your results to external benchmarks" for details, along with a list of sources that can provide you with external benchmarks.)

# Analyzing Your Overall Recruitment Marketing Strategy Success

The metrics and analysis described in the previous sections help you identify the relative cost, effectiveness, and ROI of different recruitment marketing activities. The next step is to establish a more complete assessment of the cost and effectiveness of your total recruitment marketing strategy. Such an assessment can help you to evaluate your current strategy and establish a number of overall key performance indicators (KPIs). In recruitment, as in many other areas of business, it's tempting to focus on the more quantifiable measures of success, such as cost and time, overlooking more complex (but ultimately more important) qualitative measures, such as quality of hire. Ideally you should attempt to link both types of measure to plan and budget for the future. In this section, we explain how to evaluate the overall success of your recruitment marketing strategy both quantitatively and qualitatively.

# Calculating cost-per-hire

The quantifiable measure of overall recruitment marketing success is cost-per-hire, which essentially represents your immediate return on investment. To calculate cost-per-hire for your overall recruitment marketing program or for individual campaigns or channels, use the following equation:

$$\text{Total Cost-Per-Hire} = \frac{\left(\sum(\text{Internal Costs}) + \sum(\text{External Costs})\right)}{\text{Total Number of Hires Across a Time Period}}$$

Internal costs include the following:

>> **Recruitment staff costs:** Salaries, benefits, training, and so on

>> **Office costs:** Share of office overheads

>> **Additional management costs:** The time necessary for additional management involvement in recruitment marketing events, interviewing, and selection

>> **Employee referral awards/incentives**

>> **Sign-on bonuses**

>> **Relocation and immigration fees**

>> **Time-to-fill costs:** The estimated cost involved in excessive position vacancy days, particularly in relation to key revenue generating positions

When totaling external costs, include costs for the following:

>> **Advertising:** Costs related to the creation and placement of recruitment adverts

>> **Social media:** The time involved in planning and creating social content and engaging with prospects along with the cost of any sponsored content

>> **Career site development and maintenance:** Costs related to building and maintaining the site and keeping it populated with fresh, relevant content

>> **Campus recruiting activities**

>> **Job fairs and other non-campus recruiting events**

>> **Third-party hiring agency fees**

>> **Recruitment process outsourcing (RPO) fees:** For prescreening and assessing candidates

>> **Other external candidate assessment costs:** For example, travel, eligibility checks, and drug testing

>> **Consulting services**

TIP

When possible, try to find external points of comparison to benchmark your costs, using the sources provided at the end of the chapter. You should also track cost-per-hire over time to evaluate your success in improving the overall efficiency and effectiveness of your recruitment marketing efforts.

## Measuring success in terms of quality applicants and hires

The ultimate measure of your recruitment marketing success is your ability to deliver the right quality of talent to support your organization's business goals and objectives. To determine how successful your recruitment marketing activities are in delivering quality applicants to your organization, look at the following metrics:

>> **Applicants per vacancy:** The number of applicants per vacancy provides insight into the supply and demand for different positions, shifts in talent supply and demand over time, and the effectiveness of different job-specific marketing activities.

>> **Qualified applicant ratio:** This ratio indicates the proportion of applicants who have the qualifications to fill a certain position.

>> **Submission-to-hire ratio (SHR):** This ratio shows the number of candidates submitted to the business by a third-party agency to produce one successful hire. The lower the better.

>> **Hiring manager satisfaction:** This is a subjective measure of how satisfied the hiring manager is with the candidates submitted to fill a position.

To determine how successful your recruitment marketing activities are in delivering quality hires to your organization, look at the following metrics:

>> **First-year retention:** The proportion of hires retained for a minimum of 12 months, or long enough to provide a return on the investment made in recruitment and orientation.

>> **First-year quality:** The proportion of hires meeting end-of-year performance expectations. The nature of this measure varies considerably from company to company, making it difficult to benchmark externally. However, if you can agree on a formula internally, it will serve as an important ongoing measure of your recruitment marketing success.

# Comparing your results to external benchmarks

In addition to comparing the success of your recruitment marketing activities internally by region, function, and activity type, you should also try to find comparisons with external benchmarks. Here are some helpful sources for benchmark information:

>> **ERE** (www.eremedia.com)**:** Provides excellent benchmarking tools and dashboards

>> **Career Xroads** (www.careerxrpads.com)**:** Produces regular annual reports on recruitment industry trends and benchmarks

>> **Bersin by Deloitte** (http://home.bersin.com)**:** A great resource for recruiting analytics on time-to-hire and cost-per-hire by job title and industry segments

>> **Potential Park** (www.potentialpark.com)**:** A great resource for benchmarking your online communication practices

Chapter **18**

# Monitoring and Maintaining Long-Term Impact on Employer Brand Value

As you strive to strengthen your employer brand, you need to monitor your progress to determine whether what you're doing is adding value to your brand over time. You must find out whether brand awareness is growing and whether perceptions of you as an employer are becoming more or less positive among both candidates and employees. Only through such knowledge can you gain the insight required to correct course, if necessary, or continue investing in your current strategy.

The metrics highlighted in Chapter 17 are largely focused on the immediate impact of your recruitment marketing activity on talent acquisition. Assessing the full, longer-term value of your employer branding activities requires a wider focus, including measures of your external brand reputation, internal brand perceptions, and employee engagement. If you've conducted an employer brand health check (as recommended in Chapter 3), you've already established benchmarks against which you can measure progress. The purpose of this chapter is to provide a reminder of the key metrics you need to track and some additional analyses you should perform to gauge the longer-term effectiveness of your employer brand strategy.

# Tracking Employer Brand Awareness and Reputation

Two measures of your success in building employer brand equity (value) are brand awareness and reputation. Employer brand awareness among the people you want to reach and a clear and distinctively positive reputation represent the cumulative result of your marketing efforts. This should lead to correspondingly greater returns on your marketing investment as more people within your target talent pools recognize and respond to your advertising and actively engage with the content on your career site and social domains. Once established, awareness and reputation cast a golden glow of trust and favorability across your future employer branding activities.

In this section, we explain how to gather and analyze the data necessary to evaluate your employer brand awareness and reputation. With this knowledge and insight, you'll be well equipped to fine-tune your employer branding initiatives.

REMEMBER

High levels of overall brand awareness and a fairly consistent reputation are certainly good signs, but measuring employer brand awareness and reputation among your target groups (current employees and the candidates you want to attract) provides more useful insight. In other words, assessing what people know, feel, and think about your organization should always be carefully qualified by the type of people you choose to ask.

## Measuring improvements in brand awareness, consideration, and preference

Employer brand awareness, consideration, and preference should grow in relation to the reach, frequency, and effectiveness of your recruitment communication. Before we get into a discussion of how to measure awareness, consideration, and preference, you should understand their differences:

>> **Awareness:** The percentage of people who've heard of your company (or brand name)

>> **Consideration:** The percentage of people who would consider working for your company

>> **Preference:** The percentage of people who select your company as an ideal preference (for example, amongst the top five from the total list of companies they would consider for employment)

Here are two excellent tools for gauging your employer brand awareness, consideration, and preference and tracking the impact of your employer branding activities over time:

>> **LinkedIn Talent Brand Index (see Figure 18-1):** LinkedIn's employer branding research compares the following to determine an organization's brand index:

- **Reach:** The number of people on LinkedIn who are familiar with the organization as an employer, which includes people who have viewed the organization's employee profiles or are connected with those employees

- **Engagement:** The number of people who show an interest in the organization as an employer — for example, by viewing the organization's career page, choosing to follow the organization, or viewing job openings

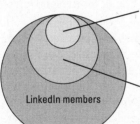

**Talent Brand Engagement**
The number of people who have proactively shown an interest in your brand, measured by:
- Researching Company and Career pages
- Following your company
- Viewing jobs and applying

LinkedIn members

**Talent Brand Reach**
The number of people who are familiar with you as an employer. This is the pool of talent you have the potential to influence, measured by:
- Viewing employee profiles
- Connecting with your employees

**FIGURE 18-1:** LinkedIn's Talent Brand Index.

**Talent Brand Index = Talent Brand Engagement/Talent Brand Reach**

*Reproduced with the permission of LinkedIn Ireland Unlimited Company*

>> **Universum Recruitment Funnel (see Figure 18-2):** Universum provides employer brand tracking data for more than 1,200 companies across more than 65 countries. If you're among Universum's listed companies, you can measure levels of brand awareness, consideration, and preference among students and young professionals (graduates with two to ten years of work

experience) and compare relative affinity with your brand against that of your key talent competitors. If your company isn't listed, you can arrange for a tailored survey to be conducted, enabling you to compare your awareness with up to five talent competitors of your choosing.

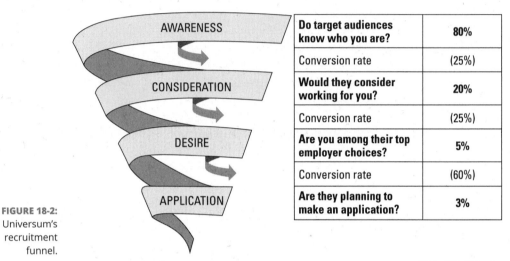

| AWARENESS | Do target audiences know who you are? | 80% |
|---|---|---|
| | Conversion rate | (25%) |
| CONSIDERATION | Would they consider working for you? | 20% |
| | Conversion rate | (25%) |
| DESIRE | Are you among their top employer choices? | 5% |
| | Conversion rate | (60%) |
| APPLICATION | Are they planning to make an application? | 3% |

FIGURE 18-2: Universum's recruitment funnel.

© John Wiley & Sons, Inc.

REMEMBER

A strong corporate or consumer brand with a global reach doesn't necessarily translate into an attractive employer brand, for the following two reasons:

>> **Familiarity with your organization's products/services and with the kind of employment opportunities you offer can be vastly different.** Potential candidates may even exclude your organization as a potential employer because they associate it only with the jobs they can see or imagine at your organization. For example, from L'Oréal to P&G, science, technology, engineering, and mathematics (STEM) graduates often fail to consider the range of scientific and engineering roles required to deliver the products and services those companies offer.

>> **Familiarity with your organization may not translate into accurate knowledge.** People may hold a negative view of your organization, because they have a misguided impression of what you or your industry does. For example, leading accountancy firms like EY, PWC, KPMG, and Deloitte are well known but often fail to attract many people because the nature of the work they do is often poorly understood.

# Examining conversion ratios

In addition to measuring improvements in overall levels of awareness, consideration, and preference, you should also look for improvements in the conversion ratio for each of these measures. *Conversion ratios* provide a measure of how well you're able to convert people from one level of brand affinity to the next. Here are some examples:

>> The ratio of people who are aware of your company as an employer to the number that would consider working for your company

>> The ratio of people who are aware of your company to those who would list it as among their top (preferred) companies to work for

>> The ratio of people who list your company as a preferred employer to the number who are actively considering applying for a job with your company

In addition to these overall measures of change in your brand affinity over time, you can also obtain a more precise measure of the effectiveness of your marketing by comparing the results in different locations where you've either made different levels of investment or tried different marketing tactics. For example, the Universum talent survey enables companies to compare awareness levels among students on target campuses where employers have been more directly active in their recruitment communication against campuses where they've made no investment in order to demonstrate the effect of these activities on awareness.

**REMEMBER**

If possible, try to determine relative levels of consideration among active job seekers versus passive targets. High levels of consideration among active job seekers could be driven by the perception that you hire a lot of people rather than your relative merit as an employer. The true test of your employer brand equity is consideration among targets who aren't currently active in seeking a job. Another good indicator is the proportion of target candidates who agree to discussing employment opportunities with a recruiter on the strength of your brand name.

# Conducting employer brand image surveys

Conducting employer brand image surveys is one of the best ways to determine what people outside your organization think about it as an employer. Here are some approaches for collecting employer brand image data:

>> **Adding employer brand questions to existing brand surveys:** Increasingly, organizations are adding employer brand questions to existing brand surveys, including corporate image surveys. Companies, including McDonald's, also use their customer satisfaction survey to track people's perceptions and

consideration of the company as a potential employer. Responses to employer brand questions provide insight into the organization's reputation as an employer.

Although you may want to include questions specifically related to your EVP pillars, here are a few essential, though more general, questions you should ask:

- How would you describe the overall reputation of this company as an employer?

- Would you describe this company as a top employer in its industry?

- How would you describe the quality of talent you'd expect this company to attract?

- Is this a company that you would ever consider working for?

>> **Conducting a new joiner survey:** New joiner surveys represent one of the most underused sources of employer brand image data. The advantage of this data collection method is that it typically represents a highly distilled sample of the people you most want to hire. The disadvantage is that it doesn't represent the broader target population, resulting, inevitably, in a positive bias.

As you develop a list of questions to ask new hires, make sure to include the following four questions:

- **What qualities did you first associate with our organization before you started looking for more information?** Responses to this question reveal the relative strength of your EVP pillars in relation to other brand image associations, including corporate and customer brand images.

- **In what ways, if any, did your image of the organization change as you gathered more information?** Responses to this question indicate how effective your recruitment advertising and content marketing were in strengthening associations with your EVP pillars.

- **Which other organizations did you consider joining?** If you're wondering which organizations you're competing with for talent, responses to this question provide the answer.

- **Why did you choose to join our organization?** Responses to this question show the relative value of your EVP pillars in convincing candidates to join your organization. You may be surprised to discover that a lower-priority pillar is valued higher by candidates.

>> **Defining and tracking your employer brand image index:** Having established a baseline for your employer brand image, use the same framework to measure whether your marketing efforts have been successful in building the desired brand associations laid out in your EVP. Ideally, your analysis should

look something like what's shown in Figure 18-3. Here, you can see that the company in question has built stronger associations with its desired EVP attributes, particularly leadership and international opportunities. It would be important in this case to identify whether this appeared to follow the relative level of investment in communicating these attributes, or whether they made a greater impact because these attributes were generally perceived to be more attractive or distinctive to the target audience and, therefore, more likely to attract people's attention. It's also important to note in this case that the aggregate improvement in the employer brand index appears to have increased consideration and preference for the employer. Whether this also translates into a tangible return on investment (ROI) would need to be considered in relation to other relative measures such as cost and quality of hire.

| External Image Survey (% ASSOCIATED) | Year 1 | Yr 2 | Yr 3 | |
|---|---|---|---|---|
| Creative and dynamic environment | 65 | 66 | 69 | +4 |
| Challenging work | 57 | 57 | 59 | +2 |
| Flexible working | 60 | 61 | 63 | +3 |
| Leadership opportunities | 55 | 58 | 63 | +8 |
| International opportunities | 51 | 56 | 60 | +9 |
| | | | | |
| Employer Brand Image INDEX | 58 | 60 | 63 | +5 |
| Employer Consideration | 35 | 37 | 40 | +5 |
| Employer Preference | 5 | 7 | 9 | +4 |

EVP Pillars *(label for rows 1–5)*

**FIGURE 18-3:** Employer brand image index.

© John Wiley & Sons, Inc.

# Drawing conclusions from external brand tracking

The two sets of data outlined earlier — improvements in awareness, consideration, and preference, along with changes in your employer brand image index — should provide a clear indication of whether your messaging strategy has produced the desired results. Improvements in awareness should broadly match your investment in the reach and frequency of your communication. If these improvements appear to be lower than anticipated, you need to either invest in ensuring more people in your target audiences are exposed to your communication or find ways of improving the impact of your marketing efforts.

Judging your consideration and preference results is more complex, because it depends more on people's response to your communication. Have they understood the messages you wanted them to understand, and if so, have these messages had the desired effect in increasing their affinity with your brand? Ideally, improvements in your brand image associations should match the broad themes and individual attributes you've focused on in your communication. If they have, then you know that you're getting your message across. If not, then you need to find ways to make your communication clearer and more engaging.

However, getting your message across is only a means to an end. The ultimate objective is to drive higher levels of consideration, preference, and application. If you've drawn the right conclusions from the research leading to your EVP, then an improvement in your desired brand associations should deliver higher levels of consideration, preference, and application. If you find this not to be the case, you may need to review your communication strategy, placing more emphasis on the most attractive elements within your EVP. You may also need to review your EVP to introduce more attractive elements into your underlying proposition.

Finally, your conversion ratios should provide a clear indication of where you need to place your communication emphasis going forward. Consider the following scenarios:

>> **Low awareness but strong conversion to consideration:** Your employer brand is attractive to those who've heard of you, potentially those working in the same industry, but generally not well known enough outside your industry. In this situation, you need to focus your investment on building reach and establishing higher levels of awareness.

>> **High awareness but weak conversion to consideration:** People have heard of your brand, potentially as a result of your products and services, but they may not be as familiar with what you offer in terms of employment. In some cases, the nature of your consumer offering may drive down consideration because people may not associate themselves with your product. In this case, you need to focus more on building familiarity with your employment offering, particularly the less visible types of roles that your business nonetheless depends on to deliver its more visible products and services.

>> **High consideration but weak conversion to preference:** You're generally well known and well regarded, but you're falling short of your talent competitors. In this case, you need to focus your efforts on differentiation and emotional engagement. You need to find ways of increasing the desirability of your brand to potential candidates through richer and more personally engaging marketing content.

>> **High preference but weak conversion to application:** You're highly rated as an employer, but your perceived status may be so exceptional that potential candidates feel too insecure to apply. Alternatively, this pattern can also result from the locations offered by your company. (For example, the LEGO Group has long been an ideal employer in Denmark, but few people want to work in its relatively remote head office location in Billund.) If you feel that well-qualified candidates are failing to apply because your high status is putting people off, you may put greater effort into promoting a more friendly and accessible image and selection process. If your locations are potentially seen as a drawback, you may (like the LEGO Group) develop and promote a more flexible approach to where employees in certain functions live and work, or invest more in promoting the desirability of your work locations.

# Tracking the Internal Impact of Your Employer Brand Strategy

**REMEMBER**

Improving the external awareness and attractiveness of your employer brand is always great, but the most important long-term effects of your employer brand strategy should be internal. Effective employer branding should ultimately result in your organization acquiring higher-quality talent, who fit your culture and engage, stay, and perform at their very best. Your employees (and alumni) should also ideally become your most powerful recruitment marketing tools, recommending your company to potential candidates within their professional networks and participating in the creation of rich, story-driven content.

This section outlines the key measures you should track to monitor your ongoing success in delivering these highly positive outcomes.

## Evaluating employee engagement

To evaluate employee engagement, the majority of employers hire an external research firm to conduct internal surveys to ensure an independent and anonymous assessment of employees' opinions. Organizations that conduct employee surveys define employee engagement in a number of different ways, but they tend to share a number of common components, including the following:

>> **Motivation:** Do employees feel motivated to go the extra mile for the organization?

>> **Loyalty:** Are employees committed to building long-term careers with the organization?

>> **Advocacy:** Would employees recommend the organization as a good place to work?

The most important measure from an external employer brand reputation and recruitment perspective is advocacy, because the readiness of employees to communicate positively about their employer through social media and refer good candidates has increasingly become the bedrock of effective social marketing. The other common term used for this measure is the *net promoter score* — the net sum of positive employee advocates and negative detractors.

**REMEMBER**

Balance your net promoter score with employee motivation to perform, because the wrong kind of advocacy could result from a comfortable but low-performing work environment. In other words, employees love the company because they're allowed to slack off.

Some people have begun to question the inclusion of loyalty in the definition of engagement, because it tends to be more influenced by the external context. Over recent years, it could be argued that employees' intention to stay with their employers has tended to be more influenced by the relatively poor economic environment and a risk-averse desire for stability than heart-felt loyalty and commitment to their employer brand. Likewise, in fast-growing emerging markets, engaged employees may still be highly vulnerable to the many alternative opportunities open to them elsewhere.

More recently, Willis Towers Watson has introduced the concept of "sustainable engagement," which includes measures of well-being. Given that employees can sometimes be too engaged, prone to overwork and burnout, this is a welcome addition to engagement thinking.

These engagement measures represent the desired behavioral outcomes of a strong employer brand in the same way that application and positive word of mouth represent the desired outcomes of a strong employer brand reputation and effective recruitment marketing.

## Tracking your employer brand experience

A number of leading companies have begun to measure the strength and consistency of their desired employer brand experience in the same way they measure the external strength of their desired brand image associations — by conducting their own surveys or participating in surveys conducted by third-party organizations. Fortunately, you can conduct this kind of research internally. Most leading organizations conduct some form of employee engagement survey, which can provide a rich source of data for evaluating the current health and vitality of the employer brand, as well as the relative performance of priority EVP attributes in comparison to industry and high-performance company norms.

TIP

Consider creating an employer brand experience index or EVP index by adding a subset of questions to your overall engagement survey that specifically relate to the EVP pillars or explicit employer brand promises your company has made to employees. Choose two to three questions describing the key dimensions of each pillar. Ideally, these questions should include one or two generic benchmark questions describing the general "territory" in which the employer brand promise is made. These questions enable you to compare your company's performance with that of other peer group companies to determine whether your company is distinctively strong in relation to comparative benchmarks. Then you can add to this one or two more unique questions to capture the more distinctive or stretching aspects of the pillar.

The questions in Table 18-1 illustrate how the LEGO Group applied this thinking to calculating its EVP index. (EB stands for *external benchmark* and refers to the generic questions that can be benchmarked externally. IB stands for *internal benchmark*, designating more-specific questions that can be benchmarked only internally.)

**TABLE 18-1**

## Calculating the EVP Index

| EVP Pillars | Questions/Statements |
| --- | --- |
| Purpose-driven | (EB) I am proud to tell other people where I work. |
| | (IB) In my daily work, the LEGO mission strongly inspires me to do my best. |
| Systematic creativity | (EB) My present job offers me a chance to learn new skills and develop my talent. |
| | (IB) In my daily work, I am highly inspired to use both my imagination and my experience. |
| Clutch power | (EB) In the LEGO Group, there is an environment of trust. |
| | (IB) I feel part of a strong LEGO community, with an extraordinary bond among people working in the LEGO Group. |
| Action ability | (EB) My job makes use of my work-related skills and abilities. |
| | (IB) People working for the LEGO Group always take accountability and deliver what they promise. |

The index is simply made up of the aggregate scores from each set of pillar questions, providing one overall metric summarizing the current health and vitality of your employer brand from an employee experience perspective.

You can receive a similar benchmark measurement by participating in best employer surveys such as those conducted by the Great Place to Work Institute.

If you set out to align your people management processes and behaviors with your EVP and employer brand promises, as we recommend throughout this book, you should see positive shifts in these scores over time, as in the example from a drinks company (shown in Figure 18-4), which made significant efforts to invest in leadership and employee development following the launch of a new EVP in 2008, and to create the right conditions for people to have more fun at work.

| Employee Engagement Survey (% FAVORABLE) | Year 1 | | Year 3 | |
|---|---|---|---|---|
| We demonstrate a passion for excellence | 75 | | 79 | +4 |
| We can make a personal difference | 77 | Internal Activation | 85 | +8 |
| We work together to win | 70 | | 76 | +6 |
| We make our company a fun place to work | 64 | | 71 | +7 |
| We enable people to realize their full potential | 51 | | 60 | +9 |

(EVP Pillars)

| | Year 1 | | Year 3 | |
|---|---|---|---|---|
| Employer Brand Experience INDEX | 75 | | 82 | +7 |
| Employee Advocacy (Recommend to others) | 65 | | 74 | +9 |
| Employee Commitment (Intend to stay) | 57 | | 70 | +13 |

**FIGURE 18-4:** Your employer brand experience index scores should rise over time.

© John Wiley & Sons, Inc.

If you're not making the necessary progress in improving those areas of employee experience that fall short of your employer brand promises, you need to either do more or adjust your EVP and messaging to more credibly reflect the reality of the employment experience.

## Evaluating the candidate experience

In addition to conducting surveys to monitor employee engagement, you should also monitor candidates' experience of the application and selection process to ensure that it leaves a positive impression. Ideally, this should also include some form of image analysis to determine whether the process has reinforced the expectations of the employer brand communicated through the company's recruitment marketing. The goals are to leave a positive impression on both successful and unsuccessful candidates and to keep suitably qualified candidates who aren't selected in your talent pool ready to consider more suitable positions if they arise in the future.

TIP

Here are some of the key question areas you should consider including in this kind of survey:

>> **Application process:** Was the application process clear and easy to follow? Was the applicant kept informed of the status of his application? What, if anything, would the applicant suggest should be changed to improve the application process?

>> **Selection process:** Did the candidate feel the interview/selection process was managed fairly and professionally? Was the company responsive to the candidate's needs (in establishing mutually convenient times for interviews, for example)? What, if anything, would the applicant suggest should be changed to improve the selection process?

>> **Employer brand image:** Did the selection process leave a positive impression on the candidate? Would she recommend the employer to others? Which of the following would she associate with the employer as a result of her experience of the application and selection process (provide a list of image attributes to choose from)?

Because only a portion of the applicants are likely to be selected for interviews, it makes sense to run two separate surveys — one for applicants and a second follow-up survey for candidates participating in the selection process.

TIP

Don't send the survey to applicants/candidates at the same time as a rejection letter. Allow for a cooling-off period to ensure you receive a more measured response.

REMEMBER

Research suggests that the overwhelming majority of candidates reporting a positive candidate experience also claim that they would refer others to apply to the company. Given the ease with which people can now broadcast a dissatisfactory experience across their personal and professional networks, the potentially negative consequences to your employer brand are also significant. Despite the clear benefits of monitoring candidate experience, the evidence surprisingly suggests that this form of research is still only conducted in a minority of cases.

# Assessing the onboarding experience

A successful onboarding experience improves retention while reinforcing your company's reputation as an employer. To evaluate your onboarding experience, you need to track satisfaction with the onboarding process and determine whether the experience is reinforcing the desired impressions of the employer brand. Ideally, feedback should span the entire orientation period, which typically takes place over the first 3, 6, or 12 months of employment, depending on the importance and complexity of the role.

The three key outcome measures that determine the overall success of onboarding and orientation are

>> **Engagement:** In many organizations, engagement levels tend to decline during the first year of employment. It's understandable for the initial honeymoon period to produce very high levels of engagement, but the organization should keep track of the decay rate and rectify sources of dissatisfaction. (For details on how to measure engagement, see the earlier section "Evaluating employee engagement.")

>> **Retention:** Attrition levels within the first 12 months can indicate a number of potential issues that may need to be addressed by the organization. These could include hiring people with the wrong cultural fit, significant gaps between employer brand expectations, the reality of employment, or a poor onboarding process.

>> **Speed to performance:** Speed to performance can be difficult to measure. Some organizations calculate how long it takes an employee to get up to speed with his new job and the time it takes to make a return on the investment involved in recruitment and onboarding someone to a new position.

# Evaluating employer branding's impact on employee performance

As we point out in Chapter 2, many general research studies have been conducted to prove a strong link between employee engagement and enhanced business performance. If you've developed an internal EVP index (see the earlier section "Tracking your employer brand experience"), you can take this kind of engagement analysis a step further by comparing the performance of business units with their respective EVP index scores, as well as their employee engagement scores (see the earlier section "Evaluating employee engagement").

As shown Table 18-2 and Table 18-3, RBS was able to demonstrate a strong correlation between EVP index scores, employee engagement, customer satisfaction, and sales. It also found that delivering on the EVP was an even stronger predictor of customer service and sales performance than was employee engagement alone. This outcome can be explained by the fact that an effective EVP (as in RBS's case) contains ingredients designed to enhance both engagement and performance.

**TABLE 18-2**    **Comparison of the RBS Employer Brand Experience Index with Other Key Performance Indicators**

| Branches | Employer Brand Index | Engagement Index | Annual Turnover | Rate of Absence | Sales Performance | Customer Satisfaction |
|---|---|---|---|---|---|---|
| Median | 71% | 55% | 10% | 3% | 99% | 84% |
| Top 10% | 10% | 13% | –2% | –1% | 35% | 3% |
| 10%–20% | 3% | 7% | –1% | 0% | 19% | 2% |
| 20%–30% | 4% | 6% | 0% | 0% | 13% | 2% |
| 30%–40% | 4% | 6% | –2% | 0% | 7% | 2% |
| 40%–50% | –1% | –1% | –1% | 0% | 2% | 1% |
| 50%–60% | –3% | –3% | 2% | 1% | –2% | 0% |
| 60%–70% | –3% | –4% | 2% | 1% | –8% | –1% |
| 70%–80% | –8% | –7% | 4% | 1% | –14% | –2% |
| 80%–90% | –8% | –10% | 5% | 1% | –22% | –2% |
| Bottom 10% | –12% | –14% | 5% | 2% | –39% | –2% |

*The data displayed show the scores above or below median. Based on analysis conducted by ISR / Towers Watson and RBS Group across their retail branch network. Reproduced with the permission of RBS Group.*

**TABLE 18-3**    **Correlation between Employer Brand Experience Index and Retail Branch Performance**

| | Customer Satisfaction | Sales Performance |
|---|---|---|
| Employer Brand Index | 0.45 | 0.41 |
| Leadership Index* | 0.42 | 0.40 |
| Engagement Index | 0.35 | 0.39 |

*\* Leadership Index is a select combination of factors indicating the quality of immediate leaders.*

*Analysis conducted by ISR / Towers Watson and RBS Group across their retail branch network in 2006. Reproduced with the permission of RBS Group.*

# Analyzing Your Employer Brand Index

An effective employer brand strategy contains many moving parts and inter-linkages. Given the complexity, you can easily lose sight of the bigger picture. To maintain focus on the goal of employer branding, it's helpful to have an overview that you can use for ongoing tracking and analysis. After you've put in place the key measures recommended for internal and external tracking of your employer brand performance, pull them all together, as shown in Figure 18-5.

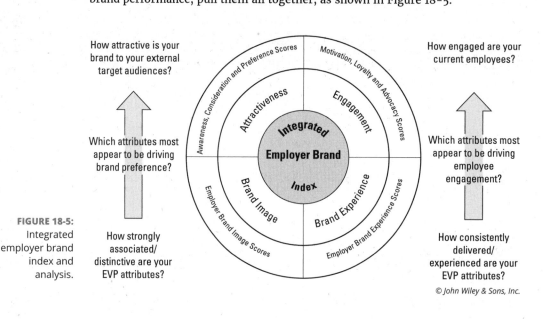

How attractive is your brand to your external target audiences?

Which attributes most appear to be driving brand preference?

How engaged are your current employees?

Which attributes most appear to be driving employee engagement?

**FIGURE 18-5:** Integrated employer brand index and analysis.

How strongly associated/ distinctive are your EVP attributes?

How consistently delivered/ experienced are your EVP attributes?

© John Wiley & Sons, Inc.

This index can be used at a company-wide level to determine the overall health of your employer brand. You can also use it to compare the status of your employer brand across different business divisions and countries.

With this index in place, you can more easily establish potentially meaningful links, correlations, and returns on investment. Here are three potential analysis pathways you should consider:

>> **Measuring the ROI of brand experience enhancements:** Given the investment made in improving the employee experience (such as additional spending on training and development), you should evaluate its impact on employee engagement and performance, as well as how it may have affected how employees rate the company on the corresponding brand attribute. Drawing conclusions from this analysis is easier if different levels of invest-ment have been made in different business units.

Timing is key. Data collected shortly after an initiative is launched may well indicate a spike in satisfaction and overall engagement based on expectation, whereas data collected later in the delivery of the program will be more reliable in determining the true quality and longer-term effects of the program on engagement and performance.

>> **Measuring the connection between internal brand experience and external brand image:** Compare your internal employer brand experience index to your external employer brand image index to determine whether any correlation exists. Over time, do higher internal experience scores seem to result in higher external image scores? If not, you may need to do more to highlight the steps you're taking internally to drive a more positive experience, and do more to encourage active employee advocacy.

>> **Measuring the ROI of a stronger employer brand image:** Compare your employer brand image scores for different countries or different subsidiary employer brands within a group. To what extent does it appear that a stronger employer brand is helping to improve the cost efficiency and general effectiveness of your recruitment marketing? If possible, compare your employer brand awareness, preference, and image scores across each country with measures such as cost, time-to-hire, and the quality of new hires.

# Keeping Pace with Talent Market Trends

Tracking the success of your own recruitment marketing activities and employer brand equity and performance is important, but keeping your employer brand strong over the longer term also requires that you keep an eye on the wider talent market to ensure you keep pace with emerging trends.

Companies tend to take a good look at their immediate talent competitors when they develop their EVP, but they often fail to take a similarly systematic approach to monitoring the competitive environment on an ongoing basis. Given the current pace of change, companies are updating their EVPs, careers sites, and communication strategies on a far more regular basis.

Here are four ways you can maintain a competitive edge in the talent market:

>> **Monitor the top employers.** Universum and several other organizations produce free annual rankings of the most attractive employers in many markets, based on surveys conducted among students and professionals. This

provides the opportunity for you to monitor your standing relative to the key talent competitors in your industry and more generally (because for many positions, the industry is less relevant than the overall status and appeal of the employer).

**TIP**

Pay particular attention to the employers who've significantly increased their position in the rankings and those that have dropped in the rankings. Then take a look at what they may have done or failed to do to achieve a higher ranking.

» **Keep an eye out for evolving best practices.** Bersin by Deloitte, ERE Media, LinkedIn, PotentialPark, and Universum all produce regular reports on the latest state of best practice in talent management and employer branding. You should also consider attending some of the conferences held on these subjects, during which leading employers make presentations on some of the new tools and techniques they've been introducing. Three of the leading conferences in this space are LinkedIn's annual Talent Connect conference, Glassdoor's annual Employer Brand Summit, and HR Tech. All three pull in big-name employers and delegates from around the world to focus on the latest trends. If your budget can't extend to attending in person, you can watch many of these events live from the comfort of your own office or home.

» **Set up competitor activity alerts.** Although you're probably already overwhelmed by the amount of email you receive, consider setting up Google Alerts (www.google.com/alerts) to keep you posted whenever one of your key talent competitors does something new or different as part of its recruitment and employer branding strategy. Use the name of each talent competitor and each company you've identified as leading talent innovator along with key phrases, such as *employer brand* or *career site,* to have Google notify you whenever these companies change what they're doing to attract talent or strengthen their employer brand.

» **Update your EVP and employer brand strategy.** Companies used to stick with the same EVP for at least five years, and sometimes as long as ten years, supported by very similar advertising campaigns. Now companies typically update and refresh their EVPs every two to three years. This doesn't necessarily require a complete overhaul. The more typical pattern is to retain a number of core EVP pillars as anchor points for the employer brand over the long term — pillars that reflect the EVP attributes closely aligned with key cultural characteristics or organizational values. These long-term attributes can then be supplemented with more short- to medium-term attributes based on changes in market conditions and talent strategy (for example, shifting from a buy to build approach to talent acquisition based on increasingly limited and, therefore, expensive-to-hire talent pools).

In terms of communication strategy, we have seen a very definite shift away from uniform, long-term, advertising-concept-led approaches to more agile, data-led content marketing. This newer type of marketing requires the implementation of the kind of short- and long-term metrics outlined in the previous chapter and earlier in this chapter, and a much more flexible and adaptive response to the insights provided by those metrics.

Given the increasingly volatile, uncertain, complex, and ambiguous world of talent, employer branding is becoming more like a jazz band than a marching band. The dynamic nature of talent acquisition has made it much more challenging, but it also makes employer branding a wonderfully diverse, creative, and stimulating occupation to pursue. Enjoy!

# 6
# The Part of Tens

Discover ten powerful success factors that will help you on your way to building a strong employer brand.

Identify ten common pitfalls that can destroy or dilute your efforts to build a strong employer brand.

Find out how to cut costs while maximizing the efficiency and effectiveness of your employer branding.

Chapter **19**

# Ten Success Factors to Embrace

When you set out to build a strong employer brand, you may feel overwhelmed by everything it involves. Here, we make employer branding more manageable by providing you with a list of ten key success factors. These ten factors serve as a framework for the more detailed activities you'll be conducting. Structure your activities around this framework, and everything else should fall neatly in place.

## Getting Your Leadership Team's Buy-In

Effective employer branding starts at the top. The executive team needs to be onboard to communicate in words and actions that delivering a positive employment experience and building a strong employer brand reputation are critically important to the success of the business. Convincing the leadership team that employer branding is worth the investment should be fairly easy. Just focus their attention on the following key points:

>> **Talent is key to achieving business objectives.** Of course, your leadership team is well aware that proper staffing is essential for operating a business, but when you're asking them to invest in employer branding, you may need to remind them how critical it is to secure talent of equal or superior quality to that of your competition.

>> **Part of being a market leader is being the employer everyone wants to work for.** Leadership is likely to take pride in being part of a company where everyone in the industry wants to work. Remind them that employer branding is key to becoming the employer of choice in your industry.

>> **A strong employer brand boosts productivity while reducing costs.** Employer branding reduces cost-per-hire, lowers the cost of attrition, and enables the company to hire and retain above-average talent without the need to fork out for top-quartile remuneration. It also boosts performance by raising the quality of new hires and ensuring they're fully engaged and committed to the company.

# Bridging the Gap between HR and Marketing

Employer branding requires the expertise and commitment of both HR and marketing to succeed. Organizations that lead the field in employer branding tend to be the ones that have built the strongest bridges between these two functions.

Unfortunately, if your organization is new to employer branding, marketing and HR may operate as entirely separate entities, and they may not recognize the need or value of working together. If you're heading up the employer branding initiative, you may need to serve as the liaison between HR and marketing to encourage and facilitate communication and collaboration. In addition, you must get the leadership team involved to encourage and promote the collaboration necessary to build a strong employer brand.

REMEMBER

Building a strong relationship between HR/recruiting and marketing should be a focus of your early employer branding efforts.

# Sizing Up Your Company's Talent Needs

The purpose of employer branding is to attract, engage, and retain the talent needed for the company to meet its business goals and objectives, so early in the process, you need to identify and clearly describe the type of talent your company needs. At a bare minimum, employees are needed to fill the various positions in the company — people who have the knowledge and expertise required for each position. Beyond that, you want people in your organization with the right character, values, and attitude, both to do the job and to reinforce the desired culture within your organization.

Gather input from your organization's leadership team and from line managers regarding the type of talent needed to meet the company's business goals and objectives. When you can clearly envision the talent you need to attract, you can begin to size up your audience to maximize reach and engagement; you can find out where they learn about opportunities in their field (media usage) and what they look for in a company and in the work they do (engagement hooks).

# Defining a Clear and Compelling Employer Value Proposition

An effective employer value proposition (EVP) defines the key qualities you most want to be associated with as an employer; it encapsulates the give and get of the employment deal and serves to differentiate your company from its competition. Think of it as the guiding star for all your employer branding and recruitment marketing campaigns and activities. To optimize impact, whatever you do to promote your employer brand should align with the EVP.

TIP

To define a clear and compelling EVP, take the following steps:

1. **Conduct brainstorming sessions to gather input from the executive leadership team, management, HR, recent hires, and other key stakeholders.**

   Generate a list of the key employee qualities needed to optimize business performance, the key cultural differentiators, the employee engagement drivers, and the attributes that make your company currently or potentially attractive to targeted talent.

2. **Pare down the list of EVP ingredients generated in Step 1 to a list of no more than five key ingredients.**

   These are your brand pillars.

3. **Based on the list of brand pillars, write an overarching positioning statement that conveys the essence of your organization as an employer — what makes it a distinctively great place to work.**

REMEMBER

The actual writing of the EVP (Step 3) is better suited to an individual or a Lennon and McCartney duo, to avoid the deadening effect of committee compromise. Steps 1 and 2 provide the steak, but Step 3 should ultimately provide the sizzle. (See Chapter 4 for details on developing an effective EVP.)

# Building Flexibility into the Framework

Consistency improves the impact of the employer brand, but your brand framework shouldn't be too rigid. It should contain enough flexibility to adapt your brand pitch to the more specific interests of different target groups. Think of your EVP as a distinctive "brand chord," with each brand pillar representing a separate note that can be played louder or softer, and more or less frequently, depending on its local importance. For example, if your EVP stresses both team spirit and career mobility, your local research and experience may indicate which of these two elements is more relevant and attractive within the local context, in which case the local business unit should make that element more prominent in its employer branding efforts.

# Getting Current Employees Onboard First

Your current and former employees can be your strongest brand advocates or detractors. What they say about your company as an employer and how they interact with prospects outside the company can have a tremendous impact on your company's reputation as an employer. Before ramping up your marketing efforts to promote your employer brand, make sure you're delivering on the promise to your current employees and that they're clear about the role they can play in promoting the employer brand.

TIP

Get employees involved. Employees can write their own profiles, participate in videos, share information about your organization through their social accounts, engage with prospects, and refer highly qualified candidates. By engaging employees in your recruitment and branding efforts, you can significantly improve the reach and impact of your employer brand.

# Making the Most of Social Media

Whether your company is a distinctively great or a distinctively lousy place to work, people will soon discover the truth through social media. Work on building a strong social media presence across a range of the most popular social media channels. Most leading companies now leverage LinkedIn, Facebook, Twitter, YouTube, and (increasingly) Glassdoor and Instagram. Make sure you post content across these channels on a regular basis. And don't just post content; engage with prospects by responding to comments and playing an active role in relevant communities.

REMEMBER

Social media can be a valuable tool for facilitating referrals. Prior to applying for a position, prospects may look up your company on LinkedIn to see whether they have any inside connections. If they have a connection, they can get in contact with that person to find out more about what it's really like to work at the company, find out whether they're likely to be a good fit, and maybe even ask their contact to recommend them for a particular position.

# Keeping an Eye on Your Competition

If another organization is constantly outcompeting you for the talent you need, find out what it's doing and then take one or more of the following actions:

>> **Do it more.** Invest more to improve the employee experience. You don't need to be highly creative; you just need to raise the bar for what's considered the industry standard, whether it's paid training, tuition reimbursement, flexible work arrangements, opportunities to advance within the company, or anything else.

>> **Do it differently.** Offer something new or take a completely different approach to the way you serve up typically generic people management processes such as management training or performance management. Google took this approach with its "20% time" program, giving software engineers one day a week to focus on their own creative projects.

REMEMBER

The goal is to create signature brand experiences — an employee experience that sets your organization apart from its talent competitors.

# Getting into the Right Shape for Talent

Before you set out to market your company as a great place to work, it needs to *be* a great place to work; otherwise, you'll run into credibility issues. You don't need to become a union rep, but you do need to make sure that your company is delivering on its end of the give–and–get deal — that your company is living up to the EVP it espouses.

**REMEMBER**

Leadership needs to model the character and behavior conveyed in the EVP, and the desired behaviors must be consistently encouraged and rewarded. For example, if your company promotes itself as a creative workplace where employee input is valued, employees must be consistently encouraged and rewarded to think creatively and share their ideas. Any manager who operates with a "my way or the highway" mind-set needs to be brought into line.

# Investing in Metrics

Because you have so many ways to promote your employer brand and enhance the employer brand experience, you need to measure what's working, what's not working, and what's working most and least effectively, so you can decide what's having the most impact and improve over time.

Most social media or career platforms (Twitter, LinkedIn, Glassdoor, Facebook) have built-in analytics that enable you to track engagement with your profile and the content you post. If you use external social media tools, such as Hootsuite or Buffer, you have access to additional analytics. You should also use tools such as Google Analytics to track activity on your career site and related websites to gain insight into your employer branding efforts.

Some of the recruitment marketing metrics you'll want to understand include the following:

>> **Source of applicant or new hire:** Which media appear to have prompted initial interest in application and which appear to be delivering the most hires?

>> **Source of application influence:** Which media appear to be most influential in forming candidates' impressions of the employer brand?

>> **Social account follower growth**

>> **Social post engagement:** Likes, retweets, comments, shares, and so on.

To evaluate the longer-term impact of your activities on employer brand reputation and experience, invest in internal and external research to measure the following:

- » **External brand affinity:** Awareness, consideration, and preference
- » **External brand image:** The extent to which your brand image reflects your EVP and messaging strategy
- » **Quality of hire:** Hiring manager satisfaction, overall bench strength
- » **Internal engagement:** Motivation, brand advocacy, and loyalty
- » **Internal brand experience:** How well you're perceived to be delivering against your employer brand promises
- » **Performance:** Productivity, customer satisfaction, and so on

Chapter **20**

# Ten Common Mistakes to Avoid

E ven when you're doing everything right, employer branding involves a considerable amount of trial and error. After all, you're dealing with people and with a host of factors that are subject to change — economic conditions, what employees value, how people conduct their job searches, and so on. However, you can lessen the amount of trial and error by avoiding the most common and serious mistakes.

We've seen what works and what doesn't, what makes an employer branding initiative rumble and what makes it crumble. In this chapter, we highlight ten common mistakes and provide guidance on how to avoid them.

## Treating Employer Branding as a Project

Companies often approach employer branding as a project — a single marketing push to boost the reach and reputation of the company as a great place to work. Unfortunately, as with any brand, developing a strong employer brand reputation requires consistent, long-term effort. It's more like an ultra-marathon than a sprint.

Take the same business-critical, long-term approach to building your employer brand as successful companies devote to building their customer brand. Monitor the long-term effects of your activities on your external employer brand reputation and internal brand engagement advocacy. Review and refresh on a regular basis to ensure you're continually improving and building in the right direction.

**WARNING**

Don't be fooled into thinking that your work is over just because your brand has demonstrated positive momentum. With so many companies competing for people's attention, as soon as you stop pumping energy and effort into your employer brand, you can lose relevance and interest very quickly. You snooze, you lose.

## Failing to Focus

Complex organizations tend to spread rather than concentrate resources in order to placate many different stakeholders. They pursue multiple objectives that are unconnected with one another, or worse, that conflict with one another. As a result, the organization's focus on employer branding becomes diluted, diminishing the impact of the company's investment in the employer brand.

To avoid this common mistake, stress the importance of the system (strategy) over individual components (branding objectives or activities). Taking a systematic approach to employer branding ensures that all components work together and reinforce one another to maximize impact.

**REMEMBER**

Focus is a product of strategy and leadership. Leadership is required to maintain a focus on strategy and ensure management is in place to coordinate efforts and evaluate outcomes.

## Promising the Sun, the Moon, and the Stars

An ambitious plan to attract, engage, and retain talented individuals is admirable, but an overly ambitious plan will be counterproductive. If you promise employees the sun, the moon, and the stars and deliver only the sun and the moon, they won't applaud your ambitions or even your efforts. Instead, they'll feel cheated and disappointed. You're more likely to lose brand advocates than gain them.

To avoid the common mistake of overpromising and underdelivering, have a plan in place to ensure you achieve and maintain a consistently high standard of delivery, as well as a few signature experiences to provide additional sizzle and spark. See the chapters in Part 4 of this book for detailed guidance on how to deliver on your employer brand promises.

# Playing It Too Safe: Corporate Bland or Industry Generic

After all the work is done, if you're not careful, your employer brand can end up looking and sounding like everyone else's. If you want your brand to stand out from the crowd, it's important to understand how and why this happens and the steps you need to take to avoid corporate bland.

When refining your EVP, you typically end up with a collection of statements that outline the key qualities you want to highlight in your proposition. The initial purpose of this exercise is to define the right qualities, to focus and clarify rather than inspire. These descriptions may be perfectly agreeable, but very often these source materials become the final product and different companies end up using very similar descriptions.

After hammering out the key qualities you want to highlight in your EVP, you need to pump in some creativity. Step beyond the obvious and generic territories such as teamwork, empowerment, innovation, and development, and find a more unique and differentiating means to describe the place your company will occupy. This takes courage. The logic of committees will always try to drag you back to words that everyone can agree to, but the words that everyone agrees to are the words every company tends to use. For this reason, it's better to regard the final EVP definition as a creative exercise best suited to one or two people, with the final say of a decisive leader, than a team exercise requiring committee approval.

**REMEMBER**

An EVP description seldom works effectively as a plain list of factual claims. The snow in Antarctica is too dry to make snowballs, which isn't much fun. If your EVP is too dry to convey the spirit of your organization, it's equally unlikely to create much excitement. You need some alchemy to translate what makes sense, from a rational point of view, into something that also feels right, something that captures the essence and not just the dimensions of the employment offer.

# Getting Obsessed with the Tagline

A clever tagline provides a great focal point for deploying a consistent, overarching campaign message. If you're trying to build brand awareness, focusing your efforts on a single advertising tagline, rather than taking a more varied approach to messaging, may initially deliver greater impact and help you stand out from your competitors. However, if you take this too far, it can backfire. After you've won people's attention, they need richer, more varied content to hold their interest and build engagement. If you just continue serving up the same message in the same way, initial interest will soon drift away. In other words, it's useful to find a catchy tagline for your employer brand, but don't get too obsessive about playing out the same message everywhere you can. These days, you need a great deal more authentic, employee-focused marketing content to avoid being branded a phony one-trick pony.

# Over-Policing Your Local Teams

A brand becomes a brand through the consistent and coherent application of brand elements, such as logos, colors, and core benefits, so consistency is a key to branding success. However, if you police brands too tightly, you inevitably squeeze the life out of them. Unless a brand adapts and flexes to the different environments in which it needs to operate, it will generally lose relevance. For example, if a bank were to apply the same employer branding approach to experienced investment bankers as it does to junior retail bank branch employees, it's likely to miss the mark with at least one of its target audiences, if not, both.

The strongest brands apply consistent design standards to maintain a coherent frame, but constantly adapt the content of the communication to stay fresh and relevant to different audiences. They also recognize that a consistent realization of the desired brand benefits among different target audiences generally requires the brand to be delivered in different ways.

**REMEMBER**

Local teams are closer to their audience than you are. Establish branding guidelines, but give your local teams some license in tailoring the content and messaging for their purpose and audience.

# Underestimating the Resources Required to Create Quality Content

Creating the content required to build a strong employer brand requires a considerable and continual investment. To do it right, you need to post fresh, relevant content online at least twice a week on every website and social channel on which you decide to establish a presence. If you let up for even one week, people are likely to lose interest, and your brand recognition will suffer. To ease the burden of content creation, here are a few suggestions:

» Use a social media management tool, such as Hootsuite, to schedule and coordinate content development and delivery.

» Distribute the responsibilities of content development throughout your organization. Every department should be involved in creating content.

» Repurpose content your organization has already developed for other purposes that may be relevant to employees and prospects.

» Hire third-party content developers or editors who are skilled in polishing raw content to make it suitable for publication.

» Use tools like RSS feeds to help you find, aggregate, and share external content related to your industry or other fields of interest with your ideal candidates.

» Follow and amplify employee social media posts.

REMEMBER

Don't overlook resources required for engagement. One or more people need to monitor your career-based social properties for comments and respond when appropriate.

# Forgetting to Connect Communication with Experience

Employer branding involves creating a great place to work and then ensuring all the right people find out it's a great place to work. Unfortunately, too often, the two initiatives are self-contained, with HR taking the lead on the first and recruitment marketing in charge of the second. As a result, a disconnect often arises between the actual work experience and communication, which results in two problems:

>> The employer promise fails to align with the employee experience leading to disgruntled employees.

>> Employer brand messaging fails to capture and convey the essence of the actual work experience and the spirit of the company's employees.

The solution is to maintain a connection with employees:

>> Obtain employee input, through surveys and focus groups, when developing the EVP, to ensure that employer promises align with the employment experience.

>> Monitor and evaluate the employee experience on a continual basis and make adjustments as necessary to ensure that the company is delivering on its promises.

>> Involve employees in content creation to give prospects a more genuine perception of what working at the company is really like.

# Turning Off Your Brand Investment When the Going Gets Tough

Branding of any kind is more like a marathon than a sprint, and you may not experience immediate benefits or be able to identify an immediate connection between branding activities and outcomes. If you see a huge increase in the number of applications or the quality of applicants immediately following a recruitment campaign, you can be relatively sure that your investment is paying dividends, but long-term benefits can be less obvious, and if you're investing considerable resources, you may get discouraged.

**REMEMBER**

Be persistent. Long-term success requires a long-term commitment. Continue to market the employer brand and engage with employees (both current and former) and with prospects. Continue to take steps to make your company a great place to work. If you look after your employees, and you continue to promote the qualities that make your brand special externally, you'll reap the many rewards associated with a strong employer brand. It takes time, but it's worth it, so keep the faith.

# Failing to Learn from Experience

A key to success in any endeavor is to find out what's working and what's not. Then do more of what's working, find ways of doing it even better, and either fix what's not working or stop doing it. The same is true for employer branding. Track outcomes. Use analytics, when possible, to track metrics for various recruitment marketing campaigns and activities. Keep track of the number of applications you receive for different types of jobs and the quality of applicants and new hires. Track and compare your cost-per-hire over time.

As you gather and analyze data over time, you begin to develop a clearer idea of what's working, what's not, and what could be working better. Use this information and insight to improve your employer branding strategy and the various activities you engage in to promote the brand. (See the chapters in Part 5 of this book for guidance on how to measure success and make adjustments.)

**REMEMBER**

As humans, we have a tendency to discount the reasons for failure, and this applies to employer branding, as well. If a former employee posts a negative review of the company, you may be inclined to blame the employee instead of trying to understand why the employee was so disappointed in the company to post the review. The same can happen with marketing activities that fail to deliver what's expected of them. Don't discount them. Don't bury them. Learn from them, and you'll soon become a much more effective employer brand manager as a result.

» Making your creative spend go
  further

» Shifting your emphasis from paid
  media to owned and earned media

» Finding smarter ways to generate
  marketing content

# Chapter **21**

# Ten Ways to Minimize Cost and Maximize Impact

Two common arguments against employer branding are: (1) It costs too much, and (2) It's hard to identify and measure the return on investment. Creating recruitment campaigns, developing or buying content, and drawing time and focus from other business activities all demand valuable resources. In Chapter 2, we make the business case for employer branding, which should convince you and your company's leadership team that investing in your employer brand delivers value in terms of better quality hires and enhanced performance, but it can also help your company to reduce the costs. In this chapter, we present ten ways to reduce the costs and maximize the impact of your investment in attracting, hiring, engaging, and retaining employees.

# Building More Talent Than You Buy

Companies have the option of buying or building talent. Buying talent involves hiring someone with the expertise to do the job, whereas building talent involves training candidates who have the potential to do the job. Building talent generally costs less, so consider investing at least a portion of your employer branding resources in reaching out to college students and graduates and developing an internship program. Some businesses may even expand these programs to local high school students.

# Maximizing Referrals

Instead of paying large bonuses to professional recruiters, incentivize current and former employees to reach out and refer qualified candidates from their personal and professional networks. Many of your employees are probably well qualified to prescreen applicants, so you can save money in several ways:

>> Reduce or eliminate the cost of recruitment advertising to fill a position.

>> Eliminate the cost of paying a professional recruiter.

>> Streamline the screening process.

# Hiring Above-Average Talent for an Average Wage

One way to deliver cost savings through employer branding is to reduce the premium you pay new hires to join your organization. Building a strong employer brand enables you to hire above-average talent for an average wage. This doesn't mean underpaying talent, but a strong employer brand means you shouldn't have to pay an above-market premium. With an employer brand, you build equity in other areas of the employment offer. The benefit that you're deriving is your ability to attract and hire high-quality candidates at a lower cost, because you have a strong career-enhancing reputation, and deliver a distinctively positive employment experience.

Conversely, if you have a poor employer brand image, you have to pay a great deal more to attract the interest of high-quality talent and convince them to join you. You may also need to pay a lot more to executive search firms to go out and hook people, because they're not coming to you of their own accord. This adds up to a fairly major additional cost in terms of attracting the right talent.

# Targeting Efforts to Attract Fewer, But Higher-Quality Candidates

Some organizations receive thousands or even tens of thousands of applications for a single advertised opening. With employer branding, you can more effectively target your recruiting efforts to attract fewer but higher-quality applicants, so you save time and money on the screening process.

TIP

Here are a few suggestions for targeting candidates who are likely to be a better fit for your company or for a particular opening:

>> Be very specific in your job descriptions when listing minimum qualifications, certifications, and skills required.

>> Be very clear when crafting your EVP to convey the character, values, and commitment your company expects from its employees.

>> Identify advertising and media sources of low-quality applicants and stop spending in those areas.

>> Leverage the profiling tools available to help you identify more specific target groups when promoting your marketing content across social media channels such as Facebook and Instagram.

>> Be open to sharing your warts. Openly conveying the pros and cons yields more informed candidates who are likely to be stickier hires because they're joining with a better insight into your company and what the opportunity entails.

# Focusing Your Creative Spend

In business, you always try to get the biggest bang for your buck. The same is true for employer branding. Use your EVP and brand framework to focus your creative spend where it's likely to have the greatest impact:

>> Create an employer brand toolkit that allows everyone across the business to use the same advertising templates rather than reinventing new ones every time advertising is needed.

>> Use design tools, such as Canva, to create employer brand creative assets in-house.

>> Invest more in evergreen creative assets that can be reused. Resist the urge to invest too heavily in a creative campaign for a short-term project, because the assets created aren't likely to deliver longer-term value.

# Shifting from Paid to Owned and Earned Media

One way to reduce marketing and advertising costs is to invest less in paid advertising and focus more attention on owned and earned media:

>> **Paid:** Promotional material you pay for. Paid advertising includes TV adverts, radio spots, print advertising, search engine marketing (SEM), sponsored social media posts, and programmatic.

>> **Owned:** Content published through your own channels. Owned media includes websites, blogs, company pages on social sites, e-books, and white papers.

>> **Earned:** Content that other people outside your company create. Earned media includes press coverage, company profile reviews, blog posts about your company, mentions on social media, shares, and retweets.

**REMEMBER**

Although you have more control over paid media, owned and earned media are likely to appear more genuine and encourage greater engagement.

# Localizing Content Creation

You may be able to cut costs by encouraging and facilitating local communication managers to create more of their own content within the employer brand framework provided. By "local" we mean a country or region, a division within the company, a business unit, a specific group, or even a job function. Various entities within your organization may welcome the opportunity to contribute content and reap the benefits of a stronger, more engaging, local employer brand communication.

**REMEMBER**

An additional benefit of localizing content creation is that locally relevant content is likely to resonate with more narrowly targeted audiences.

# Encouraging Employee-Generated Content

In respect to employer branding, employee-generated content may be the most effective in attracting the desired talent and convincing them to apply. It's also the cheapest to produce. Here are a few ways to encourage employees to contribute content:

>> Provide clear guidance on the kind of content you're looking for, and share great examples to encourage others to follow.

>> Start small and simple. Ask for team photos or for a short description of the employee's proudest moments at work. Don't initiate employee involvement by requesting a major production, such as a video.

>> Make use of some of the content management apps now available for smartphones to help employees capture, edit, and share content with the employer brand team. In other words, make it easier for employees to share content.

>> Create team projects — for example, showcasing a project that a particular department or team is working on. Some employees may feel more comfortable contributing something as part of a team than by themselves.

>> Sponsor contests or giveaways. Cash prizes, time off, and even company-wide recognition can be enough to motivate participation in the company's efforts to build a strong employer brand.

# Creating Your Own Talent Pools

A great way to build brand awareness, recruit candidates, and increase referral hires is to build talent pools (talent communities/networks) — forums where individuals with shared skill sets and interests can gather and interact with one another and with the company's leadership, management, and HR personnel. (See Chapter 10 for detailed instructions on how to create your own talent communities.) Once established, these communities can significantly reduce the cost involved in identifying and communicating with target candidates.

**TIP**

Maintain a low profile, serving the community as a gracious host and encouraging peer-to-peer discussions. The best approach is to have someone in your company who does the same sort of work serve as the host or moderator. Whatever you do, don't treat the group as a passive audience for company updates and job openings.

# Learning from Failure and Building on Success

Invest some time reflecting on what you've learned from your employer brand marketing activities. If something has failed to deliver a return or has run significantly over budget, make sure you identify what caused these failings to prevent them from happening again. It's also important to recognize what you're doing well and build on that success. Success secrets can be hidden in a marketing campaign that produced incredible results, a certain social channel that has proven to be very effective, or a specific message that has resonated with the target talent. Don't just celebrate. Figure out which elements within the marketing mix were the most effective in delivering great returns, so you can efficiently continue to deliver similar results.

# Index

## A

Aberdeen Group, 37, 244

Abram, Carolyn (author)

*Facebook For Dummies,* 6th Edition, 187

active job seekers, connecting with, 148–149

ad-blocking software, 102

adcepts (advertising concepts), 96

Adidas, 65–66, 74, 159

Adobe's career microsite (website), 214

advertising

budgeting for, 181

job openings on Glassdoor, 185

recruitment advertising and costs of, 267–268

advertising concepts (adcepts), 96

advocacy, 290

agencies, selecting, 93–95

aligning

with business goals/objectives, 11–12

with corporate brand, 25–27, 84–88

with corporate communications and marketing, 126–127

with customer brand, 27–29, 84–88

website with employer value proposition, 159

alumni talent networks, building, 171

Amazon, 84

American Express, 26

analytics, 183–184, 187

analyzing

competitors' visual positioning, 59–60

effectiveness of recruitment advertising, 269

employer brand index, 296–297

Apple, 12, 84, 145, 234

applicant tracking software (ATS), 192

applicants, interviewing, 239–241

applicants per vacancy, 279

application process, 238–239, 293

applications

for current openings, 162–163

number of, 268, 271

tailoring, 242–243

at risk, 257

ATS (applicant tracking software), 192

attracting candidates, 17–18, 321

audience exposure

career site content and, 273

recruitment advertising and, 268

referral effectiveness and, 276

social campaigns and, 270

audiences

evaluating your, 142–145

motivation of your, 149

prioritizing segments of, 143–144

segmenting, 142–143

traits of your, 149

Audiense (website), 191

average time on page, 274

## B

Bacardi, 86

backlinks, 201–202

balancing

competing perspectives, 73–76

global and local considerations, 75–76

immediate engagement with long-term brand building, 104–105

inbound and outbound marketing activities, 150–151

targeting with diversity, 217

banner, on landing page, 155

Ben & Jerry's, 28

benchmarking

competitor media presence, 55–56

in engagement survey action planning, 250

current openings
  advertising on Glassdoor, 185
  applications for, 162–163
  on landing page, 155
  prioritizing hiring needs based on, 143
current strengths, weighing with future aspirations, 74
customer brand, aligning with, 27–29, 84–88
customer experience, applying to HR processes, 226–230
CX. *See* candidate experience (CX)
cycle, of employer branding, 9–10

# D

data, drawing insights from, 67–68
Deiss, Ryan (author)
  *Digital Marketing For Dummies,* 202
delivering
  content, 158–164
  employer brand briefing, 70
  facts, figures, and infographics, 112–113
Dell, 167, 168–169
Deloitte, 110, 227
demographics
  for creating talent personas, 145
  in employee engagement surveys, 44
design elements
  about, 17
  on landing page, 154
  visual brand identity and, 89
designing
  graduate programs, 216–217
  orientation processes, 248
  signature experiences, 233–235
desire for increased compensation, as a behavioral indicator, 259
desire to move, as a behavioral indicator, 259
Deutsche Bank, 60, 78
development cost, 273
Diageo, 86
Diamond, Stephanie (author)
  *Social CRM For Dummies,* 115

Dice (website), 207
differentiation, 30, 76–77
differentiators, in employee engagement surveys, 45
*Digital Marketing For Dummies* (Deiss and Henneberry), 202
direct engagement, 208–210
direct sourcing, as a cost-cutting benefit, 35
Disney, 77
dissonance, potential, 86
distinctive strengths, of employer brand image, 53
diversity
  balancing targeting with, 217
  of content stream, 179
  targeting, 32
drive, culture fit and, 30
Dummies (website), 3

# E

early-warning systems, establishing, 258–259
earned media, 322
earning employee trust and engagement, 20–21
EB. *See* employer branding
Edelman, 88
EDF, 58
Elad, Joel (author)
  *LinkedIn For Dummies,* 4th Edition, 182
emotional engagement, 135–136
employee advocacy, 276
employee diversity, 221
employee engagement, 44, 289–290
employee engagement survey, 43–45
employee favorability scores, in engagement survey action planning, 250
employee feedback, 43, 45–46
employee generated content (EGC), 114–117
employee performance, evaluating employer branding's impact on, 294–295
employee profiles
  about, 17–18
  on LinkedIn, 184
  as a method of pitching your story, 106–110

# F

marketing and, 304

strategy of, 11, 13, 24

Hussain, Anum (author)

*Twitter For Dummies,* 3rd Edition, 190

OgilvyOne, 145

on brand, 238

onboarding processes, 246, 294

online meeting places, 171

online surveys, testing creative concepts using, 97

opportunities, spotting, 57–60

optimizing

    engagement on LinkedIn, 183–184

    for mobile, 157

    parent-subsidiary house of brands framework, 87–88

    recruitment advertising, 199–210

    social media, 307

organizational change, maintaining attraction and engagement during, 260–261

organizational transformation, senior leadership and, 38

orientation, 243–248

outbound marketing activities, balancing with inbound marketing activities, 150–151

overall recruitment marketing strategy success, measuring, 277–280

overarching recruitment advertising campaigns, developing, 90–95

over-policing teams, 314

owned media, 322

# P

Page, Larry (Google founder), 256

page views, 274

*PageFair Mobile Ad Blocking Report,* 102

paid media channels, 203–207, 322

paired/team profile, 108–109

Palantir, 156–157

Papirfly (website), 128

parent-subsidiary house of brands framework, optimizing, 87–88

participation rate, 276

passion profile, 18, 107–108

passive job seekers, connecting with, 148–149

peer advancement, as a behavioral indicator, 259

people, influencing, 38–40

people-management conversations, 256–257

Pepsico, 67, 86

perception, evaluating, 14

performance benefits, 36–37

performance scorecard, in employee engagement surveys, 45

Periscope, 194

person, as a behavioral indicator, 259

personality test, 221

personalizing

    messages, 208–209

    response letters, 163–164

P&G, 12, 26, 29, 78, 86, 115, 284

pharmaceutical companies, competitors' visual positioning for, 59

Ph.Creative, 145

photography, 17, 18, 89, 155

pillars, of EVP, 242, 291

Pinterest, 19

pitch process, 92–93, 105–114

playing it safe, 313

plugins, 157

policies, developing, 116–117

Porras, Jerry (author)

    *Built to Last,* 26

posting status updates on LinkedIn, 183

potential candidates, engaging, 178–180

potential dissonance, 86

Potential Park (website), 280

potential resonance, 85–86

preboarding new hires, 246–247

preference, evaluating, 47–49

preferred media/communication channels, 149

presenting insight platform, 70–71

principles, of content marketing, 103–105

prioritizing

    audience segments, 143–144

    employee referrals, 169

process, of employer branding, 9–10

programmatic media, 20, 146, 206–207

promises, 312–313

promoting

    employee generated content (EGC), 114–117

    hiring awareness, 167, 169

proof points, 79–81

prospects, engaging, 191

pull actions, 150

pull power, 36

purpose, using in aligning with corporate brand, 25

push actions, 150

push marketing, 190–191

push messaging, 176

# Q

QQ, 195

qualified applicant ratio, 279

quality, of talent, 320–321

QueSocial (website), 116

Quicken Loans, 235

QZone, 195

# R

Rach, Melissa (author)

*Content Strategy for the Web,* 2nd Edition, 118

reach, 268, 270, 283

Read, Scott (Associate Director), 115

rebranding merger of equals, 261

recruiting

about, 17–18

on Facebook, 187–189

on Glassdoor, 184–187

on LinkedIn, 182–184

on Snapchat, 192–193

on Twitter, 190–192

on YouTube, 194–195

recruiting tagline, on landing page, 154

recruitment, as a benefit of employer branding, 9

recruitment advertising

about, 199

direct engagement, 208–210

job boards, 207

measuring effectiveness of, 267–269

optimizing, 199–210

paid media channels, 203–207

replacing, 102–103

search engine results, 200–203

recruitment advertising agency, 147

recruitment community, briefing, 124

recruitment marketing plan

about, 141–142, 213, 266–267

constructing, 141–152

evaluating target talent media preferences, 146–149

evaluating your audience, 142–145

setting out your plan, 149–152

recruitment teams, 127–132, 245

referral applicants, 276

referral costs, referral effectiveness and, 275

referral effectiveness, 275–277

referrals, 166–167, 220, 320

regional channels, 195–196

regional differences, evaluating, 215

rejected candidate referrals (RCRs), 173–174

rejection, handling, 241–242

relevance, maintaining, 137

Remember icon, 3

remote recruiting, 220

reputation

evaluating, 47–54, 185

*versus* reality, of employer brand image, 53

request for information (RFI), 93

request for proposal (RFP), 93

resonance, potential, 85–86

resources, underestimating, 315

responding to retention risks, 257–258

response letters, personalizing, 163–164

response rate, increasing, 208

responsive design, 148

retention

as a benefit of employer branding, 9

onboarding and, 294

retention risks, identifying and responding to, 257–258

revenue production, prioritizing hiring needs based on, 143

reviewing current employment experience, 227–230

# About the Authors

**Richard Mosley:** Richard is head of strategy at the global talent research and employer branding firm Universum. He's widely recognized as one of the leading world authorities on employer brand development and management. Richard's thinking draws on over 25 years of experience in both brand management and HR consulting. He has led major employer brand development projects for many leading global employers, including BP, Coca-Cola, Ferrero, GSK, HSBC, LEGO, L'Oréal, PepsiCo, Santander, and Unilever. This work has involved a significant focus on core values, employee engagement, and culture change, as well as the more externally focused dimensions of reputation and talent attraction. He has written two previous books on the subject: *The Employer Brand* (2005) and *Employer Brand Management* (2014), both published by Wiley. Richard is a regular keynote speaker and chairman at employer brand events around the world, and his work appears regularly in leading business newspapers and journals, including *Harvard Business Review*, the *Wall Street Journal*, *Financial Times*, and the *Economic Times* of India.

Email: richard.mosley@universumglobal.com

LinkedIn: http://uk.linkedin.com/in/richardmosley

Twitter: @rimosley

**Lars Schmidt:** Lars is the founder and principal of Amplify Talent, a consulting agency that helps companies like Hootsuite, NPR, and SpaceX reimagine the intersection of culture, talent, and brand. Before founding Amplify, he developed talent strategies at NPR that were recognized by Mashable, the *Wall Street Journal*, the *Washington Post*, and others. In prior roles, Lars was responsible for creating scalable high-growth global recruiting strategies at Ticketmaster, Magento, and several startups in Los Angeles. Lars is also the co-founder of HR Open Source (www.hros.co), a global initiative to drive collaboration and innovation in HR. He's a global keynote speaker and contributor to *Fast Company*, *Forbes*, *TechCo*, the LinkedIn Talent Blog, *SHRM*, and *ERE*, sharing views and insights around the intersection of talent, culture, brand, digital engagement, and technology. He was named a Top 100 Influencer by *HR Examiner*, included in the *Huffington Post* Top 100 Most Social HR Experts on Twitter, and LinkedIn's 50 Most Popular Recruiting Influencers.

Email: lars@amplifytalent.com

LinkedIn: www.linkedin.com/in/larsschmidt

Twitter: @Lars

# Dedication

We would like to dedicate this book to all the employer brand leaders who are taking risks and pushing the boundaries of the field. We hope this book helps inspire a new generation to continue moving the field forward and inspiring others.

We would also like to thank our amazing wives, Fiona and Janet, for their support, patience, and love.

# Authors' Acknowledgments

Although we wrote the book, several other talented individuals contributed to its inception, conception, and perfection. Special thanks go to Executive Editor Katie Mohr, who chose us to author this book and guided us patiently from start to finish. Elizabeth Kuball, our project editor, deserves an all-expenses paid vacation to the destination of her choice for being a very patient and adept choreographer — shuffling chapters back and forth, shepherding the text and images through production, and serving as unofficial quality-control manager. Thanks also to our "Dummifier," Joe Kraynak, who has helped ensure the book is as clear, precise, and practical as possible.

This book is the result of a combined 45 years of experience in recruiting, branding, marketing, and HR. It was inspired by countless mentors, friends, teachers, and peers we've had the pleasure of working with during our respective careers.

**From Richard:** Many people have played a part in shaping the thinking in this book. I would first like to thank those who gave up their time to contribute their perspectives on employer branding. This includes: Steve Fogarty and Nanci Hogenboom (Adidas); Dominik Hahn (Allianz); Bernard Kunerth (Amazon); Helmut Schuster (BP); Miranda Kalinowski (Facebook); Dennis de Munck (Ferrari); Fabio Dioguardi and Charu Malhotra (Ferrero); Troels Wendelbo (the LEGO Group); David Fairhurst (McDonald's); Scott Read (P&G); Brigitte Franssen (Philips); John Fikany and Frank Riviera (Quicken Loans); Greig Aitken (RBS); Viviane De Paula (Santander Brazil); Rosa Riera and Chris Knorn (Siemens); John Leader and Helene Parent (Suez); and Gerry Crispin (CareerXroads).

I would like to thank my team at Universum, particularly Claudia Tattanelli, Lars-Henrik Friis-Molin, Petter Nylander, Jonas Barck, Karl-Johan Hasselstrom, Jacinta Waak, and Stefan Muller-Nedebock, whose support and encouragement made this book possible.

Finally, I'd like to thank my co-author, Lars Schmidt, who has brought a great deal of light and joy to the writing process.

**From Lars:** I would like to thank and acknowledge Janet Ciciarelli, Rob Harol, Beverly Carmichael, Bob Schwartz, Laurie Ruettimann, Craig Fisher, Stacy Zapar, Matt Charney, Bill Boorman, Will Staney, Celinda Appleby, Susan LaMotte, Matthew Jeffery, Gerry Crispin, John Sumser, and Jeff Perkins for providing inspiration and support for this book. I'd also like to thank Hootsuite, Dell, Oracle, CA Technology, LinkedIn, and Virgin Media for inspiring parts of this book through their HR Open Source contributions. There are many more of course, and I'm grateful for all of them.

Special thanks to my HR Open Source co-founder and dear friend, Ambrosia Vertesi, for sharing a vision for what HR can be and having the courage to see that through. Thanks also to all the HROS community members around the globe for adding your voices and expertise to this initiative.

Lastly, I'd like to thank my co-author, Richard Mosley, for inspiring me and many others to take risks and embrace innovation in the field of employer branding.

## Publisher's Acknowledgments

**Executive Editor:** Katie Mohr

**Project Editor:** Elizabeth Kuball

**Copy Editor:** Elizabeth Kuball

**Editorial Assistant:** Serena Novosel

**Sr. Editorial Assistant:** Cherie Case

**Production Editor:** Siddique Shaik

**Brand Consultant:** Joe Kraynak

**Cover Image:** ©Rawpixel.com/Shutterstock

## Apple & Mac

iPad For Dummies,
6th Edition
978-1-118-72306-7

iPhone For Dummies,
7th Edition
978-1-118-69083-3

Macs All-in-One
For Dummies, 4th Edition
978-1-118-82210-4

OS X Mavericks
For Dummies
978-1-118-69188-5

## Blogging & Social Media

Facebook For Dummies,
5th Edition
978-1-118-63312-0

Social Media Engagement
For Dummies
978-1-118-53019-1

WordPress For Dummies,
6th Edition
978-1-118-79161-5

## Business

Stock Investing
For Dummies, 4th Edition
978-1-118-37678-2

Investing For Dummies,
6th Edition
978-0-470-90545-6

Personal Finance
For Dummies, 7th Edition
978-1-118-11785-9

QuickBooks 2014
For Dummies
978-1-118-72005-9

Small Business Marketing
Kit For Dummies,
3rd Edition
978-1-118-31183-7

## Careers

Job Interviews
For Dummies, 4th Edition
978-1-118-11290-8

Job Searching with Social
Media For Dummies,
2nd Edition
978-1-118-67856-5

Personal Branding
For Dummies
978-1-118-11792-7

Resumes For Dummies,
6th Edition
978-0-470-87361-8

Starting an Etsy Business
For Dummies, 2nd Edition
978-1-118-59024-9

## Diet & Nutrition

Belly Fat Diet For Dummies
978-1-118-34585-6

Mediterranean Diet
For Dummies
978-1-118-71525-3

Nutrition For Dummies,
5th Edition
978-0-470-93231-5

## Digital Photography

Digital SLR Photography
All-in-One For Dummies,
2nd Edition
978-1-118-59082-9

Digital SLR Video &
Filmmaking For Dummies
978-1-118-36598-4

Photoshop Elements 12
For Dummies
978-1-118-72714-0

## Gardening

Herb Gardening
For Dummies, 2nd Edition
978-0-470-61778-6

Gardening with Free-Range
Chickens For Dummies
978-1-118-54754-0

## Health

Boosting Your Immunity
For Dummies
978-1-118-40200-9

Diabetes For Dummies,
4th Edition
978-1-118-29447-5

Living Paleo For Dummies
978-1-118-29405-5

## Big Data

Big Data For Dummies
978-1-118-50422-2

Data Visualization
For Dummies
978-1-118-50289-1

Hadoop For Dummies
978-1-118-60755-8

## Language & Foreign Language

500 Spanish Verbs
For Dummies
978-1-118-02382-2

English Grammar
For Dummies, 2nd Edition
978-0-470-54664-2

French All-in-One
For Dummies
978-1-118-22815-9

German Essentials
For Dummies
978-1-118-18422-6

Italian For Dummies,
2nd Edition
978-1-118-00465-4

**Available in print and e-book formats.**

## Math & Science

Algebra I For Dummies,
2nd Edition
978-0-470-55964-2

Anatomy and Physiology
For Dummies, 2nd Edition
978-0-470-92326-9

Astronomy For Dummies,
3rd Edition
978-1-118-37697-3

Biology For Dummies,
2nd Edition
978-0-470-59875-7

Chemistry For Dummies,
2nd Edition
978-1-118-00730-3

1001 Algebra II Practice
Problems For Dummies
978-1-118-44662-1

## Microsoft Office

Excel 2013 For Dummies
978-1-118-51012-4

Office 2013 All-in-One
For Dummies
978-1-118-51636-2

PowerPoint 2013
For Dummies
978-1-118-50253-2

Word 2013 For Dummies
978-1-118-49123-2

## Music

Blues Harmonica
For Dummies
978-1-118-25269-7

Guitar For Dummies,
3rd Edition
978-1-118-11554-1

iPod & iTunes
For Dummies, 10th Edition
978-1-118-50864-0

## Programming

Beginning Programming
with C For Dummies
978-1-118-73763-7

Excel VBA Programming
For Dummies, 3rd Edition
978-1-118-49037-2

Java For Dummies,
6th Edition
978-1-118-40780-6

## Religion & Inspiration

The Bible For Dummies
978-0-7645-5296-0

Buddhism For Dummies,
2nd Edition
978-1-118-02379-2

Catholicism For Dummies,
2nd Edition
978-1-118-07778-8

## Self-Help & Relationships

Beating Sugar Addiction
For Dummies
978-1-118-54645-1

Meditation For Dummies,
3rd Edition
978-1-118-29144-3

## Seniors

Laptops For Seniors
For Dummies, 3rd Edition
978-1-118-71105-7

Computers For Seniors
For Dummies, 3rd Edition
978-1-118-11553-4

iPad For Seniors
For Dummies, 6th Edition
978-1-118-72826-0

Social Security
For Dummies
978-1-118-20573-0

## Smartphones & Tablets

Android Phones
For Dummies, 2nd Edition
978-1-118-72030-1

Nexus Tablets
For Dummies
978-1-118-77243-0

Samsung Galaxy S 4
For Dummies
978-1-118-64222-1

Samsung Galaxy Tabs
For Dummies
978-1-118-77294-2

## Test Prep

ACT For Dummies,
5th Edition
978-1-118-01259-8

ASVAB For Dummies,
3rd Edition
978-0-470-63760-9

GRE For Dummies,
7th Edition
978-0-470-88921-3

Officer Candidate Tests
For Dummies
978-0-470-59876-4

Physician's Assistant Exam
For Dummies
978-1-118-11556-5

Series 7 Exam For Dummies
978-0-470-09932-2

## Windows 8

Windows 8.1 All-in-One
For Dummies
978-1-118-82087-2

Windows 8.1 For Dummies
978-1-118-82121-3

Windows 8.1 For Dummies,
Book + DVD Bundle
978-1-118-82107-7

**Available in print and e-book formats.**

Available wherever books are sold. **For more information or to order direct visit www.dummies.com**